Seductive Flavours of the Levant

Seductive Flavours of the Levant

HOME COOKING FROM LEBANON, SYRIA AND TURKEY

NADA SALEH

ROBSON BOOKS

First published in Great Britain in 2001 by Robson Books, 64 Brewery Road, London, N7 9NT

A member of Chrysalis Books plc

British Library Cataloguing in Publication Data
A catalogue record for this title is available from the British Library.

ISBN 1 86105 446 7

Typeset by SX Composing DTP, Rayleigh, Essex
Printed in Spain

CONTENTS

ACKNOWLEDGEMENTS

Seductive Flavours of the Levant has been possible to write only because of the assistance of many people, to whom I wish to express my immense gratitude and heartfelt thanks.

For Lebanon:
Nour Saleh; Nayla Comair Obeid; Laudi Taleb, whose hospitality is beyond description; Anna Captan; Aida Foustok; Leila Marzagao; Nelly Ghorayeb; for her great family recipes; Nelly Kikano, for her support and for introducing me to the Cordon Bleu cook, Nelly Ghantous; Mazen and Boushra Salha; Farouk Ghandour; the distinguished journalist Salim Nasser and his wife Renée; Zeina Tony Kiwan; my sisters, Rafat Bu-Chacra and Samira Sayegh; my brothers, Nabil and Riaya Kanso, for their support during the writing of the book, and to Mustafa and Fouad Kanso; my eldest sister, Nazira Makarem; Michel Genin, President and founder of the International Academy of Gastronomes; Dell Osso, President of the Italian Academy of Gastronomes; Randa Gazi Youssef.

For Aleppo:
To Maguy Zobian, whose kindness, generosity and sincerity cannot be surpassed, and her daughter Gina Zobian, for her illuminating stories about the area; François Broccard, for his comments on my introduction.

For Damascus:
To a wonderful lady, Hind al-Adem Yafi, Syrian-born and wife of the ex-Prime Minister of Lebanon, for her recipes from the capital of the Umayyads; Lucien Dahdah, President of the Lebanese Academy of Gastronomes; Avo Deir Stephinian, of Sham Palace Hotel; Rabih Ala el-Din, writer and Manager of Functions and to Elias Nehmeh for their hospitality; the chef, Abd al-Kader Shbat, who I will always remember for his generosity and delicious recipes; Abdallah and Bambi Ziadeh, the former Minister of Defence and his wife, who kindly received me in their lovely home and discussed at length the origins of many recipes; Aboudi and Reem Jallad.

For Turkey:

My heartfelt thanks to Ghassan Shaker, his sister, Ghada Shaker, and her daughter, Dina Topbas, who took care of me, entertained me generously, and gave me details of Ottoman Palace fare; Ghazi Shaker, who introduced me to the best fish restaurant in Istanbul and many others; my friends Ali and Gülfem Esad Göksel, who made me feel at home in Istanbul and paved the way for my culinary experiences – Gülfem for her never-failing help; Vedat Basaran of the Feriye Restaurant, for sharing his knowledge of Ottoman *sarai* cuisine and his hospitality; Sevil Develier, for generously sharing her knowledge of Turkish cuisine; Aylin Tan, wife of the former Minister of Tourism, for her unusual recipes; the top chef, Feridun Ugüviü, for his family recipes and his hospitality; Mahmut Veziroglu, General Manager of the Falez Hotel in Antalya, for his hospitality in this beautiful hotel and his chef for his valuable information.

For London:

Sonia Land, Jeremy Robson and Joanne Brooks, my editor; Suzanne Walsh; the great time working with Allan Brooke and Mary Remnant; John Mansbridge for his beautiful drawings; Sue Atkinson for her photographs; the Michanicou brothers, Chris and Andy, who supplied me with the freshest of vegetables, and whose warm welcome reminded me of home; Michael Rowe and Tim Gritton at Lidgates, who took time to prepare meat and chicken to my liking; as well as John and the rest of the staff; Leslie Pilbrow.

In general for their advice and support:

To my husband Nabil Saleh, for his valuable support; Michel Génin, president and founder of the International Academy of Gastronomes; Guiseppe Dell Osso, president of the Italian and International Academies of Gastronomes; Diane and Michel Klat; Sir Colin Southgate.

Note on Photographs

All the dishes were prepared by Nada and co-styled by her.

INTRODUCTION

Searching for a Lost Way of Life

The smell of a flower or the taste of a cake sometimes brings back nostalgic memories. That is what Marcel Proust, that most sensitive of early 20th-century French writers, made us particularly aware of. Well, nostalgia is my lot and that of many of my Lebanese compatriots, who long for a way of life that was lost as a result of 15 years of war.

Eating figs takes me back to my father's house, to an old tree in our garden and to a ritual that occurred every September when the figs were ripe. In the early morning before the heat of the blazing sun, my uncle would begin the delicate operation of picking the figs. With the handle of a small wicker basket over his forearm, he would climb into the tree. As usual my grandmother would stand on the veranda, her lookout post, sending out her orders. I was always amused by the sight of my uncle, perched high among the leaves, arguing with his mother, who gave him no respite until she had her last word. Figs were my favourite fruit, especially for their sap.

Other instances of food-induced nostalgia come all the time. For instance, whenever I am in Beirut, my sister brings me *manakish*, the famous Lebanese breakfast that consists of a round, flat pastry, topped with *zaatar*. We indulge and reminisce about our daily, early-morning gatherings round the table in our parents' house, which was spread with *foul medamas*, *kishk*, hot bread, *manakish* and the inevitable pot of Lebanese coffee, called Turkish coffee yet different in flavour. Lebanese coffee is thick, strong and just as delicious as Turkish coffee. While my father poured the coffee over the milk (no instant coffee was then available), my mother would go back and forth to the kitchen, looking beautiful and graceful with her white veil falling to her shoulders.

Another memory is of every last Wednesday of the month of April, which celebrates the recovery of the prophet Ayoub (Jacob) from a skin disease. In the early morning we would awake to a unique fragrance that filled the house and you wished for life to come to a standstill. For this was a holy day and, at my father's request, the bath tub would be filled with fragrant Seville orange blossoms, their leaves and rose petals, as part of a purification ritual. As was customary in our house on that religious day, we splashed ourselves with the scented water. The blossoms and rose petals fell over our face and neck, caressing them before they fell again. At the same time a different sort of perfume was coming out of the cauldron – the aroma from *Mufataqua*, a dessert made of rice, tahini and turmeric. It was customary to eat this dessert at this time, probably because it needed to be stirred for hours to show sympathy with the prophet Ayoub's ordeal, who needed all the patience of the world to heal his skin. Another suggestion is that turmeric was used for medicinal purposes.

I am the youngest of eight in my family and am lucky to have lived part of my life during the best years in Lebanon. My parents, who had spent most of their lives in Mexico, had returned home. Our daily routine was governed by my father, a benign patriarch who took care of his family's welfare. Those were magical days. Like most of his contemporaries, my father was a traditionalist. We became used to these traditions and overcame their restrictions because we were a close family and did not need the presence of strangers for our entertainment. Indeed, little else was needed at this time to make us happy. Going to the cinema was one of our regular outings and American films were our favourite. They depicted a rosy way of life that we thought to be the norm.

We were always very excited by the eagerly-waited-for religious feasts and our Sunday trips outside of Beirut. Weather permitting – and the weather in Lebanon often obliged – we would usually leave early in the morning to have lunch in one of the rustic restaurants scattered in the Shouf mountains, my father's birthplace. On other outings another popular choice were fish cafés that were strewn on the littoral. When frying Mediterranean red mullet in my London house (which I seldom do because of the smell that persists afterwards), my mind travels to Khaizaran, a modest eating place by the sea outside Saida (the modern name of the Phoenician city, Sidon). We would be served different kinds of fish, fried or grilled over charcoal. Also we would have fried potatoes and aubergines, an oriental salad and, inevitably, hoummos.

Our return to Beirut late in the afternoon also had its own particular ritual. All along the road were villages and small farms. The produce of their orchards were displayed on the edges of the narrow road, inviting the people in cars to stop and buy. The many cars that stopped alongside the heaps of oranges, lettuces, radishes and other wonderful fruit and vegetables often generated quite a traffic jam. My mother had her usual suppliers who would not give her what was on display but kept the best quality produce hidden for their favourite customers. That made her happy but she did not discuss prices, losing what was considered by some as the best part of the bargain. These frequent pauses at the street vendors was a magical experience that I greatly miss.

A fragrance that often jogs my memory with the sweetest of recollections is that of oranges and Seville orange blossom. In the garden of my parents' house we had several fruit trees scattered about: lemons, figs, loquats and clementines. There was also a gigantic palm tree bearing dates, from which we made tasty preserves. As was customary, a sample would be sent to the neighbours. As for the Seville orange trees, they stood side by side and their beautiful blossoms were designated for distillery operations, which were always supervised by my grandmother, Adma, to produce *ma'al-zahr* (orange flower water). Flower water is an essence no Lebanese household can live without. This essence was, and still is, used in the preparation of sweets. It was also added to hot water and used as a panacea – not unlike the great cup of tea for the British. Whenever a delicate woman fainted – this was at a time when fainting was the last resort in complicated or compromising situations – she would be splashed with flower water to revive her. Whenever we Lebanese established homes abroad, and before the spread of the Lebanese shops, we would always bring back from Lebanon bottles of *ma'al-zahr*. When we received a guest we would ask, 'Do you prefer coffee or white coffee?' (In our vocabulary, white coffee was simply boiling water, with a little orange-flower essence.)

Like many Lebanese, in summer we would retreat to the mountain, leaving behind the capital, Beirut, with its blazing heat and dusty atmosphere. Every day I waited eagerly for the seller of *gazl al-banat*, a sweet similar to candy floss, a most delicious angel-hair shaped in small squares. It was not pink but white in colour, topped with ground pistachios. If you ever pass by a Lebanese food shop, ask for some *gazl al-banat* and give it a try.

I have been interested in food from an early age, and when I arrived in London I decided to study nutrition and compare it with what we learned about the preparation of food from our parents and grandparents. I do not recall exactly when I began comparing Lebanese and Syrian cuisines. This may have been triggered by my numerous visits to Damascus with my parents or it may simply have been as a result of my passion I had for food. My interest in Turkish food came later.

Many people believe that the countries of the Levant have the same cuisine. Although there is a strong resemblance between many dishes, having sampled recipes of these countries, I know there are many variations. Of course, similarities are bound to be found. The Ottomans lived in our area for 400 years and they contributed to the cuisine of the region. However, the origins of a recipe from the Levant, be it from Aleppo, Damascus, Lebanon or Turkey is altogether a different matter, much disputed and difficult to settle.

Author's note: All recipes in this book serve 4 unless otherwise stated

Lebanon

PART 1

Lebanon

I decided to start my culinary survey with Lebanon, the country that I left more than 20 years ago in order to establish a permanent home in England. I still have family and a home there, so I am still in touch with the people there.

For 15 years, this small country was engulfed in an armed conflict described by some as 'a violent internal struggle' and by others as 'a foreign war on Lebanese soil'. The fighting ended in 1991 and the reconstruction of the country began. For years, its inhabitants had lived mainly confined to the one area in which they felt secure. After the war, many of them were pulled by an irresistible desire to visit other regions they had often never seen, and they started a tour of their own country.

Baalbek, Byblos, Saida, Tyre and many other historical places were favourite destinations. Soon foreign visitors followed, a timid flow, then a steady and ever-increasing one.

The economy has been badly hit. As a result the Lebanese, resilient as ever, have had to find new sources of income. The food industry is just one growth area. Scores of restaurants, coffee shops and sandwich bars have mushroomed in the space of a few years. Areas that used to be entirely residential, where outsiders were looked on suspiciously, have now opened up to newly-established eating places.

Ashrafieh is one of these areas. It has a few thousand inhabitants, and before the war it hosted no more than a dozen modest restaurants and eating places. That is no longer the case. In my district alone there are at least 30 restaurants. Some, such as the Rabelais, offer French cuisine, the *Mijana* specializes in Lebanese food, while others offer Italian, Chinese, Japanese and other cuisines. Well, this is cosmopolitan Beirut. For specific Lebanese dishes other than the conventional *mezzé*, you have to venture outside Beirut. For my tour, I decided to follow the path of 19th-century travellers on their way to the Holy Land and revisit historical places that I had seen long ago – but this time with a gastronomic aim.

Mountain food can sometimes be frugal, as this story illustrates. A sheikh was the faithful customer of his village's grocer, who persistently extended to him an open invitation to share his dinner any day he wished. One day, while out, the sheikh decided it was about time he took up the kind invitation. So that evening the sheikh knocked on the grocer's door. In truth, the grocer never thought that his invitation would be taken seriously. Annoyed, he masked his feelings and spoke nonsense in the hope of tiring the sheikh and making him leave without supper. The unsuspecting guest stood fast, smoking his host's tobacco on an empty stomach. The grocer saw that he had no choice and eventually laid a miserly table of three small plates, on which were thyme (*zaatar*), olives (*zaytoun*) and oil (*zeit*) – the three Zs. The sheikh realized that this was all he would be offered to eat. When the time came for him to leave, he staggered and fell unconscious on the ground. The alarmed grocer revived him, wiping his face with a moist towel and asking anxiously 'What happened? Are you hurt? Can I get you anything?' The sheikh answered angrily, 'No, no, for God's sake, leave me alone.' He then lifted his head and said, 'After a dinner composed only of the three Zs, what do you expect the effect to be, you fool?'

Byblos, Tripoli, Baalbek and Beit el-Deen are the four places I visited. There are certainly other interesting places but I selected those four because, apart from their historical importance, their cuisine is influenced by their respective religious communities. The inhabitants of Byblos are mostly Christians, those of Tripoli are mostly Sunni Muslims, those of Baalbek are mostly Shii Muslims, and those of Beit el-Deen are mostly Druze. There are also significant differences in altitude and climate which also affect what is grown and eaten.

Byblos

This enchanting town by the sea boasts of being the oldest continually-inhabited city in the world. The first settlement dates back to approximately 5,000 BC and since then has been occupied by many cultures, including Phoenician, Assyro-Babylonian, Persian, Hellenistic, Roman, Byzantine, Umayyad, Abbasid, Frankish (crusaders), Mameluke and Ottoman. All those who occupied this relatively small area have left a legacy which can be seen from the top of the south-west tower of the crusader castle. From the castle, there is a magnificent view of the port and the sea, and a panorama of antique ruins and traces of settlements that became superimposed on each other – the oldest being deep in the ground. Several years of excavations allow the present-day visitor to see at a glance an historical span of more than 7,000 years.

Every time I visit Byblos, I am overwhelmed by the beauty of the place and, more particularly, by an atmosphere charged with memories of the past. I can imagine the Genoese Lord of Gibelet, Guy II, holding court in his crusader castle, towards the end of the 13th century before being savagely put to death by another Frankish lord. Any white rose in any of the many small gardens can suddenly be turned red in my mind by the blood of Adonis gored to death by the wild boar. Seated in one of the cafés overlooking the port, I can see the fishing boats leaving the harbour and these are metamorphosed in my mind's eye into Phoenician boats sailing towards Egypt with their cargoes of cedar timber, intended to perpetuate forever Pharaonic splendours.

'Are you ready to order?' Roused, on this particular occasion by the voice of the waiter asking what we wanted to eat, I said, 'Fish, of course,' while my eyes were still mesmerized by the radiant lustre of the sea. I ordered my favourite simple *mezzé* of hoummos, *fattouche* (bread salad) with lots of fresh mint, fried aubergines and potatoes. A plate of olives and flat bread invariably accompanies those dishes. To follow we had a most delicious platter of small red mullet, fried and lying on a bed of Lebanese fried bread surrounded with lots of lemon wedges. Then we refreshed ourselves with succulent *batikh* (water melon) and finished off with Lebanese coffee.

Tripoli

After lunching among the ruins of Byblos, we headed further north up the coast to visit the crusader fortress which stands on a hilltop that overlooks the old city of Tripoli. It was built by Raymond of St Gilles who, for a number of years in the early 12th century, was unable to capture the town of the Banu Ammars; instead he settled for control of the countryside. The citadel is in an excellent state of preservation; it shows signs of having undergone some changes under the Mamelukes and the Ottomans without destroying the overall Frankish style.

After the fortress, I headed for the food that Tripoli is most famous for: fine sweets that are best prepared by its Sunni inhabitants. We had some *mafroukeh*, for which Tripolitans are renowned, and *aish al saraya* – delicacies to be savoured without counting calories.

I decided to take up a long-standing invitation to stay a couple of days with friends from Tripoli. I had warned them of my intended visit and requested specific Tripolitan specialities to be cooked for me – in the name of research. These special dishes, including *Djaj bi-zaitoun* (Chicken with olives, see page 68), *Aswad ala aswad* (aubergines and lamb, see page 43), and *Samakeh harra* (chilli fish, see page 46), were all prepared in the authentic homely way. Some have seldom travelled outside Tripoli.

While in Tripoli I was told this amusing story about a pasha and a drunkard. The pasha was very strict about the prohibition of drinking alcohol. One day, when he was touring the town ensuring that his strict instructions were being followed to the letter, he encountered a drunkard who was already known to him. The man, who had a bottle of red wine hidden behind his back, stopped and bowed respectfully to the pasha. The pasha knew from the man's behaviour and past history that he was not innocent. He signalled him to approach and show both his hands. Thus the bottle came into full view of the pasha, who asked 'What do I see?' 'A bottle of oil,' replied the man with a bravura that only a drunk could show in such circumstances. 'A bottle of oil? What about its colour?' asked the pasha. 'Your Excellency,' replied the drunkard, 'it just turned red from shame.'

Baalbek

The next expedition took me to the town of Baalbek, which lies at the foot of the Anti-Lebanon mountains, 1170 metres (3,850 feet) above sea level and 80 kilometres (50 miles) from Beirut. It is there that the magnificent ruins of the largest Roman temple still in existence can be seen. The best view of the ruins is from a distance. The six, still-erect, columns emerge from among orchards and poplar trees beneath a sky that is blue for most of the year, with mountain peaks crowned with snow in the background. I tell my friends to stand beneath the gigantic columns and fix their eyes on them for 30 seconds; they will be transfixed as their minds relive the glory of the past.

To the south of the Temple of Jupiter is a smaller one dedicated to Bacchus. It is the finest and best-preserved temple in the Middle East. About 600 feet to the south of this is the much smaller temple of Venus. The worship of Venus ranked high among the pagan inhabitants of Baalbek until the reign of Constantine the Great, who closed the Roman temples in the 4th century AD.

Baalbek's name comes from two Phoenician words: *Baal* which means sun, and *bek* which means town. An Arab legend says that Cain built Baalbek as a place of refuge after God had cursed him. According to another legend, King Solomon in 1,000 BC built the temple as a gift to Balkis, the Queen of Sheba.

Our visit to the temples was followed by lunch at a nearby rustic restaurant. I had a *mezzé* which included *lahm bi-ajeen*, and *balila*, a salad of cooked chick peas tossed in a garlicky sauce of lemon and olive oil sprinkled with cumin. To eat *balila*, use pieces of bread to pick up the sauce and chick peas. As is the custom, I sipped arak, an anise drink that Lebanese have with their *mezzé*. Roasted chicken, the pride and speciality of the restaurant, french fries and oriental salad followed. After this delicious meal, I relaxed against a pile of cushions, sipping coffee in the hope of seeing a passing Bedouin who would read my fortune.

At the end of the meal I checked whether a sweet that Ibn Batuta (a famous Arab explorer) had described in the account of his travels as a speciality of Baalbek was still being made there. Ibn Batuta writes: 'A kind of molasses is made out of grape juice, which is put in special jars and left until it becomes so thick that when a jar is broken, the molasses comes out in one piece'. Today, a sweet called Malban made with molasses, either with almonds or pistachios, is found in Lebanon, Aleppo and Damascus.

On the way back we saw street vendors selling fruit and vegetables. Most of them were from Damascus, which is less than half an hour away from Syria. On the way back to Beirut we passed through the famous town of Shtoura, renowned for its dairy products.

Beit el-Deen

For me, driving into the rugged Shouf mountains was going home. My father's birthplace is there, and it was in one or other of the cafés here that we usually had Sunday lunch. The whole family used to leave our Beirut home early in the morning in two cars – there were many of us – and visit my uncle in the village of Mokhtara. We would head for *ain Mershed*, a rustic restaurant where I have spent memorable hours in its huge, beautiful garden. *Shish kebab*, or grilled lamb meat, was prepared in front of us over a wood fire and the smell wafted through the air while we would run all over the grounds of this lovely wooded café.

Before sundown, we would return to Beirut, passing orchards and the occasional house. There was a mountain that seemed uninhabited until we heard the trotting of a donkey mounted by a Druze sheikh. The magical and mystical atmosphere of the place will stay with me as long as I live.

My planned trips through Lebanon included a visit to the palace of Beit el-Deen in the Shouf mountains. This was built by Emir Beshir II in the early 19th century, when the ruler of Mount Lebanon decided to move his seat from the town of Deir Al-Kamar (Convent of the Moon) 5 kilometres (3 miles) away.

The palace has beautiful terraced gardens and a large courtyard where today a summer festival takes place. There are quarters which, in the past, opened for travellers to rest and sleep, a section for the Emir's workers, a harem with sumptuous bathrooms and stables which today display Byzantine mosaics.

The 19th-century French poet and statesman, Alphonse de Lamartine, wrote about his visit to the palace of Beit el-Deen in 1832 in his *Voyages en Orient*. He reported that he had spent the night in the magnificent palace in rooms that were very poorly furnished. Slaves brought in rush mats, which they spread on the floor then covered with carpets from Damascus. Then they had brought a low table, inlaid with mother of pearl, on which a tray was placed. The meals served to Lamartine were very simple. He had courgettes with yogurt (*Koussa bi-laban*), and courgettes stuffed with a mixture of rice and minced meat.

Rice is an ingredient that has become a staple all over the Levant ever since the Arab conquerors encountered rice in Iraq in the 7th century, when Persian soldiers fleeing before them left behind a basket containing grains of rice. The Arab soldiers looked at the basket with suspicion, in case the rice had been poisoned by the Persians and left intentionally to kill them. They were reassured only when one of their horses started eating rice from the basket with no harm to its health.

My visit to Beit el-Deen ended at a nearby palace, Kasr Emir Ameen, which is now a hotel. With my sisters Rafat and Samira, absorbed by the serene beauty that surrounded us, we sipped our coffee, reminiscing about the past.

Lebanon

Starters

Ejjet al shommar

DILL FRITTERS

This is a century-old recipe for delicious fritters flavoured with dill. Few people remember the recipe today in Lebanon – perhaps only a few of the older generation, and certainly not the Beirutis. My grandmother always prepared it. It is tasty and economical, and makes an excellent and unusual snack for friends. It can also be served as a starter with an Oriental salad (p. 35). This is an unusual dish because, unlike Turkish cuisine, Lebanese dishes rarely use dill.

Ingredients
85g (3oz) 1 bunch fresh dill, finely chopped
100g (3½ oz) onion, finely chopped
1¼ teaspoon salt
¼ teaspoon black pepper
1–2 eggs
85g (3oz) flour
200ml (7fl oz) water
extra virgin olive oil

In a bowl combine the dill, onion, salt and pepper. Add the eggs and beat well. Put the flour in another bowl and gradually add the water, whisking constantly until smooth. Pour slowly over the dill and egg mixture, stirring until blended.

In a large pan, heat enough oil to cover the bottom of the pan. When hot, take a tablespoon of the mixture and drop in the oil. Cook 4–5 fritters at a time. Let the underneath set for a minute then turn over with a small spatula. Cook till the other side is done. Remove and drain over kitchen paper. Repeat with remaining mixture.

Serve as a starter with a mixed salad or with cocktails.

Houmous

CHICK PEA DIP

This dish is rich in B vitamins and minerals. It is extremely popular in the Middle East and known all over the world. It is simple to make and freezes well when made without the garlic. The chick peas are combined with the white variety of tahini, a creamy paste of sesame seeds and oil that is sold in health shops and supermarkets. Another way to serve houmous is to stir in a handful of finely chopped parsley, then sprinkle with cayenne and drizzle with olive oil. Or you can serve it with lamb. Sauté 4 tablespoons of pine nuts in olive oil. As they turn pale golden, add 225g (8oz) minced lamb, brown until thoroughly cooked, then season with ¼–½ teaspoon of cinnamon, a pinch of allspice and black pepper, and a little salt. Remove and spread over the houmous. This makes a perfect starter or even a main dish. Follow with the refreshing dessert of Aleppo, *Khoshaf al-rumman* (see page 141) or a chilled *Firin sütlac* (page 275).

Ingredients
200g (7oz) dried chick peas, soaked overnight
1.5–1.75 litres (2½–3 pints) water
100ml (4fl oz) white tahini
2 garlic cloves
75–100ml (3–4fl oz) lemon juice
1½ teaspoons salt, or to taste
75–100ml (3–4fl oz) cooking liquid (from chick peas)

To garnish
½ teaspoon cayenne pepper (optional)
2 tablespoons extra virgin olive oil

Drain and rinse the beans and place in a large pan with the cold water. Bring to the boil, skim, then reduce the heat to low, cover and simmer for about 2–3 hours or until the chick peas are very soft, reserving some of the cooking liquid and keeping about 2 tablespoons of whole chick peas to garnish.

Place the beans, tahini, garlic, lemon juice, salt and some of the cooking liquid in a food processor. Purée until smooth, adding more of the reserved cooking liquid if necessary. Taste and adjust the seasoning. Serve on a plate garnished with the reserved chick peas, sprinkled with cayenne pepper, if using, and a drizzle of extra virgin olive oil.

Serve with wholemeal bread and cos lettuce.

Tabbouleh

CRACKED WHEAT SALAD

An exotic and mouth-watering salad which is vibrant in colour and provides a wealth of antioxidants (A, C, E). Parsley, one of its main ingredients, was used by the Greeks for medicinal purposes and it is mentioned by Homer in *The Odyssey*. For the mountain people of Lebanon, tabbouleh has long been a source of energy. In cosmopolitan Beirut, however, the dish has become more sophisticated and the ladies use less burghol and more parsley so as not to gain weight. Today, tabbouleh is eaten all over the world. For those who are sensitive to wheat, quinoa or millet are excellent substitutes. Cook according to the instructions in the packet, allow to cool, then follow the recipe as below.

The Lebanese prepare *tabbouleh* for any occasion, but it has long been a favourite for Sunday picnic lunch.

Ingredients
2 bunches of parsley (225g / 8oz)
2 large handfuls of mint leaves
100g (3½oz) fine burghol
450g (1lb) ripe tomatoes, finely chopped
1 small size onion, finely chopped
1 teaspoon salt, or to taste
¼ teaspoon black pepper
pinch of cinnamon (optional)
4 tablespoons lemon juice
4–5 tablespoons extra virgin olive oil

Gather the sprigs of parsley into small bundles so that the leaves are packed together at the same level. Place each bundle on your chopping surface, grip the upper part of the parsley firmly with one hand and use the other to cut off the stalks with a sharp knife. You can keep the stalks to flavour stock. Chop the rest of the parsley and place in a mixing bowl. Chop the mint and add to the parsley.

Rinse the burghol, leave for a few minutes in the sieve then add to the parsley and mint. Add the tomatoes. Sprinkle the onion with the salt, black pepper and cinnamon (if using) and rub with your fingers (the salt and pepper reduce the sharpness of the onion). Add this with the lemon juice and oil to the other ingredients. Toss, taste and adjust the seasonings. If the *tabbouleh* is not moist enough, mix in about 1½ tablespoons of cold water.

Serve immediately with leaves of cos lettuce, raw cabbage or, if available, tender vine leaves.

Fattouche

BREAD SALAD

Fattouche is a substantial salad and as popular as tabbouleh. It contains purslane, a pale green herb with a unique mild, peppery flavour. It is said to be very rich in Omega 3s (usually found in oily fish). The other ingredients also provide a wealth of nutrients and antioxidants.

Although it takes a little time to prepare *fattouche* is easy to make. I have added some rocket leaves and a few cauliflower florets cut into tiny pieces the size of chick peas; this is not authentic but it does give the salad a deeper flavour, especially when purslane is out of season. Purslane can be found at all Lebanese and Greek grocers. Fresh Lebanese thyme is a wonderful addition, when available. In northern Lebanon, a little pomegranate syrup lifts the flavour.

The various components of *fattouche* can be prepared in advance, but do not combine them until just before serving.

Ingredients
1 garlic clove
1¼ teaspoons salt, or to taste
4–5 tablespoons lemon juice
6–7 tablespoons extra virgin olive oil
1 tablespoon **sumac**
285g (10oz) ripe tomatoes cut into 1cm (½in) cubes
6 large spring onions, finely sliced or
1 large onion, finely sliced
6 radishes, finely sliced
1 green pepper, seeded, coarsely chopped
1 baby cucumber, rinsed, cut lengthways and sliced
1 large handful of rocket leaves (about 45g / 1½oz) chopped
¼ teaspoon freshly milled black pepper
85g (3oz) parsley, stalks removed, leaves left whole or coarsely chopped
1 bunch purslane, stalks removed
1 large handful mint leaves, chopped
½ head cos lettuce (6 leaves) sliced into 1cm (½in) ribbons
1½ medium pitta breads, toasted until crisp and torn up into small pieces
2 cauliflower florets, cut into tiny pieces (optional)

In a large salad bowl, crush the garlic with ¼ teaspoon of salt, until smooth and creamy. Add the lemon juice and 1 tablespoon of oil. Add the *sumac* and the tomatoes, and sprinkle with the remaining salt to bring out their full flavour. Add the spring onions or onions, radishes, green pepper, cucumber, rocket leaves and season with the black pepper. Add the parsley, purslane, mint and lettuce. Set aside.

In a separate small bowl, toss the toasted bread in the remaining oil, coating it on all sides – this will keep it crunchy for longer. Add to the reserved salad mixture along with the cauliflower florets, if using, and toss well with the other ingredients. Taste, adjust the seasonings and add more oil, if necessary.

Serve immediately as a starter or as an accompaniment to other dishes.

Batata bil-fitr

POTATOES WITH MUSHROOMS

This is a simple mountain dish from Kura in northern Lebanon. In season, the mushrooms are picked freshly from the fields, then prepared in a multitude of ways by the village housewives, who exchange recipes among themselves and take pride in the success of a dish. Rinse, but do not soak, the mushrooms. They are excellent for health, low in fat, high in phosphorus and rich in B vitamins.

This dish is suitable for vegetarians. It can be served as a starter or as a main course for the family. Serve in a buffet with other vegetarian dishes such as *Fattouche* (see page 18), Olive salad (page 105) and *Muhammara* (page 95). End the meal with the delicious dessert, *Mafroukeh* (page 78).

Ingredients
175ml (6fl oz) extra virgin olive oil
5 medium potatoes (about 1kg / 2¼lb) scrubbed and cut into 5mm (¼in) pieces
1 medium size onion, finely chopped
4 garlic cloves, crushed
550g (1¼lb) mushrooms, finely sliced
1 bunch of coriander, chopped, with stalks removed
1½ teaspoons salt, or to taste
½ teaspoon cinnamon
¼ teaspoon allspice
pinch of black pepper
juice of half a lemon (about 50ml / 2fl oz)

Put the oil in a large, deep frying pan. When the oil is hot but not smoking, add half the potatoes and fry over medium heat. Cook the potatoes, turning them from time to time until they reach a deep golden colour. Remove with a slotted spoon and place on a dish. Add the second batch of potatoes, repeat as before, remove and set aside.

Add the onions to the remaining oil in the pan and sauté for 3 minutes or until translucent. Add the garlic, stir for a few seconds, then add the mushrooms, stirring occasionally. The high water content in the mushrooms will produce some liquid. Allow the mushrooms to simmer in their juice over a medium to low heat until the water evaporates. Stir in the coriander then the fried potatoes. Sprinkle with salt, cinnamon, allspice and black pepper and stir once more. Turn the heat off, stir in the lemon juice and serve hot or cold.

Koussa bi-zeit

COURGETTES IN OIL

Lebanese courgettes are nearly seedless, have a light green colour and a lovely delicate flavour. However, any variety can be used in this recipe. In Lebanon, courgettes are sometimes simply boiled (preferably steamed) and then tossed in olive oil, lemon juice and a hint of garlic. This particular way of preparing them was a favourite of my mother. She never ate meat, although she cooked the most delicious meat dishes, she never tasted them. This dish makes a good starter eaten with wholemeal bread, radishes and green olives.

Ingredients
3–4 tablespoons extra virgin olive oil
350g (12oz) onions, finely sliced
7 large cloves of garlic, finely sliced
20g (¾oz) fresh mint leaves, chopped
1½ teaspoons dried ground mint
450g (1lb) courgettes top and tail trimmed, diced in equal small shape
1¼ teaspoons salt, or to taste
¼ teaspoon black pepper
2–3 tablespoons lemon juice

Heat the oil in a medium size pan. Add the onions, sauté over medium heat for 3 minutes. Add the garlic, sauté for 2–3 minutes more *or* until onions and garlic are golden in colour, stirring occasionally. Stir in the fresh and dried mint and add the courgettes, salt and pepper. Reduce the heat to medium-low, cover and simmer for 15 minutes. About a minute before the end of cooking add the lemon juice. Turn the heat off and keep the pan covered for 15–20 minutes. Serve warm or at room temperature.

Houmous bi-shommar

CHICK PEAS WITH DILL

Lebanon is renowned for its wealth of vegetarian dishes. In this dish, the secret lies in the balance of fresh herbs, chick peas and in the freshness of the produce. This dish couldn't be simpler to prepare and has a wonderful combination of flavours. It also makes a great addition to a vegetarian buffet. Chick peas are excellent for health. They contain a substance that mimics the function of the hormones that decrease during the menopause. Dill aids the digestion, relieves gas and induces more milk in nursing mothers.

Serves 5–6 as a starter.

Ingredients
4 tablespoons extra virgin olive oil
400g (14oz) onions, finely sliced
1½ teaspoons salt, or to taste
280g (10oz) chick peas, soaked overnight, drained and pre-cooked
20g (¾oz) fresh dill leaves, finely chopped

Place the oil in a frying pan over medium heat. Add the onions then sprinkle with salt. Sauté for 5 minutes or until onions are translucent and pale in colour. Cover the pan but check the onions every 1–2 minutes to make sure they do not overcook, stirring if necessary. Stir in the chick peas, sauté for a few minutes, stirring occasionally. Then add the dill, reduce the heat and cook for a further 10 minutes.

Serve hot, and eat on its own or with yogurt.

Baba-ghanouj

AUBERGINE DIP

A Lebanese classic, this dip is served as part of the *mezzé*. Aubergines can be grilled, charred over an open fire (an excellent way to keep the white colour of the aubergine pulp) or even steamed. However it is cooked, it will always retain its distinctive taste. This dish is extremely simple to prepare, and has a good combination of texture and flavour.

Tahini, a sesame paste, is stirred into the puréed aubergine flesh along with lemon juice, which enhances its flavour. As tahini is high in calories, you may like to follow the Turkish way by substituting yogurt for the tahini.

Ingredients
675g (1½lb) aubergines
1 garlic clove (optional)
¾ teaspoon salt, or to taste
3–4 tablespoons lemon juice
2½ tablespoons white tahini

To garnish
1 tablespoon parsley leaves, chopped
¼ teaspoon cayenne pepper (optional)
1–2 tablespoons extra virgin olive oil (optional)

Slit the skin of each aubergine once or twice. Put them on a baking sheet and place under a preheated grill 10cm (4in) away from the heat. Grill for 20 minutes, or until the skin is blackened and blistered and the pulp is soft, turning them once. Remove from the oven.

Meanwhile, mash the garlic (if used) with the salt in a glass bowl. When the aubergines have cooled slightly, scrape the pulp from the skin. Place the pulp and lemon juice in a blender. Puré for a few seconds (or use a vegetable mill). Remove from the blender, add to the garlic (if used) then stir in the tahini to blend. Taste and adjust the seasonings.

Garnish with parsley and sprinkle with cayenne pepper, if using. Pour olive oil all over, if using. Serve and eat with wholemeal bread or cos lettuce leaves.

A nice finishing touch is to decorate the surface of the aubergine dip evenly with the seeds of sour or semi-sour pomegranates when these are in season.

Kibbeh batata al-jabal

MOUNTAIN POTATO KIBBEH

This simple vegetarian mountain dish is one of many prepared by Lebanese Christians during Lent and is quickly assembled. Burghol is an essential ingredient in Lebanese cuisine that can be prepared in a multitude of ways. Spring onion and mint are picked from the garden and potatoes are bought cheaply. These basic ingredients produce a delicious, economical and satisfying dish. It serves 6 as a starter. Eat with bread and a tomato salad sprinkled with finely chopped onions and chopped walnuts, and tossed with lemon juice and olive oil.

Ingredients
675g (1½lb) potatoes
100g (3½oz) onion
2 tablespoons water
1¾ teaspoons salt, or to taste
75g (2½oz) fine burghol (preferably white)
¼ teaspoon black pepper

To garnish
2 spring onions, finely sliced
handful of mint leaves, chopped
¼ teaspoon cayenne pepper, or to taste
extra virgin olive oil

Cook the potatoes in a pan of boiling, salted water until soft. Drain then leave to cool. Peel and mash the potatoes or pass through a vegetable mill. Put to one side. Place the onion, water and salt in a blender. Blend until the onion forms a creamy paste. Alternatively, grate the onion and rub into the burghol. Add to the potatoes, sprinkle with black pepper, knead to a smooth consistency, then spread into a serving dish. Garnish with spring onion and mint. Sprinkle with cayenne pepper and generously drizzle oil all over. Serve to eat with bread.

Makmour al-malfouf

CABBAGE WITH CHICK PEAS

This ancient mountain recipe is made with one of the oldest vegetables in the world. The Romans regarded the cabbage as a medicine and a neutralizer of alcohol and today's nutritionists approve of its therapeutic powers. This recipe makes use of the outer leaves that you might otherwise want to throw away. Whenever possible, I buy organic cabbage to help farmers produce more in the hope that prices will become cheaper.

Makmour al-malfouf can be served as part of a *mezzé* along with *Tabbouleh* (page 17) and *Mortadella* (page 106). It makes an informal meal to have with friends.

Serves 5 as a starter.

Ingredients
4 tablespoons extra virgin olive oil
450g (1lb) onions, finely sliced
115g (4oz) chick peas, soaked overnight, drained and pre-cooked
8–10 cabbage leaves, coarsely chopped
1¼ teaspoons salt, or to taste
150ml (¼ pint) hot water
5 garlic cloves, finely crushed
1½ teaspoons dried mint
50–75ml (2–3fl oz) lemon juice

Heat the oil in a shallow pan and when it is hot add the onions. Stir for a minute over medium-high heat, then reduce to medium and cook for 4 minutes or until a pale golden colour. Add the chick peas and sauté for 3 minutes, stirring occasionally. Add the cabbage and cook for a further 5 minutes or until it reduces in size.

Sprinkle with salt, add the water and bring to the boil. Cover and simmer over low or medium-low heat for 10–15 minutes. In the meantime, mix the garlic, mint and lemon juice, and add this mixture to the cabbage a few minutes before the end of the cooking time. Turn the heat off and leave the pan covered until it reaches room temperature.

Spoon over 2 tablespoons of yogurt, which gives a lift to the flavour, before serving.

Mjadra bi-loubieh

KIDNEY BEANS WITH BURGHOL

Mjadra is the name of a famous Lebanese lentil dish eaten during Lent. However, *Mjadra bi-loubieh* is a mountain dish prepared in the north of Lebanon that has nothing to do with lentils. It uses a special bean similar to the kidney bean. Coarse burghol is added, producing a simple, homely dish that is economical, low in fat but rich in fibre and B vitamins. Here we use kidney beans instead. *Mjadra bi-loubieh* can be served for 5 as a starter or 4 as a main dish. Eat with an Oriental salad (page 35). If you wish to cut down on oil, when the beans have softened, add the onions, the burghol, salt and ½–1 tablespoon of olive oil and simmer as below.

Ingredients
285g (10oz) kidney beans, soaked overnight, rinsed and drained
2 litres (3½ pints) water
450g (1lb) onions, very finely chopped
4–5 tablespoons extra virgin olive oil
200g (7oz) coarse burghol
2 teaspoons salt, or to taste

Put the beans and water in a pan. Bring to the boil, skim and cook over medium-high heat for 10 minutes. Reduce the heat to medium-low and leave for about 1¼ hours or until the beans are soft.

In the meantime, fry the onion with oil until golden brown. Stir into the cooked beans. Add the burghol and salt, reduce the heat to medium-low, cover and leave to simmer for a further 20 minutes or until the liquid has evaporated but the consistency of the dish is still quite moist. Season with the salt.

Serve hot with radishes, olives and spring onions.

Kasbet djaj bi-sumac

CHICKEN LIVERS WITH SUMAC

In this dish, the sourness of the sumac and pomegranate syrup makes an extraordinary combination, giving a boost to the dryness of the liver. This dish is simple to make for any occasion, whether you are on your own, or with friends or family. It makes an ideal starter, served with *Baba-ghanouj* (page 23), *Kibbeh al-hammam* (page 96), and finish with the refreshing *Mouhallabieh* (page 82).

Ingredients
450g (1lb) organic chicken livers
pinch of black pepper
pinch of cinnamon
pinch of allspice
3–4 tablespoons extra virgin olive oil
350g (12oz) onion, finely sliced
1½–2 tablespoons sumac, mixed with 6 tablespoons hot water
1 tablespoon sour pomegranate syrup
1–2 tablespoons lemon juice
1¼ teaspoons salt, or to taste
handful of parsley, chopped

Clean and discard the fat and greenish parts, if any, from the liver. Cut in small pieces of about 3mm (¼in). Sprinkle with pepper, cinnamon, and allspice. Set to one side.

Heat the oil in a heavy frying pan but do not allow it to smoke. Add the onions and sauté over medium-low heat, stirring occasionally until translucent and pale in colour. Add the liver and sauté for 2 minutes, then turn over and continue cooking until the liver looses its blood colour. Mix the sumac and water with the pomegranate syrup and lemon juice. Stir this into the liver and onions in the pan and sprinkle with salt. Cover and simmer over very low heat for a further 8–10 minutes. Sprinkle with parsley, stir gently, turn the heat off and serve hot with wholemeal pitta bread.

Koussa bi-banadoura

COURGETTES WITH TOMATOES

Courgettes have been cultivated in the Lebanon for hundreds of years and are prepared in a myriad ways. They go well with most things – seasonal vegetables or the contents of your kitchen, such as dried mint and tomato purée. Authentically, the courgettes are sautéed in oil beforehand, but it is omitted here. This is a particularly unpretentious, healthy and tasty dish.

Courgettes with tomatoes, served with pitta bread and green olives, makes an unusual starter. Follow with the Damascene *Ouzi* (page 173) and the Turkish *Kaymakli kuru kayisi* (page 272).

Ingredients
3 tablespoons extra virgin olive oil
300g (10½oz) onion thinly sliced
450g (1lb) tomatoes, peeled and finely chopped
1 heaped teaspoon tomato purée
1 teaspoon flour
2 teaspoons dried ground mint
1¼ teaspoons salt, or to taste
¼ teaspoon black pepper
½ teaspoon allspice
750g (1lb 10oz) courgettes, topped and tailed, and finely sliced widthways
1 red mild chilli, halved and deseeded
150ml (5fl oz) hot water

Heat the oil in a medium size pan and when it is hot add the onions and sauté for 5 minutes or until golden brown. Add the tomatoes, tomato purée, flour, mint, salt, black pepper and allspice. Stir for a few seconds, add the courgettes and chilli and stir occasionally for 2 minutes. Then add the water.

Bring back to the boil, cover and simmer over medium-low heat for 30 minutes. Turn the heat off and leave the pan covered for at least 10 minutes.

Serve warm or at room temperature.

Kibbeh kataa

VEGETARIAN *KIBBEH* WITH CHICK PEAS

Chick peas, besides being the basic ingredient for making *Houmous* (page 16), are also used in many other mountain dishes, adding flavour, bulk and nutrients. The women take great pleasure in preparing these splendid dishes. For them, the most important thing is to supply a delectable meal that pleases their husbands after a long working day. There is an old Arab saying: *Al rijal janna wal-mara banna* (the man provides and the woman builds). What would modern women think of that? Yet in the Levant, this is still the custom, especially in the villages, where a woman may spend a whole day preparing food.

Vegetarian kibbeh is easy to make and is a good starter for 5, served with Oriental salad (page 35). Follow with Chicken and olives (page 68) as a main course.

Ingredients
75ml (3fl oz) extra virgin olive oil
140g (5oz) chick peas, soaked for 18 hours, drained
85g (3oz) fine burghol
2 large spring onions
85g (3oz) onion, halved
45g (1½oz) parsley leaves
30g (1oz) mint leaves
40g (1¼oz) plain flour
zest of 1 orange
1 large red mild chilli, deseeded
1¼ teaspoons salt
1 teaspoon cumin
½ teaspoon allspice
¼ teaspoon black pepper
¼ teaspoon cayenne pepper

Using 1 tablespoon oil, oil the base of a 26cm (10½in) round baking pan. Set aside.

Place the rest of the ingredients in a food processor. Blend for 2 minutes or until you have a smooth, soft dough, then remove. (If you don't have a food processor, grind the chick peas or pass through a vegetable mill, then mix with other finely chopped ingredients).

With moist hands flatten a layer against the base of the oiled baking pan. Smooth the surface, moistening your hands again with water. Drizzle the rest of the oil all over and run a pointed knife around the edge of the baking dish. Then cut through into medium-size squares or lozenges.

Bake in a preheated oven at 180°C (350°F/gas mark 4) for 35 minutes or until the top is nicely browned. Remove and place the squares in a serving dish.

Serve warm or at room temperature. Eat with Tahini sauce (see page 39 or 70) or for a delicious alternative, Aubergine dip (page 23).

Taridet batinjan

AUBERGINES WITH AROMATIC SPICES

This is a delectable old recipe that has been forgotten by the younger Lebanese generation. It is worth trying since it is so simple to prepare and it really is delicious. Authentically the aubergines are poached, but once I grilled them by mistake and the resulting smoky flavour was such a success that I left it as it was.

This recipe makes an unusual starter. It can also accompany other *mezzé* dishes such as Olive salad (page 105) and Red pepper salad (page 107).

Ingredients
530g (1lb 4oz) aubergines
2 teaspoons sumac
½ tablespoon boiling water
1 garlic clove, finely crushed
1 teaspoon dried mint
1 teaspoon salt, or to taste
½ tablespoon lemon juice
1 medium pitta bread split in two

To garnish
1½ tablespoons finely chopped parsley leaves
large handful of coarsely chopped walnuts
½ teaspoon cayenne pepper
extra virgin olive oil
1 medium size Lebanese bread

Slit the aubergines in several places. Put them on a baking sheet and place under a preheated grill. Cook for 20 minutes, turning once, until the skin is blackened and blistered, and the pulp is soft. Alternatively, place on a grid over a gas flame.

Meanwhile, thoroughly mix the sumac and water, then place in a bowl with the garlic, mint, salt and lemon juice. Remove the aubergines from grill and leave to cool. Scrape the pulp from the skin and add to the ingredients in the bowl, using a fork to mix and mash it into a medium-smooth consistency.

Split the bread and place the pieces next to each other on a flat serving dish, then spread with the aubergine mixture. Garnish with parsley, walnuts and cayenne pepper. Drizzle with oil, slice and serve.

Fattet batinjan

AUBERGINES FATTEH

This dish is an unusual one that looks impressive on a table. The combination of aubergines and pomegranate syrup are heavenly, while the yogurt, tomatoes, peppers, parsley, cucumber and bread intensify the flavours.

This quantity makes an excellent starter for 4 or 5 people. Double the portion and it will be the star of your buffet, your friends will call you the following day to demand the recipe. Prepare ahead of time and assemble before serving.

Ingredients
900g (2lb) aubergines
extra virgin olive oil (as required)
1–1½ medium size pitta breads, cut in small squares
1–2 tablespoons sour pomegranate syrup
1 teaspoon salt
4 tablespoons chopped parsley leaves
2 halves finely diced red and green peppers
1 medium size tomato, peeled and finely chopped
450ml (15fl oz) yogurt
1 small garlic clove, finely chopped (optional)
1 small cos lettuce leaf thinly sliced (optional)
1 tablespoon finely diced cucumber

Slice the aubergines, sprinkle with salt and leave to sweat for one hour. Heat 50ml (2fl oz) oil in a heavy frying pan until hot but not smoking, then add the bread, preferably in two batches. Fry each batch, stirring frequently until the bread turns golden brown in colour. Remove with a slotted spoon and drain over kitchen paper. Add more oil to the same frying pan for the aubergines. When the oil is really hot, rinse and dry the aubergines, then fry, stirring constantly until they are nicely browned. Remove and leave to drain over triple kitchen paper, changing it frequently. (Alternatively, cube the slices of aubergine, mix with 4 tablespoons of olive oil and roast in a preheated oven at 180°C (350°F/gas mark 4) for an hour and ten minutes, or until completely browned.)

When the aubergines reach room temperature, place in a bowl and mix with the pomegranate syrup, ½ teaspoon of salt and parsley. Spread over a deep serving dish, cover with the peppers, tomatoes and bread. In another bowl, combine the yogurt with the garlic, if using, and the remaining ½ teaspoon of salt, lettuce, if using, and cucumber.

Pour the yogurt over the aubergine mixture in the pan or serve separately.

Kibbeh batata

POTATO KIBBEH

This delicious vegetarian dish is a regional speciality of the northern Lebanon (Tripoli), which is famed for the succulence of its dishes. It is economical and full of healthy ingredients, with the added bonus that it can be prepared in advance. It makes a perfect addition to a buffet since it can be eaten at room temperature, or a good starter for 8 with tomato salad. Serve as a hot main dish with *Lahm bi-ajeen* (see page 162).

For the stuffing
75ml (3fl oz) extra virgin olive oil
85g (3oz) pine nuts
450g (1lb) onions, finely sliced
¼ teaspoon salt

For the potato dough
285g (10oz) fine burghol rinsed, drained and squeezed of excess water
100g (3½oz) onion
115g (4oz) bunch of coriander
1¼ teaspoons salt
1 teaspoon ground coriander
1 tablespoon flour
4–5 medium size potatoes (about 750g / 1lb 10oz), boiled until soft
75ml (3fl oz) extra virgin olive oil

Heat the oil in a pan but do not allow to smoke. Add the pine nuts, stir continuously until golden brown, remove with a slotted spoon and spread over a rectangular pan 26 x 20cm (10½ x 8in). Add half the onions to the oil in the frying pan and sauté, over a high heat, stirring occasionally, for 2–3 minutes, then lower the heat to medium and cook until golden. Using a slotted spoon, remove the onions and mix with the pine nuts. Add the remaining onions to the pan and repeat as before. Place these and the cooking oil over the pine nuts and onions. Sprinkle all over with salt.

Place the burghol in a large bowl. In a blender, blend the onion and the fresh coriander until creamy (or grate the onions and chop the coriander very finely). Place over the burghol in the bowl, then sprinkle with salt, ground coriander and flour. Rub well into the burghol. Peel the potatoes and press through a sieve, or mash to a soft, smooth texture. Add to the burghol in the bowl, knead thoroughly to blend and form a dough. Leave for 5 minutes.

Flatten the dough to a medium-thin layer, to cover the onions and pine nuts in the baking pan. Moisten the hands with cold water and gently smooth the surface. Drizzle the oil all over and quickly run a thin, pointed knife around the edge of the potato *kibbeh* to loosen it. Then cut a criss-cross pattern down to the onions, allowing the oil to seep through.

Heat the oven to 180°C (350°F/gas mark 4). Bake the potato *kibbeh* for 40 minutes or until the top is nicely browned. Remove from the oven and allow to cool slightly for 15–20 minutes. Using a palate knife remove the pieces of *kibbeh*, following the criss-cross pattern. Place in a serving dish with the onions facing upwards.

Serve warm or cold, either on its own or with a salad.

Salsa harra

CHILLI AND HERB SAUCE

Salsa harra is one of numerous different chilli sauces that accompany the famous regional *Samakeh harra* (page 46) of Tripoli. This sauce uses a mixture of fresh spices that is well balanced without being excessive, to produce a very fine, pungent bite. I believe that the tomatoes play the equalizer in this recipe.

This tasty sauce makes a perfect vegetarian starter to be eaten with bread or crackers, or even cos lettuce or sweet peppers. It can also be ideal for cocktail parties, served on small toasted slices of French or wholemeal bread.

Ingredients
1–2 tablespoons extra virgin olive oil
4 large garlic cloves, finely chopped
1 teaspoon ground coriander
1 teaspoon ground cumin
¼ teaspoon ground cinnamon
¼ teaspoon ground allspice
75g (2½oz) fresh coriander, finely chopped
75g (2½oz) parsley, finely chopped
140g (5oz) walnuts, chopped medium fine
½ teaspoon cayenne pepper
75ml (3fl oz) lemon juice
750g (1lb 10oz) tomatoes, peeled and finely chopped

Heat the oil in a deep frying pan. Sauté the garlic for a few seconds, then add the rest of the ingredients. Cover and simmer over a medium or medium-low heat for 15 minutes or until the liquid has evaporated. Turn off the heat.

Serve warm or at room temperature. May be served with grilled aubergine slices.

Salata arabieh

ORIENTAL SALAD

This is one of my favourite salads because it played such a major part throughout my youth when the tomatoes were juicy, full of flavour and a deep red colour. We called them *baal*, which is similar to the Phoenician name of the God of Fertility. Oriental salad is so-called because of the locally available ingredients: mint, parsley, cucumber, white onions, garlic, lemon and olive oil. This is the classic combination but nowadays sweet peppers, spring onions and radishes may be added. Oriental salad can be one of several dishes as a starter, or it makes a perfect accompaniment to many main meat or chicken dishes.

Ingredients
1 garlic clove
1¼ teaspoons salt
2 tablespoons lemon juice
4 large red tomatoes, peeled
1 large white onion, or 4 large spring onions, coarsely sliced
handful of mint leaves
handful of parsley leaves
3 radishes, coarsely diced
1 baby cucumber, sliced
3 tablespoons extra virgin olive oil

Place the garlic in a salad bowl with ½ teaspoon salt, gently pound with a pestle until creamy and then stir in the lemon juice. Cut the tomatoes into 2.5cm (1in) pieces and add to the bowl. Sprinkle in the remaining salt to bring out the full flavour of the tomatoes. Add the onions, chop the mint or leave whole if the leaves are small, and add with the parsley, radishes, cucumber and olive oil. Gently toss and serve.

Shorba al-adas wal-khodar

LENTIL AND VEGETABLE SOUP

Lentil soup is so welcome in winter – it is satisfying, nutritious and inexpensive. It is said that the famous Arabic poet, Abi al-Alaa al Maari, whose poems were unrivalled, lived on lentils.

Lentil and vegetable soup is simple to prepare, using ingredients that can be found in your kitchen cupboard. Once you have prepared one of the soups in this book, you will be hooked because they are so delicious and appetizing. This soup will last in the fridge for up to 4 days; it also freezes well.

Ingredients
325g (11oz) brown lentils
1.7 litres (3 pints) water
1 medium potato (about 150g / 5½oz), roughly chopped
3 carrots (about 250g / 8½oz), roughly chopped
1 stem of parsley, with leaves
1 large onion (about 350g / 12oz), roughly chopped
2 teaspoons salt, or to taste
cumin to taste
lemon wedges

Place the lentils with the water in a pan. Bring to the boil, then add the potato, carrots, parsley and onion. Sprinkle with salt, reduce heat to medium-low, cover and simmer for 40 minutes or until the lentils are tender.

Place the lentil mixture in a food processor or pass through a vegetable mill. If using a food processor, blend until it reaches a creamy texture. Return the soup to the same pan and bring to the boil. Simmer for 1 minute and sprinkle with cumin.

Serve hot with toasted bread and lemon wedges to squeeze on the soup. This will enhance its flavour.

Lebanon

Main

courses

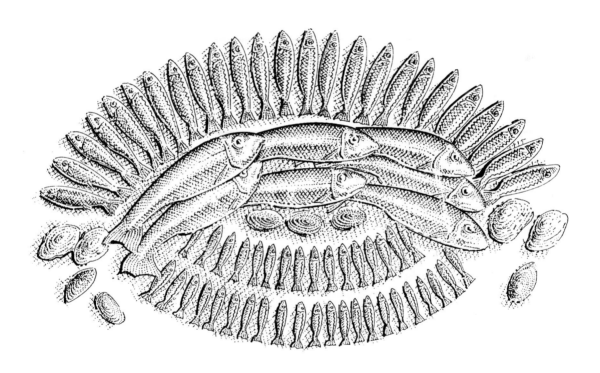

Kibbeh massalik

VEGETARIAN KIBBEH WITH SWISS CHARD

This is a dish that travelled by word of mouth from Lattakia in Syria to my parents' home in Beirut. The various components of this recipe offer a tasty, nutritious and well-balanced vegetarian meal. The robust flavours of coriander, walnuts and Swiss chard mix deliciously with the creamy tahini sauce. The recipe may appear long and elaborate, but it is actually simple to follow.

The chilli, coriander and pine nuts are my addition. I found that the pine nuts go particularly well with this mixture; they also increase the protein content. I hope this recipe will arouse your curiosity, as it did mine, and tempt you to try it. It is an ideal meal for the cold winter months, providing warmth and energy.

It makes 18–20 *kibbeh* and serves 5–6.

For the filling
bunch of Swiss chard (about 5 or 6 leaves, ribs cut off and leaves finely chopped)
1¼ teaspoons salt, or to taste
2 tablespoons extra virgin olive oil
1 onion (100g / 3½oz), finely chopped
85g (3oz) walnuts, medium to finely chopped
1 tablespoon sumac
½ teaspoon cinnamon
a pinch of allspice
¼ teaspoon black pepper
70ml (2½fl oz) lemon juice

For the kibbeh *shells*
140g (5oz) fine burghol
140g (5oz) flour
1¾ teaspoons salt
600ml (1 pint) water, or as necessary
200ml (7fl oz) organic cider vinegar

For the tahini sauce
250ml (8fl oz) white tahini
125ml (6fl oz) lemon juice
125ml (6fl oz) water
1 teaspoon salt

To garnish
½ tablespoon extra virgin olive oil
30g (1oz) pine nuts
1 fresh red chilli pepper, seeded and finely chopped (optional)
a generous handful of coriander, roots cut off, chopped (optional)
55g (2oz) walnuts, finely ground

To prepare the filling, sprinkle the Swiss chard leaves with half the salt and rub with the fingers until reduced in size. Squeeze to extract excess water.

Place a frying pan over medium-high heat and add the oil. When the oil is hot but not smoking, add the onions. Sauté until translucent and yellowish in colour. Add the Swiss chard to the onions in the pan, then add the walnuts and sumac. Season with cinnamon, allspice, black pepper and the remaining salt. Stir thoroughly. Stir in the lemon juice. Remove from heat and set aside.

To prepare the *kibbeh* dough, rinse the burghol and squeeze out any excess water. In a mixing bowl combine the burghol with the flour and 1 teaspoon salt. Gradually add 100ml (4fl oz) of the water and knead to form a dough. Cover with a clean cloth and leave for 30 minutes. Put the remaining water, salt and vinegar in a medium-size pan.

Meanwhile, prepare the tahini sauce. Place the tahini in a medium-size bowl and add the lemon juice a little at a time, whisking continuously to prevent any lumps forming. Slowly add the water and salt. Keep whisking until the mixture reaches the consistency of single cream. Set aside. When Seville oranges are in season, use their juice in conjunction with the lemon as this gives a wonderful flavour. (If you wish, slice the ribs of the Swiss chard, boil until tender and add these to the tahini sauce.)

To prepare the *kibbeh* shells, take a small portion at a time of the *kibbeh* dough and, working with moist hands, roll it between the palms to form a short cigar shape. Hold firmly in the left hand and with the right index finger, poke a hole in the centre of the dough. Work the inside to form a thinnish shell.

Place 1 teaspoon of the Swiss chard filling in each *kibbeh* shell. Reshape into an oval shape to enclose and seal the filling. If this proves difficult, roll into a round ball. Place on a dish. If any filling remains, set aside.

Bring the pan of water and vinegar to the boil and gently drop in the stuffed *kibbeh* balls. Simmer over medium heat for 5 minutes. Remove with a slotted spoon.

To make the garnish, heat the oil in a pan, sauté the pine nuts until golden brown, then remove with a slotted spoon and set aside. Add the chilli and coriander, if using, to the same oil in the pan and sauté for a few seconds. Add the tahini sauce, the walnuts and any remaining filling. Pour this over the hot *kibbeh* shells and allow them to fully absorb the sauce.

Serve sprinkled with pine nuts. Eat warm or – better still – cold.

Foulieh

BROAD BEAN STEW WITH YOGURT

This delicious Lebanese dish uses coriander, a herb used in Lebanon and Syria but not in Turkey. Vedat Basaran, a top chef who is highly knowledgeable about the palace cuisine of the Ottomans, told me that dried coriander was once used but most probably the Sultan didn't like it and since then it has vanished from Turkish cuisine.

This dish uses broad beans with their shells. In southern Lebanon, specifically Saida, this dish is called *Fostokia* (Arabic for pistachio). This is because after peeling, the inner bean is the colour of a pistachio nut.

For the stew
350g (12oz) diced lamb
100g (3½oz) onions, finely chopped
1½ tablespoons extra virgin olive oil
500g (1lb 2oz) broad beans, topped and tailed, string removed, quartered
1–2 garlic cloves
1½ teaspoons salt, or to taste
75g (2½oz) coriander, chopped
300ml (10fl oz) water

For the yogurt
450ml (15fl oz) yogurt
1 egg
1 teaspoon cornflour

Sauté the lamb and onion with oil over medium-high heat for 3–4 minutes, stirring occasionally. Add the beans, reduce the heat, cover and leave for 8 minutes to simmer in their juices. Crush the garlic with salt and add to the pan, along with the coriander. Add the water, bring to the boil, cover and simmer for 40 minutes or until the meat is soft.

In the meantime, thoroughly combine the yogurt with the egg and cornflour. Strain over a bowl. When the broad beans are cooked and the liquid has reduced to 250ml (8fl oz) or less, add the yogurt, stirring constantly in the same direction with a wooden spoon. Turn up the heat to medium and keep stirring until the yogurt starts to boil. Reduce the heat and leave to bubble uncovered for 2–3 minutes.

Serve hot with rice.

Nouille

CHICKEN AND TAGLIATELLI

A homely Lebanese dish inspired by Italian and French cuisines, this is often prepared with left-over chicken. It is a satisfying combination of pasta, chicken, béchamel sauce, grated cheese and sometimes ham, arranged in alternate layers. When cooked, there is a beautiful golden crust on the surface of the dish. *Nouille* is very tasty and can be prepared ahead of time. It lasts for up to 4 days in the fridge and freezes well. This dish is a perfect main course for 8 and is also delicious without the meat.

For the chicken
½ chicken, with the skin on
1.1 litres (2 pints) water
bouquet garni, consisting of celery stick, cinnamon stick, 1 stem of parsley, 2 bay
**   leaves, 2 cardamoms and 1 small onion studded with 2 cloves**
300g (10½oz) tagliatelli, pre-cooked
¼ teaspoon grated nutmeg
1 slice of ham, cut into bite sizes (optional)

For the sauce
30g (1oz) butter
8 tablespoons flour
1 litre (1¾ pints) milk
1 litre (1¾ pints) chicken stock
1¼ teaspoons salt, or to taste
85g (3oz) yellow cheese

Place the chicken in a pan with the water. Bring to the boil, skim, add bouquet garni, then cover and simmer over medium heat for 50–60 minutes or until chicken is tender. Arrange the tagliatelli evenly in a baking dish 28 x 20cm (11 x 8in) and sprinkle with the nutmeg. Transfer the cooked chicken to a side dish. Cut into bite-sized pieces and arrange over the tagliatelli, along with the ham, if using. Strain the chicken stock and measure the amount required for the sauce.

To prepare the sauce, place the butter in a medium-size pan. When it is hot, add the flour and cook for a minute but do not allow to burn. Gradually add the milk, whisking all the time. Now add the chicken stock, whisking until it boils. Reduce the heat to low and allow 2–3 minutes for it to thicken slightly. Remove from the heat and stir in the salt. Gradually pour over the tagliatelli, chicken and ham, if using, making sure that the sauce reaches the bottom of the dish.

Sprinkle with grated cheese and bake in a preheated oven at 180°C (350°F/gas mark 4) for 20–30 minutes or until the top is golden brown. If it is not sufficiently browned, place under a hot grill for a minute or two. Remove and allow to rest for 5 minutes, then serve.

Aswad ala aswad

STEWED LAMB WITH STUFFED AUBERGINES

Aswad ala aswad literally means 'black on black' and refers to the dark colour of the aubergines. The title might not be tempting but I promise that this dish is unusual and tasty. It is a speciality prepared by the Greek Orthodox Christians of Tripoli. An old recipe that is passed from mother to daughter, it has become a part of daily home cooking in many families.

As the baby aubergines are stuffed with a mixture of rice and meat, a side rice dish is not strictly required though it contrasts well with the dark stew.

For the stewed lamb
2 tablespoons extra virgin olive oil
285g (10oz) diced lamb, preferably from the chump
255g (9oz) onions, finely chopped
600ml (1 pint) hot water
1 teaspoon salt
pinch of black pepper

For the stuffed aubergines
8 baby aubergines
55g (2oz) round-grain (pudding) rice, rinsed
100g (3½oz) minced lamb
1 tablespoon water
pinch allspice
pinch black pepper
¼ teaspoon salt

For the coriander mixture
2 or 3 tablespoons extra virgin olive oil
6 garlic cloves, crushed
bunch coriander about 225g (8oz), finely chopped
1 aubergine about 375g (13oz), cut into 1cm (½in) cubes

Heat the oil in a pan. Add the diced lamb and onions, sauté over medium-high heat for 3–4 minutes, reduce the heat slightly and continue cooking until golden brown. Add the water, then sprinkle with salt and pepper. Bring to the boil, cover and simmer over low heat for 30 minutes or until the lamb is tender.

In the meantime, place the baby aubergines on a hard board and press and roll under the palm of your hand until they are soft. Cut across the top of each aubergine and hollow it out, leaving a thin shell. Thoroughly combine the rest of the stuffing ingredients. Loosely fill the aubergines and set to one side.

In a frying pan, heat the oil, add the garlic, sauté for a few seconds, stir in the coriander, and sauté until reduced. Add the cubed aubergines and sauté for a few minutes.

Add the stuffed aubergines along with the coriander mixture to the cooked lamb in the pan. Return to a boil, cover and simmer over medium-low heat for a further 30 minutes. Turn the heat off, then leave to stand for 5 minutes covered.

Serve hot with rice or pitta bread.

Sabidej

SQUID STEW WITH CORIANDER

This enchanting dish makes a great family meal but is also elegant enough for entertaining. It needs time to prepare but it is so simple to follow. The flavour is so good that it makes the work worthwhile. The squid needs to be peeled and the tube cleaned of all its mucus. If you cannot do this yourself, ask your fishmonger to do it to save yourself the trouble. I am very lucky, Les at the fishmongers in Notting Hill Gate skilfully cleaned and peeled the squid for me, saving its ink bag.

Squid with coriander is ideal as a main course for 5 hungry people, served with plain rice. It tastes clean and fresh. To end the meal, serve a refreshing dessert such as Rice pudding with lemon zest (page 75) or, if pomegranates are in season, *Khoshaf al-rumman* (page 141). Alternatively, try *Mafroukeh* (page 78) for a yummy ending to the meal.

Ingredients
1.5kg (3¼ lb) squid, cleaned, peeled and ink bag saved
1kg (2¼ lb) onions, chopped
1 whole head of garlic, sliced
1½–2 bunches of coriander, leaves only, 75g (2½oz)
100ml (4fl oz) extra virgin olive oil
3–4 bay leaves
3–4 slices of orange peel
¼ teaspoon black pepper
pinch white pepper
1 teaspoon sea salt, or to taste
juice of 1 lemon (about 85g / 3fl oz)

Slice the squid and set aside. In a pan layer the onions, garlic, coriander and squid, then pierce the ink bag over the top. Add the olive oil, bay leaves and orange peel. Cover and place over low heat. Leave to cook for 1½ hours. About two or three times gently move but not stir to help release the liquid. Remember to cover the pan each time.

Towards the end of cooking, sprinkle with the black and white peppers, add the salt and the lemon juice. Bring to the boil, then turn off the heat. Pour into a bowl and serve with plain rice and a dish of lemon wedges.

Samakeh harra

CHILLI FISH IN CORIANDER SAUCE

This is a famous dish from Tripoli. As this version with walnuts is expensive, it is usually made at home. Restaurants make a less costly version using chillies and ground coriander and sometimes tahini.

Fish in coriander sauce is unusual, filling, nourishing and easy to put together. Because of the colours of the sauce it is sometimes called *takhdira*, from *akhdar* meaning green. It is quite delicious, and its flavours penetrate the fish without overpowering it. This makes an excellent main course and the sauce is different from *Salsa harra* (page 34). Hake, halibut or cod can also be used.

Ingredients
1 sea bass about 900g (2lb), gutted and scaled
sea salt
30g (1oz) walnuts
4 tablespoons extra virgin olive oil
½ bunch of parsley (about 100g / 3½oz), finely chopped
½ bunch of coriander (about 115g / 4oz), finely chopped
1 tablespoon ground coriander
¼ teaspoon cayenne pepper
¼ teaspoon cinnamon
¼ teaspoon black pepper
½ tablespoon tomato purée
2 tablespoons water

Wash the fish with cold water and pat dry. Score 2–3 diagonal cuts on each side. Sprinkle with ¾ teaspoon salt. Blend the walnuts until smooth in a blender (or grind with a mortar and pestle). Remove and mix thoroughly with half the olive oil and the rest of the ingredients.

Fill the cavity of the fish with some of this mixture and put the remainder around the fish. Drizzle the remaining oil all over the fish. Bake in a preheated oven at 190°C (375°F/gas mark 5) for 5 minutes, then reduce the heat to 180°C (350°F/gas mark 4) and continue baking for a further 15 minutes. Serve hot.

Mouhabbaleh

TARO WITH CHICK PEAS IN SESAME CREAM

Taro (*Colocasia antiguorum*) is a tuber vegetable with a rough skin. It is thought to be one of the oldest vegetables ever cultivated. In the Lebanon, the mountain people have a tight budget, are practical and make the best use of anything that grows on the land. Known as *kelkass* in Lebanon, taro is used to give substance and bulk to a dish, and brings a pleasant variety to everyday meals. Above all, it is inexpensive, which suits the villagers. Potatoes can be used as a substitute.

Mouhabbaleh is vegetarian but it is similar to *Kibbeh arnabieh* (see page 283), which uses meat. The aroma of the citrus fruits intermingles with the tahini, taro and chick peas, creating a dish that gives great pleasure and satisfaction. It makes an excellent main course for 5.

For the taro
7 tablespoons extra virgin olive oil
900g (2lb) taro cut into thin segments 3mm (⅛ in) wide
450g (1lb) onions, sliced
85g (3oz) chick peas, soaked overnight, drained and pre-cooked
450ml (15fl oz) hot water

For the sauce
250ml (8fl oz) white tahini
300ml (10fl oz) Seville orange juice
150ml (5fl oz) grapefruit juice
50ml (2fl oz) lemon juice
75ml (3fl oz) clementine or orange juice

Place the oil in a heavy pan, heat for a few seconds then add the taro and onions. Sauté over medium heat, stirring occasionally, for 5 minutes or until the onions are translucent and the taro has become a pale golden colour. Add the chick peas and sauté with the other ingredients in the pan for a further 8 minutes. Add the water and bring to the boil. Reduce the heat to medium-low and simmer for 15 minutes or until the taro is tender.

To prepare the sauce, place the tahini in a bowl and gradually add the juices whisking constantly. (When Seville oranges are not in season, use 150ml/5fl oz lemon juice and combine equal amounts of clementine, orange and grapefruit juice to make 150ml/5fl oz.) At first the mixture will thicken, but as you add more juice the sauce will acquire the consistency of single cream. Using a wooden spoon, stir the tahini sauce into the pan containing the taro mixture. Keep stirring until it boils, then allow to simmer over medium-low or low heat for 8–10 minutes.

Serve hot with rice or vermicelli (see page 108) and radishes.

Makloubet djaj

UPSIDE-DOWN CHICKEN

This succulent chicken dish is ideal for the winter months when you need warmth and comfort. Eaten with Oriental salad (page 35), it makes a satisfying main course for 5–6 for Sunday lunch. Whenever possible, I use organic chicken.

Ingredients
5 tablespoons extra virgin olive oil
55g (2oz) pine nuts
4 medium size pieces of chicken, each cut into 2 pieces
450g (1lb) onions, sliced
6 garlic cloves, finely chopped
225g (8oz) minced lamb
350g (12oz) long grain rice, rinsed once
½ teaspoon cinnamon
¼ teaspoon black pepper
½ teaspoon allspice
pinch of grated nutmeg
2 bay leaves
700ml (1¼ pints) hot water
1¼ teaspoons salt, or to taste

To garnish
pine nuts

Heat the oil in a pan over a medium heat and when it is hot stir in the pine nuts and keep stirring until they turn golden brown. Remove with a slotted spoon and set aside. Add the chicken pieces to the same oil and cook for 5 minutes. Then turn over and cook for a further 5–6 minutes or until the chicken pieces are golden brown all over. Using a slotted spoon, transfer the chicken to a dish and set aside.

Add the onions and garlic to the remaining oil in the pan, using more oil if necessary. Sauté for 3–4 minutes or until golden brown, remove and set aside. To the same oil add the minced lamb and cook through until lightly browned.

In the same pan, arrange a layer of onions over the minced lamb, then lay the chicken pieces on top. Mix the rice with the cinnamon, black pepper, allspice and nutmeg, and place this over the chicken. Add the bay leaves, water and salt, making sure the water reaches down to the bottom. Bring to the boil, lower the heat to medium-low or low, cover and simmer for 30 minutes. Turn off the heat, cover the pan with a thick towel and leave to stand for 5 minutes to allow the flavours to blend.

To serve, uncover the pan, remove the bay leaves and gently invert over a serving dish. Garnish with pine nuts. Serve with a salad, and grilled aubergines and yogurt.

Kafta bil-banadoura

MEATBALLS IN TOMATO SAUCE

A dish of minced lamb meat and delicately spiced pine nuts, these stuffed meatballs are grilled until golden brown, then cooked in an aromatic tomato sauce that has an interesting punch to it. This dish can be made in advance. It is ideal to serve as a main course along with *Baba-ghanouj* (see page 23), Potato salad (page 157) or *Batinjan bourek* (page 99).

Makes 16 meatballs.

For the meatballs

450g (1lb) minced lamb meat

1 teaspoon salt

¼ teaspoon cinnamon

¼ teaspoon black pepper

½ teaspoon allspice

2 tablespoons olive oil

75g (2½oz) pine nuts

55g (2oz) onion, finely chopped

extra pinch of cinnamon

For the sauce

1 tablespoon extra virgin olive oil

115g (4oz) onion, finely chopped

1 teaspoon tomato purée

500g (1lb 2oz) tomatoes, peeled and finely chopped

pinch of white pepper

¼ teaspoon of black pepper

¼ teaspoon cinnamon

15–20g (½–¾oz) finely chopped parsley

1 tablespoon lemon juice

Mix the lamb with the salt, cinnamon, black pepper and allspice, and set aside. Put the oil in a small frying pan, add the pine nuts and sauté until golden brown. Using a slotted spoon, transfer to a side dish. Add the onion to the pan and sauté for 3 minutes or until golden brown. Sprinkle with the cinnamon. Take off the heat and stir in the pine nuts.

Taking a small portion from the meat mixture at a time, flatten and place 1 teaspoon of the pine nuts and onion in the centre and shape into a sausage. Repeat with the remaining meat mixture, pine nuts and onion. Place on a hot oven tray and grill for 3–4 minutes or until brown all over.

To make the sauce, heat the oil in a medium-size pan and sauté the onion until golden brown. Add the tomato purée, tomatoes, white and black peppers, cinnamon and meatballs, cover and allow to simmer over a low heat for 15–20 minutes. Halfway through the cooking, add the parsley. Turn off the heat and stir in the lemon juice. Cover with a thick towel and leave to stand for 5 minutes.

Serve hot with bread, roasted potatoes, radishes and green olives.

Riz bi samak el-ton

RICE WITH TUNA FISH

This easily assembled dish is a newcomer to the Lebanese menu. It can be prepared very quickly in advance and cooked when you arrive home after a long working day. Canned tuna is used to save time. However, fresh fish would be even better. Salmon, cod or even left-over fish can be used.

This dish is a perfect 'quick-fix'. Usually it is eaten with tahini and parsley sauce, but I think lemon wedges would do just as well.

Ingredients
3 tablespoons extra virgin olive oil
325g (11oz) onions, finely sliced
225g (8oz) green pepper, seeded and finely diced
1 red chilli pepper, seeded and finely diced
55g (2oz) pitted black olives
2 medium cans of tuna, drained, or 450g (1lb) fresh fish
225g (8oz) rice, soaked in hot water for 20 minutes
¼–½ teaspoon cinnamon
¼ teaspoon black pepper
1 teaspoon cumin
1¼ teaspoons salt, or to taste
300ml (10fl oz) hot water

Heat the oil in a small pan and sauté the onions until golden brown. Add the green and chilli peppers and stir for 1 minute. Add the olives and top evenly with tuna (or fresh fish, sautéd for 30 seconds on each side, if using).

Drain the rice and mix thoroughly with the cinnamon, black pepper, cumin and salt. Place this mixture over the tuna in the pan. Add the water and bring to the boil, cover and simmer over a medium-low heat for 5 minutes or until the rice is tender and the water has been absorbed. Turn off the heat, cover the pan with a thick towel and leave to stand for 5 minutes. Then turn upside down and serve with Tahini sauce (see page 39 or 70) or lemon wedges.

Macaroni bil-forn

SPAGHETTI IN THE OVEN

The Lebanese way of making spaghetti is truly delicious. As a young girl I have fond memories of the spaghetti prepared by my mother, who had a wonderful culinary touch.

Bepy Tomé, an Italian businessman who is a gastronome and connoisseur of food, taught me that the secret of good pasta is to stir it constantly for 3 minutes to stop it sticking together. He said, 'Pasta reacts depending on its quality, the water, the type of heat, the altitude, whether you are by the sea or in the mountains, if you are happy, and so on.' I laughed and thought to myself, 'This is how an Italian treats his food – with passion, poetry and art.'

This dish is simple and can be prepared in advance. It has a good, honest taste and is a great comfort food. I can assure you that it will be applauded by everyone who tastes it. *Kashkaval*, a cheese made of sheep's milk, is sprinkled on top of the spaghetti. (If *Kashkaval* is not available use any yellow cheese.) It melts and envelops the dish, complementing it without overpowering it. Serve as a main dish for 6 with *Fattouche* (page 18) as a starter. *Keskül* (page 273) would be a soothing dessert with which to end the meal.

Ingredients
400g (14oz) spaghetti
1½ tablespoons olive oil
125g (4½oz) onion, finely chopped
3 large garlic cloves, finely chopped
450g (1lb) lamb minced meat
3 heaped tablespoons tomato purée
125g (4½oz) tomatoes, peeled and finely chopped
30g (1oz) pine nuts
3 bay leaves
¼ teaspoon black pepper
1½ teaspoons salt, or to taste
700ml (1¼ pints) hot water
85g (3oz) mild yellow cheese, preferably **Kashkaval**

Cook the spaghetti in 4 litres (7 pints) of salted boiling water, stirring constantly for 3 minutes. Allow to cook for a further 4 minutes or until *al dente*. Drain and place in a deep baking dish 30 x 20cm (12 x 8in). Set aside.

Heat the oil in a medium pan, add the onions and sauté over a medium heat for 2 minutes. Add the garlic and sauté for a few seconds. Then add the lamb, stirring constantly for 3 minutes further or until it has lost its red colour. Stir in the tomato purée, then the tomatoes, pine nuts, bay leaves, black pepper and salt. Simmer for 1–2 minutes, then add the water and bring to the boil. Cover and simmer for 10 more minutes over medium-low heat then pour this sauce over the spaghetti and mix gently. Sprinkle on the cheese and bake in a preheated oven at 180°C (350°F/gas mark 4) for 20–30 minutes or until the top is golden brown. Serve hot.

Djaj bi-basal wa sumac

CHICKEN WITH ONIONS AND SUMAC

This is a heavenly dish and a novelty in the Lebanese culinary repertoire. It is influenced by the delicious Palestinian dish, *Musakhan*, meaning 'heated'. An aromatic mixture of sumac, chicken stock and onions mingles with the chicken, which is baked to maximise its succulence.

Extremely nutritious and simple, this recipe has made its way into my everyday cooking. It makes a perfect main course. Double the quantities and this will have a pride of place on your buffet table. Pickles such as baby turnips and cucumbers go well with this dish.

Ingredients
1.5 kg (3¼lb) chicken, cut into 4 pieces
2 tablespoons flour
½ lemon
2.25 litres (4 pints) water
1–2 celery sticks
1 onion, studded with 6 cloves
1 large cinnamon stick
a few black peppercorns
5 tablespoons extra virgin olive oil
55g (2oz) pine nuts
675g (1½lb) onions, finely sliced
2–2½ tablespoons **sumac**
2 teaspoons salt, or to taste
¼ teaspoon black pepper
¼ teaspoon allspice
½–¾ teaspoon cinnamon
175ml (6fl oz) lemon juice
300ml (10fl oz) chicken stock
1 large Lebanese or pitta bread

Clean the chicken pieces the Lebanese way, by sprinkling them with flour and rubbing them inside and out with half a lemon. Rinse them with cold water, discarding all the bloody bits. Place in the pan with the water over high heat. Skim, then add the celery, onion studded with cloves, cinnamon and peppercorns, and bring to the boil. Reduce the heat to medium, cover and simmer for 50 minutes or until the chicken is tender.

In the meantime, heat the oil in a frying pan and sauté the pine nuts, stirring constantly until golden. Remove with a slotted spoon and set aside. To the same oil, add the onions and sauté over medium heat for 5 minutes or until translucent and pale in colour, reducing the heat if they darken.

Stir in the sumac, salt, black pepper, allspice and cinnamon. Turn off the heat. Stir in the lemon juice and chicken stock, and set this onion mixture aside.

Remove the pieces of chicken and with your fingers break the chicken meat into small-medium elongated pieces. Place in a baking dish. Mix the chicken pieces with the onion mixture and bake in a preheated oven at 180°C (350°F/gas mark 4) for 30 minutes or until the stock is reduced and the top is browned.

In the meantime, gently split the bread into 2 pieces, and place one of these in a large, deep dish. Place the chicken mixture over the bread and sprinkle evenly with the reserved pine nuts. Cover with the other slice of bread and serve immediately.

Makloubet al-arnabit

UPSIDE-DOWN CAULIFLOWER

This dish is made with cauliflower, a vegetable that became popular in Europe in the 17th century after it had been cooked for Louix XIV. Cauliflower is available all year round. It is low in fat, rich in vitamins B, C and K and contains minerals such as selenium, magnesium, potassium, sulphur and silicon. One of my favourite ways of preparing it is to steam the florets until tender and then deep fry them in oil until golden brown in colour and crispy, ready to eat with pitta bread dipped in Tahini and parsley sauce. The authentic method of making *Makloubet al-arnabit*, is to boil the florets until tender, then deep fry them before including them with the other ingredients. This gives a very rich flavour to the dish.

This dish makes a tasty main course, which is simple to make, economical and can be prepared in advance. *Fattouche* (see page 18) served with it would make a refreshing starter.

Ingredients
1 kg (2¼lb) cauliflower
3–4 tablespoons extra virgin olive oil
3 tablespoons pine nuts
450g (1lb) minced lamb
3 large garlic cloves, crushed
85g (3oz) chopped coriander
200g (7oz) long-grain rice, rinsed once
¼ teaspoon cinnamon
pinch of black pepper
1¼ teaspoons salt, or to taste
450ml (15fl oz) boiling water

Rinse the cauliflower thoroughly. Using a sharp knife, trim the stem and separate gently into small florets. Leave to drain.

In the meantime, put the oil in a pan over a medium heat and when hot stir in the pine nuts. Sauté until they turn slightly golden in colour, remove with a slotted spoon and set aside. Add the florets to the oil in the pan and sauté until they colour. Leave aside.

Sauté the lamb in the remaining oil for 5 minutes or until nicely browned, then add the garlic, coriander, the reserved pine nuts and stir for a few seconds. Over this mixture spread the cauliflower, then the rice, and sprinkle with cinnamon, black pepper and salt. Add the water, bring to the boil, cover and simmer over low heat for 8–10 minutes or until the water has been absorbed. Turn off the heat, cover the pan with a thick towel and leave to stand for 10 minutes in order to allow the flavours to blend.

Serve hot with radishes.

Riz bi samak

RICE WITH FISH

This recipe from the ancient city port of Trablos (Tripoli) is a perfect combination of fish and rice. For years Tripoli fended off one of the leaders of the First Crusade, Raymond of St Gilles, who built a fortress facing the city he longed to occupy. However, he died in 1105 before he could fulfil his dream and it was left to his illegitimate son, Bertrand, to seize the city. The well-preserved remnants of this fortress can today be visited. In 1292, Tripoli was retaken by the Mamelukes. Since then, Tripoli has had the largest Suni population after Beirut. The charming old port has many restaurants strewn along the littoral, offering wonderful fish dishes. This dish, though, is strictly home cooking.

Riz bi samak is an indication of the honest passion for food of the people of Tripoli; it also reflects their economical cuisine. Families are large so clever cooks put together ingredients that will produce a delicious dish which is kind to the pocket. In this recipe, rice is used to make the fish go further. The rice simmers in a fish stock with a hint of *osfour*. It has a mild flavour that will appeal to most palates (if not available, use ¼–½ teaspoon turmeric). In this recipe, I have used cod. For a treat, use sea bass.

For the fish stock
1 fish head and bones
1.1 litres (2 pints) water
bouquet garni, consisting of parsley stem and leaves, lemon pieces, 2 bay leaves, 6
    black peppercorns, 2 cardamoms, 1–2 sorrel leaves (optional)
1 teaspoon salt

For the stew
2 tablespoons extra virgin olive oil
285g (10oz) onions, finely chopped
1½ teaspoons salt
½ teaspoon cinnamon
¼ teaspoon black pepper
500g (1lb 2oz) cod or any other white fish, cut in medium-size pieces
2 bay leaves
1 teaspoon **osfour** threads
285g (10oz) long grain rice, rinsed once and drained

To garnish
1 teaspoon olive oil
30g (1oz) pine nuts or almond flakes

To make the fish stock, place the fish bones and fish head in a pan. Add the water and bring to the boil, skimming until the water is clear. Add the bouquet garni and salt, reduce the heat to medium-low, cover and simmer for 30 minutes. Turn off the heat and let the pan stand for at least 20 minutes before straining so that the flavours intensify.

In the meantime, place the oil in a medium-size pan, and gently rub the onions with the salt, cinnamon and black pepper. Add the onions, fish pieces, bay leaves and fish stock to the pan. Bring to the boil, cover and simmer over medium heat for 4–5 minutes or until the fish flakes. Gently remove the fish pieces to a plate, cover and keep warm.

Sprinkle the *osfour* over the onions and stock in the pan. Add the rice. Bring to the boil, reduce the heat to low, cover and simmer for 8–10 minutes or until the rice is tender and the liquid has been absorbed. Turn off the heat. Cover the pan with a towel and leave to stand for 5 minutes.

Heat the oil and sauté the pine nuts or almond flakes until golden brown.

To serve, place the rice in a dish, arrange the fish pieces on top and garnish with the pine nuts or almond flakes.

Kelkass bi-adas

TARO WITH LENTILS

In this earthy dish, taro and lentils are combined, and their flavours enhanced with mint and lemon juice.

Taro grows in the Lebanon and is cheap to buy. It is often used during Lent. As it is bland, it is usually fried and added to lentils, chick peas, Swiss chard or any other vegetable, depending on what the season has to offer. This recipe is an excellent example of how cheap ingredients can be utterly delicious and have a high nutritional value. If taro is not available use potatoes instead.

Served as a starter and with *Kanafeh* (page 79) as a dessert, this would make a perfect informal dinner for friends.

Serves 5.

For the taro
3 tablespoons extra virgin olive oil
285g (10oz) onions, chopped
675g (1½lb) taro cut into 1cm (½in) cubes
3 garlic cloves, finely crushed
225g (8oz) green lentils
700ml (1¼ pints) hot water
1½ teaspoons salt, or to taste
3 tablespoons lemon juice
1 teaspoon dried mint

To garnish
Lebanese or pitta bread
fresh mint

Heat the oil in a pan and sauté the onions on a high heat, stirring constantly for a minute. Reduce the heat to medium, add the taro and sauté with the onions for another 2 minutes. Add the garlic, stir for a few seconds, then add the lentils and water. Sprinkle with salt, bring to the boil, cover and simmer over medium heat for 25 minutes or until the lentils are soft. Add the lemon juice and mint 5 minutes before the end of cooking.

Serve hot. To garnish, brush the surface of bread that has been split in two with olive oil. Cut into small squares and bake in oven until golden brown. Place these around the dish with a few mint leaves.

Djaj bi-kamoun

CHICKEN WITH CUMIN

This is a very unusual dish – you have to be really very fond of garlic. The bonus is that garlic is very healthy. *Djaj bi-kamoun* makes a good, warming winter meal for 5 or 6. Begin with a starter such as *Kibbeh al-hammam* (page 96) and end with *Khoshaf al rumman* (page 141), as they are both very refreshing.

Ingredients
1.5kg (3¼ lb) chicken cut into 8 pieces
2.2 litres (4 pints) water
bouquet garni consisting of 2 celery sticks, 2 bay leaves, 1 small onion studded with 5
*   cloves, 2–3 cardamoms, 6 black peppercorns, 1 large cinnamon stick and a stem*
*   of parsley*
1½ heaped tablespoons tomato purée
1¼ teaspoons salt, or to taste
1 whole head of garlic, crushed until creamy
1¼ teaspoons cumin

Place the chicken and water in a large pan over medium high heat. Bring to the boil, skim, add the bouquet garni and reduce the heat to medium. Cover and simmer for 50 minutes or until the chicken is tender.

Strain and measure 300ml (10fl oz) of chicken stock. Mix the stock with the tomato purée, salt, garlic and cumin. Remove the chicken pieces from the pan and place in a baking dish. Pour the stock mixture over the chicken pieces to cover and bake in a preheated oven at 180°C (350°F/gas mark 4) for 30 minutes or until the chicken pieces are nicely browned. Half way through baking turn the chicken pieces over and baste. Serve hot with steamed carrots, broccoli, grilled aubergine and roasted potatoes.

Fakhdeh Istanbouli

ISTANBUL LAMB

The name of this dish (Istanbouli, from the Turkish capital Istanbul) shows its Turkish influence. This is not surprising as Lebanon was part of the Ottoman Empire for about 400 years.

This is an easy recipe to prepare on Sundays for the family or to enjoy with friends. It requires few ingredients but it is most important to have good-quality meat.

Serve with Lebanese bread and fried or roasted potatoes. An Oriental salad (page 35) and fresh, seasonal fruit will crown the meal.

Ingredients
1.5kg (3 lbs 3oz) leg of lamb
2 litres (3½ pints) water
bouquet garni consisting of 3 bay leaves, 1 onion studded with 6 cloves, 5 cardamoms,
1 celery stick, 1 large cinnamon stick and 6 black peppercorns
1¼ teaspoons salt, or to taste
1–2 garlic cloves, crushed until creamy
1–1½ tablespoons tomato purée
4–5 tablespoons thick yogurt.

Place the leg of lamb and water in a pan and bring to the boil, skim and add the bouquet garni. Cover and simmer over a low heat for 2–2½ hours or until the meat is tender. A few minutes before the end of cooking, sprinkle with salt. Remove the meat from the pan, cut into medium-size pieces and place on a dish. Ladle 200ml (7fl oz) of the meat stock and mix together with the garlic and tomato purée, pour this over the lamb pieces. Add a dollop of yogurt in 3–4 different places among the pieces of meat. Serve immediately.

To eat, dip a piece of bread in the stock, then take a piece of lamb and a little yogurt.

Samakeh harra bi-tahini

CHILLI FISH WITH TAHINI SAUCE

This is another interesting recipe from Tripoli, famed for its fish dishes. It is prepared in many fish restaurants and at home for special occasions. The fish is served with a delicious coriander sauce. As well as sea bass, you can use other fish such as cod, hake, red snapper and turbot. You can also use the sauce as a dip to eat with bread, lettuce or cabbage leaves. It serves 4 or 5 as a main course.

For the fish
1 sea bass (1.25kg / 2lb 8oz), gutted and scaled
1¼ teaspoons salt
¼ teaspoon black pepper
¼ teaspoon cinnamon
2 thin slices of onion
2–3 thin slices of lemon
1 stem of parsley
1 stem of coriander
3–4 tablespoons extra virgin olive oil

For the nut mixture
30g (1oz) almonds
85g (3oz) pine nuts
100ml (4fl oz) water
50ml (2fl oz) lemon juice
75ml (3fl oz) tahini
55g (2oz) onions
1½ teaspoons salt, or to taste

For the sauce
2 tablespoons extra virgin olive oil
3 large garlic cloves, finely chopped
1 teaspoon ground coriander
75g (2½oz) fresh coriander, finely chopped
½ teaspoon cayenne pepper
1 medium-size red tomato peeled, finely chopped (optional)

Rinse the fish in cold water and pat dry. Place in a baking dish. Score 2–3 diagonal cuts on each side. Sprinkle with salt and black pepper inside and out. Rub the cavity with cinnamon and fill with the onions, lemon, parsley and coriander. Smear the oil all over the fish. Bake in a preheated oven 180°C (350°F/gas mark 4) for 18–20 minutes.

To make the nut mixture, place all the ingredients in a blender and blend until smooth.

To prepare the sauce, put the oil in a frying pan and sauté the garlic over medium-low heat for a few seconds. Stir in the ground coriander, then add the fresh coriander. Do not stir and allow to cook for 1–2 minutes. Stir in the cayenne pepper and the chopped tomato, if using. Stir in the nut mixture and combine thoroughly. Allow 2–3 minutes to heat through, then turn the heat off. Take the fish out of the oven, leave or remove the skin according to preference and place on a serving dish. Spread the nut mixture over the fish or serve separately in a bowl.

Fattouche (Bread salad)

Houmous bi-shommar (Chick peas with dill)

Kafta bil-banadoura (Meatballs in tomato sauce)

Samakeh harra bi-tahini (Chilli fish with tahini sauce)

Mafroukeh (Rose-scented semolina)

Kanafeh (Kataifi with cheese)

Kibbeh al-hammam (Burghol and tomato kibbeh)

Salatet flifleh hamra (Sweet red pepper salad)

Hrisseh

LAMB WITH WHEAT GRAIN

This traditional and popular dish, which is reputed to go back to the time of the Abbassid caliphate, is prepared for large family gatherings, to honour guests and at religious festivals. One church on the Lebanese mountain of Bhamdoun distributes *Hrisseh* to the congregation every year on 15 August to commemorate the Virgin Mary's ascension. *Hrisseh* derives from the word *mahrous* (crushed) because the ingredients are cooked and stirred until they dissolve into a creamy porridge-like texture. It is thought by many Lebanese to be an elaborate and delicate dish. In fact, it is simple to prepare and is at its best when using good-quality ingredients and allowing ample time to cook. Avoid over-stirring so as to keep a little of the ingredients' identity. You can buy the whole-wheat grain from Lebanese or health shops.

This recipe uses lamb but you could use chicken or a mixture of the two. It serves 8–10 for a party.

Ingredients
1kg (2¼lb) diced lamb
7–8 lamb bones
4 litres (7 pints) water
3–4 cinnamon sticks
350g (12oz) whole-wheat grain
4 teaspoons salt, or to taste
1½ teaspoons powdered cinnamon

Rinse the meat and bones several times and drain. Place in a large pan with bones and water. Bring to the boil and skim. Add the cinnamon sticks, cover and simmer over medium heat for 30 minutes. Add the whole-wheat grain and reduce the heat to very low and allow to simmer for a further 7½ hours. Remove the bones after 5–6 hours otherwise they disintegrate. Cover the pan during cooking.

Uncover the pan 10–15 minutes before the end of the cooking time and sprinkle with the salt and cinnamon. Using a wooden spoon, stir continuously until the meat dissolves and amalgamates with the grain to give a uniform texture. For an authentic creamy texture, you will need to stir for 30 minutes. Serve hot.

Kibbeh bi-sayniyeh

BAKED KIBBEH

Baked *kibbeh* is a favourite of mine – it reminds me of relaxed family gatherings over a traditional Sunday lunch. It does take time to prepare but the effort is worthwhile. Eaten hot, with a cold salad of yogurt, sliced cucumber and a little garlic, it is a soothing, comforting dish. It freezes well and is delicious eaten cold straight from the fridge, as my daughter, Nour, will testify.

The stuffing can be varied by cutting out the mincemeat and adding more onions and pine nuts, and ½–1 tablespoon of *sumac* or ½ tablespoon of lemon juice.

Serves 6–8.

For the stuffing
2–3 tablespoons extra virgin olive oil
30g (1oz) pine nuts
1 large onion (about 285g / 10oz), finely chopped
150g (5½oz) lean minced meat, preferably lamb
¾ teaspoon cinnamon
½ teaspoon salt, or to taste
¼ teaspoon black pepper

For the **kibbeh** *dough*
1 onion (about 100g / 3½oz)
1¾ teaspoons salt, or to taste
½ teaspoon allspice
½ teaspoon cinnamon
½ teaspoon black pepper
285g (10oz) fine burghol, rinsed and drained
450g (1lb) lean ground meat, preferably lamb
75–100ml (3–4fl oz) extra virgin olive oil

Heat the oil in a heavy-bottomed frying pan until hot but not smoking. Add the pine nuts and sauté, stirring constantly until golden brown. Remove with a slotted spoon and set aside.

Add the onions to the pan and sauté over medium-high heat for about 2 minutes until soft and pale in colour, then add the meat and cook until it is lightly browned. Return the reserved pine nuts to the frying pan, season with cinnamon, salt and black pepper and stir well. Remove from the heat and set aside.

Grease a baking tray (26 x 26cm / 10¼ x 10¼in) with 1 tablespoon of oil and set aside. Heat the oven to 190°C (375°F/gas mark 5).

To make the *kibbeh* dough, blend the onion in a food processor until it forms a creamy paste.

Remove from the blender and place in a large bowl, sprinkle and mix with the salt, allspice, cinnamon, and black pepper. Squeeze any excess water from the burghol, add to the onion mixture and mix thoroughly until the burghol has absorbed all the seasonings. Add the ground meat and mix well, adding 2–3 tablespoons cold water or more to achieve a smooth paste. Continue kneading until the mixture blends well, using a food processor for a few seconds if necessary. Take small portions of the mixture at a time and make a thin layer 5mm (¼in) on the baking tray.

Spread the stuffing evenly on top, cover with the remaining *kibbeh* mixture and press to smooth it down. You may find it easier to moisten your hands with cold water. Drizzle the oil all over and quickly run a thin-pointed knife around the edge of the baking dish. Then cut through the *kibbeh*, dividing it into 4–8 portions (similar to pizza slices), allowing the oil to seep through. To decorate make a criss-cross pattern on the surface of each portion.

Bake in a hot oven for 40 minutes or until browned. Remove from the oven and, while the oil is still bubbling, carefully pour off any excess. Arrange on a platter and eat with a yogurt and cucumber salad or Oriental salad (see page 35).

Djaj bi-zaitoun

CHICKEN WITH OLIVES

This dish originates from Tripoli. It has been prepared for generations and is certainly a great favourite of mine. I simply love cooking it.

Whenever possible, I buy new season Lebanese green olives from a Lebanese delicatessen, because I find that the flavour of this dish is more succulent. Otherwise any green ones will do. Authentically, the dish is served with very little broth but I have increased the quantities for the tasty sauce so that you can enjoy dipping your bread into it.

A perfect main dish that serves 5 with pitta bread.

Ingredients
4 tablespoons olive oil
1.5kg (3¼oz) chicken, cut into 8 pieces
675g (1½lb) onions, chopped
4 garlic cloves
½ teaspoon cinnamon
¼ teaspoon black pepper
pinch of grated nutmeg
700ml (1¼ pints) water
1 teaspoon salt, or to taste
bouquet garni, consisting of 2 bay leaves, 2 cardamoms, 5 black peppercorns
1 large cinnamon stick
140g (5oz) green olives, pitted

Heat the oil in a pan and when it is hot add the chicken pieces. Sauté for 4 minutes to brown on all sides. To the same pan, add the onions and garlic, and sauté until golden brown. Sprinkle with the cinnamon, black pepper and nutmeg. Add the water, salt, bouquet garni and cinnamon stick. Bring to the boil, cover and simmer over medium heat for 30 minutes. Remove the chicken to a side dish and discard the bouquet garni.

Place the onions, garlic and liquid in a blender, then run the motor for a minute or until the mixture reaches the consistency of cream. Alternatively, pass through a vegetable mill. Return the mixture to the pan, add the chicken and the olives. Bring to the boil, cover and simmer over medium-heat for 20 minutes or until chicken is tender. Serve hot with pitta bread. To eat, dip the bread in the sauce, and pick up some chicken and olives with it.

Kafta

FRAGRANT LAMB

Kafta is a popular Middle Eastern combination of minced lamb meat, parsley, mint, onions and spices. For a barbecue, the mixture is pressed closely on to metal skewers then cooked over an open fire of intensely hot charcoal. When the trees start blossoming and the earth smells of spring, people start picnicking on Sundays and *Kafta* is a favourite picnic food.

This dish is simple to make, serve accompanied by Aubergine dip (page 23), Oriental salad (page 35) or *Tabbouleh* (page 17). It makes an excellent main course and is delicious sandwiched with Lebanese or pitta bread spread with Aubergine dip.

Makes 24 portions.

Ingredients
115g (4oz) onion, chopped
55g (2oz) parsley
8–10 mint leaves
500g (1lb 2oz) minced lamb
30g (1oz) bread, crust removed
¼ teaspoon cinnamon
¼ teaspoon allspice
¼ teaspoon black pepper
1 teaspoon salt

Place the onion, parsley and mint in a food processor. Blend for 30 seconds or until smooth. Add the rest of the ingredients. Blend until thoroughly mixed together (if a food processor is not available, grate the onion, chop the parsley and mint very finely, and mix with the other ingredients). Divide this mixture into 24 portions, then press each gently between forefinger and palm. Place over a hot, lightly oiled oven sheet. Grill for 5–6 minutes or until browned on both sides.

Shawarma djaj

SPICED CHICKEN STRIPS

Whenever you go in the Levant, you will see *shawarma* stalls with gigantic skewers of chicken meat pressed tightly together. The skewers turn round slowly, close to an upright fire until the chicken is thoroughly cooked.

This dish is the simpler home version, using boneless chicken breasts because they are easier to slice. This makes an ideal main dish and is perfect when accompanied by tahini sauce and small dishes of chopped tomatoes, diced radishes and spring onion. Finally, take some Lebanese bread, so that you have a piece of bread with a piece of chicken, topped with a little of each of the relishes. These spiced chicken strips make an excellent addition to a buffet. This dish can also be prepared with lamb.

Ingredients
4 boneless chicken breasts, skin removed
2 garlic cloves, finely crushed
125ml (4½ fl oz) lemon juice
2 tablespoons extra virgin olive oil
1¼ teaspoons cider vinegar
2–3 bay leaves, broken in 3 pieces
3 small shreds of orange peel
1 cinnamon stick, broken into quarters
1¼ teaspoons salt
¼ teaspoon ground cloves
1 ¼ ground cardamom, or 4–5 whole cardamoms broken into 2–3 pieces each
¼–½ teaspoon ground cinnamon
¼ teaspoon white pepper
pinch of grated nutmeg
about 2–3 pieces of miskee, *ground to a powder in a mortar with a pestle*

For the tahini sauce
a small garlic clove, crushed
½ teaspoon salt, or to taste
150ml (¼ pint) white tahini
6–7 tablespoons lemon juice
6–7 tablespoons water
handful of parsley, finely chopped (optional)
5 green olives, pitted and finely diced (optional)
a little diced pickled cucumber (optional)

Slice the chicken into strips about 5mm (¼in) long and place in a bowl with the rest of the ingredients. Cover and refrigerate overnight, or for at least 8 hours.

Remove the chicken from fridge, mix and allow to reach room temperature for about 10 minutes before baking. Meanwhile, preheat the oven to 200°C (400°F/gas mark 6). Spread the chicken in a baking dish with the aromatic juices and bake for 30 minutes.

To make the tahini sauce, place the garlic, salt and tahini in a mixing bowl and whisk. Gradually add the lemon juice and water, whisking to prevent any lumps of tahini forming. Keep whisking until the sauce reaches the consistency of cream. If using, stir the parsley, olives and pickles into the tahini sauce.

Remove the pan from the oven and place the chicken under a hot grill to brown slightly. Remove and place in a large Lebanese bread pocket. If you do not have a large loaf of bread, open up 3 small ones and fill. Eat with pickles, tomatoes, radishes, spring onion and plain tahini sauce.

Lebanon

Desserts

Riz bi-haleeb

RICE PUDDING WITH LEMON ZEST

A very nourishing and refreshing dessert, rice pudding is very popular with the Lebanese and is often prepared in the mountain regions. It satisfies a sweet tooth and is inexpensive to prepare. It is also a delicious way of making children eat food containing milk, which is so important for their growth. This recipe includes the lemon zest that some Lebanese like to add to the dish. Serves 8.

Ingredients
1.1 litres (2 pints) water
200g (7oz) round grain rice, rinsed
600ml (1 pint) milk
285g (10oz) sugar
½ teaspoon miskee pieces
1½ teaspoons lemon zest
1 tablespoon orange flower water

Put the water and rice in a pan. Place over medium heat and simmer for 10–15 minutes, stirring occasionally with a wooden spoon. Stir in the milk and simmer for 25 minutes more, or until the milk mixture coats the spoon. This means that the pudding is ready.

While the milk mixture is simmering, take 1 teaspoon of the sugar to cover the miskee, and crush gently with the pestle, moving your hand clockwise until you have an almost powder-like consistency. Put to one side.

When the milk and rice pudding coats the spoon, stir in the sugar and leave to bubble for 30 seconds. Gradually sprinkle in the *miskee* while stirring, then stir in the lemon zest and the flower water. Turn the heat off and pour into a deep serving dish or into small serving bowls. Eat warm or, better still, chilled.

Aish al saraya

PALACE BREAD

This recipe is for true devotees of sweets. It is made with bread and the result is an unparalleled triumph. This delicious dessert, which has been created from basic ingredients, is fit for a palace. The caramelized syrup and cream crowned with pistachio nuts makes a sensational combination. My sister, Rafat, adds a teaspoon of ground Nescafé when soaking the bread with the caramelized sugar. She tells me the colour and flavour are much deeper. This recipe is simple to follow and makes an excellent party dessert for 10–14 people. *Aish al saraya* reminds me of the delicious Turkish dessert, *Ekmek kadaifi*. It is made with bread that is drenched in a sugary syrup and eaten with *kaimak* (similar to clotted cream).

For the bread
425g (15oz) white sandwich loaf, crusts removed
600ml (1 pint) water
725g (1lb 9oz) sugar

For the cream topping
300ml (½ pint) double cream
300ml (½ pint) single cream
3 teaspoons cornflour
1 tablespoon water
4 slices of white bread (150g / 5½oz), crusts removed, broken into small-medium crumbs
½ tablespoon orange flower water
½ tablespoon rose water

To garnish
115g (4oz) pistachio nuts, soaked and skinned

In two batches, place slices of bread in a food processor. Blend for a few seconds or until ground into medium-fine crumbs, then place evenly in a deep, rectangular serving dish about 34cm (14in) long. If a food processor is not available break the bread into small pieces with your fingers.

Combine the water and 500g (1lb 2oz) of sugar in a pan and place over medium heat. Stir until the sugar dissolves completely, boil for a few seconds, then turn off the heat. Place the remaining sugar in a frying pan over low heat until it melts and reaches a dark brown colour; make sure that the sugar has melted and is not granular. Add this to the boiled sugar and water in the pan – if the sugar stiffens do not worry as it will melt again as you stir. Bring to the boil, and simmer over low heat for 10 minutes. Pour over the breadcrumbs, mix thoroughly and spread evenly. Allow the bread to absorb all the liquid and to cool.

Heat the double and single creams in a saucepan. Thoroughly mix the cornflour with the water, strain and add to the cream, stirring constantly until the cream mixture boils and thickens. Add the pieces of bread, and the orange flower and rose waters. Leave to cool slightly. Spread over the bread mixture in the serving dish, garnish with pistachios, then chill.

Mafroukeh

ROSE-SCENTED SEMOLINA

This impressive regional dessert which is made of semolina, butter and scented rose water, comes from Tripoli. In Tripoli it is customary to eat it warm, perhaps because it traditionally contains a large amount of butter which solidifies when cold. However, my recipe uses much less butter so it can be eaten warm or cold. In Tripoli, it is decorated with fried pine nuts and almonds. I only use almonds because they harmonize perfectly with the flavour and texture of this dessert. *Mafroukeh* makes an excellent addition to a buffet. It serves 12–14.

For the semolina
575g (1lb 5oz) sugar
450ml (15fl oz) water
100ml (4fl oz) rose water
140g (5oz butter)
500g (1lb 2oz) fine semolina

For the cream
300ml (10fl oz) milk
30g (1oz) plain flour
60ml (2½fl oz) rose water

To garnish
4–5 tablespoons olive oil or peanut oil
140g (5oz) whole almonds

In a medium pan, combine 400g (14oz) sugar and water. Stir until the sugar is fully dissolved and bring to the boil. Stir in the rose water and straight away turn off the heat. Put to one side.

Place a pan over medium heat and melt the butter. When it is hot, add the semolina and the remaining sugar. Cook for at least 15 minutes, or until the semolina is reddish-brown in colour (the colour is important for flavour), stirring occasionally with a wooden spoon. Gradually add the reserved syrup while stirring. Continue to stir until the semolina has absorbed all the liquid, starts bubbling and thickens. Place into a serving dish and prepare the cream.

In a small pan, whisk the milk, flour and rose water thoroughly. Place over medium heat and stir constantly for 5 minutes or until it boils. Leave to bubble over low heat for 2 more minutes. Remove from the heat, wait a few seconds then pour over the semolina.

Heat the oil in a frying pan. When hot, add the almonds and sauté over medium heat for 2 minutes or until they are deep brown in colour but not burned. Garnish by placing the almonds in a spiral pattern and serve.

Kanafeh

KATAIFI WITH CHEESE

This is a great delicacy in Lebanon and a national favourite. The patisseries are packed in the early hours of the morning with people eating *kanafeh* with sesame ring-shaped bread rolls called *kaakeh*, while reading the newspaper or talking to a friend. These relaxed mornings are still one of the lovely features of Lebanon and other countries of the Levant. *Kanafeh* is so much liked that it adorns the table during the holy month of Ramadan. For the Lebanese, *kanafeh* is the croissant of the French and the bacon, eggs and sausages of the English.

This recipe is a quick version and just as delicious. It is made with *kataifi* (fine-shredded wheat), which can be purchased from Lebanese, Greek or Turkish delicatessens. Serve this at any time – for dinner, lunch or at teatime.

For the kataifi
75g (2½oz) kataifi
250g (8½oz) mozzarella cheese, finely sliced
1 tablespoon flower water
45g (1½oz) butter

For the syrup
285g (10oz) sugar
200ml (7fl oz) water
1 teaspoon lemon juice
1½ teaspoons orange flower water
1½ teaspoons rose water

Loosen the *kataifi* and spread over a medium-size buttered oven pan. Rinse the cheese and pat dry between kitchen paper. Spread over the *kataifi* and sprinkle with orange flower water. Cover the cheese completely with the remaining *kataifi* and dot with melted butter to coat the entire surface of the *kataifi* threads. Bake in a preheated oven at 200°C (400°F/gas mark 6) for 12–15 minutes or until the top is golden. If the *kataifi* has not become a good golden colour, place it under a hot grill for about 30–60 seconds, keeping an eye on it because it can quickly burn.

To prepare the syrup, in a small pan, dissolve the sugar with water and bring to the boil. Add the lemon juice and leave to simmer over medium heat for 5 minutes or until it reaches syrupy consistency. Stir in the orange and rose waters.

Serve the *kataifi* immediately with the syrup in a separate bowl. Eat, spooning about 1–2 tablespoons of the syrup over each *kataifi* portion.

Helou joz el-hind

COCONUT CAKE

When I was a child, it was fun to break open a coconut and to quarrel with my sisters and brothers over who would drink the liquid that was found inside it. Then, as now, coconuts were plentiful and sold by street vendors who used to scream *batikh yajoz el-hind* (watermelon-oh-coconut). Maybe what they meant was that their coconuts were as juicy and delicious as watermelons. My mother loved buying them and I think I have inherited her passion.

This wonderful recipe was given to me by my friend, Marie Taktouk, who is a connoisseur of food and a most charming hostess. It is one of the most delicious desserts I have ever had. It is excellent for parties, but a small piece is more than enough as it is full of calories. There is an Arabic saying *Kalil min al khamr youfreh kalb al insan*, which means 'A little wine makes your heart happier'.

For the syrup
400g (14oz) sugar
175ml (6fl oz) water
¾ tablespoon lemon juice
½ tablespoon orange flower water (optional)

For the cake
2 tablespoons white tahini
255g (9oz) flour
225g (8oz) fine-shredded coconut
200g (7oz) butter, melted
300ml (10fl oz) milk
1 teaspoon baking powder

In a pan combine the sugar with the water, place over a high heat and stir until the sugar is completely dissolved. When it boils, add the lemon juice and lower the heat to medium. Simmer for 4–5 minutes, or until the consistency is slightly thick. Stir in the orange flower water, if using, and turn off the heat. Set aside to cool.

Preheat the oven to 180°C (350°F/gas mark 4). Spread the tahini in the bottom of a medium size baking dish (it prevents sticking and gives a special flavour to the base of the cake). For the cake, in a bowl, mix together thoroughly the rest of the ingredients. Pour the batter over the tahini in the baking dish and spread evenly. Cook for 40–50 minutes, or until the top is browned. Remove from the oven and pour the cooled syrup all over the cake. Cut into squares and serve warm or at room temperature.

Kamar el-din bi-nasha

APRICOT PUDDING WITH NUTS

Kamar el-din are apricots which have been flattened into thin sheets and dried. They can be purchased from Lebanese shops. My memory takes me back to my mother's kitchen when she prepared a drink with them. She would soak the sheets of *kamar el-din* in fresh water for 18 hours, strain them, then add whole pine nuts which were also soaked for several hours. This concoction is also excellent when a little is added to fruit salads. The recipe below is an immensely soothing and unusual one, and is very quick to make.

Ingredients
285g (10oz) of kamar el-din sheets
1.5 litres (2½ pints) water
115g (4oz) cornflour
225g (8oz) orange juice
115g (4oz) sugar
55g (2oz) pine nuts, soaked
55g (2oz) almonds, soaked
55g (2oz) pistachio nuts, soaked

Soak the *kamar el-din* sheets overnight in the water, leaving 120ml (4fl oz) of water aside for later use. The following day, strain over a pan. Dilute the cornflour in the remaining water and strain over the *kamar el-din* in the pan. Add the orange juice and sugar. Set the pan over medium heat, stir to dissolve sugar and bring to the boil. Leave to bubble over medium-low heat until thick. Pour into a serving dish and allow to cool. Drain the pine, almond and pistachio nuts and spread over the dessert to decorate. Serve chilled.

Mouhallabieh

MILK PUDDING

This refreshing and soothing milk pudding is found on most Lebanese restaurant menus. Taste and goodness vary, depending on the ingredients used. This is a simplified, home-made version, which is much quicker to make than the one which uses ground rice. It is excellent at any time of the day and on any occasion. It can be prepared and chilled just one hour before friends are due. When the surface sets, it appears velvety. This pudding looks beautiful when it is sprinkled with coarsely ground pistachio.

In the past *mouhallabieh* was served with home-made date and Seville orange preserve. Nowadays, the preserve can be bought ready-made. Serves 6–8.

Ingredients
850ml (1½ pints) milk
55g (2oz) cornflour
85g (3oz) sugar, or to taste
1 tablespoon orange flower water
*¼–½ teaspoon **miskee** pieces, ground with ½ teaspoon sugar (optional)*
2–3 tablespoons coarsely ground pistachio

Measure about 5 or 6 tablespoons of milk into a teacup. Add the cornflour and dissolve completely.

Place the remaining milk in a pan that has been rinsed just beforehand to stop the milk burning. Strain the cornflour and milk mixture and add to the milk in the pan. Add the sugar and stir thoroughly with a wooden spoon for a minute or two. Place the pan over medium heat. Stir constantly in the same direction until the milk becomes thick and coats the spoon. Reduce the heat and allow to bubble for about 2 minutes. Stir in the orange flower water and sprinkle in the ground *miskee*, if using, while still stirring. Remove from the heat and pour the milk pudding into a serving dish or in separate small bowls. Chill until set. Before serving, garnish the surface with the ground pistachio. If you omit *miskee*, serve with any jam of your choice.

Syria:
ALEPPO

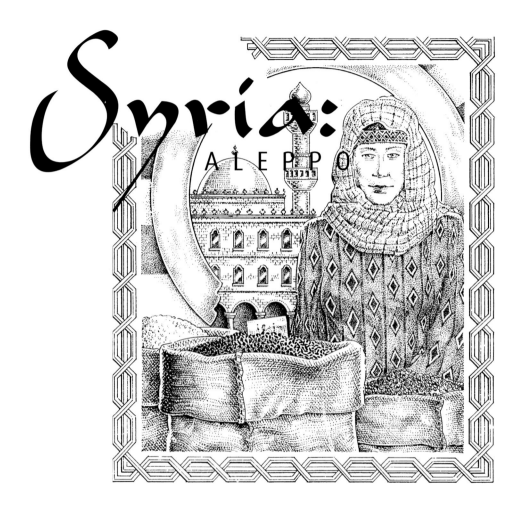

PART 2
Syria: Aleppo

The old rivalry between Damascus and Aleppo reaches its peak when it comes to food, with each city claiming that it has a better cuisine than the other. The fact of the matter is that they have different cuisines, each as delicious as the other.

Aleppo was on the caravan route from the East. It controlled the spice trade that went through Syria and channelled it towards the port of Antioch. Its cuisine is very delicate. While researching this book, a visit to the city was a must, even though the only time I had available was during the summer. All I had to do was to convince my husband, my daughter and my two sisters that the scorching month of August was the ideal travelling time.

On the road to Aleppo, we visited Qalaat al-Husn and the Krak des Chevaliers, which is the largest and best-preserved fortified castle from the time of the Crusades. This mighty Hospitallers' castle commanded the passage from the seashore at Lattakieh into the hinterland. Eventually, in 1271, Crusaders surrendered to the Mameluke Sultan, Baybars, thus sounding the death knell for the Frankish occupation of the Levant.

After our visit to the castle, our guide suggested a light lunch at the al-Safir hotel in Homs and the meal started with the *mezzé*. There were *boreks* (balls of dough stuffed with meat or cheese and parsley), a refreshing tomato and cucumber salad, and aubergine dip and *Kibbeh sajieh* (page 128), which is a regional speciality. A selection of grilled meats followed. This supposedly 'light' lunch ended with a selection of fruit, including a sweet, juicy watermelon, and the meal was washed down with the inevitable coffee.

From the al-Safir hotel, we journeyed on to Aleppo. There were stretches of desert that looked completely lifeless, as well as endless orchards of pistachio (so delicious to eat when freshly picked), olive trees and the occasional fig tree.

In Aleppo we dined at the exclusive Aleppo Club at the invitation of the art collector, Myriam Antaki. As tradition dictates, a *mezzé* of at least 18 dishes was instantly spread before us. It gave us the opportunity to discuss the differences between Lebanese and Syrian food. Aleppo is famous, in particular, for its red pepper paste and the red hot pepper that makes its food so spicy, and the tangy, succulent syrup made from pomegranate juice.

The following day, we drove south from Aleppo towards the ruined Hellenistic city of Apamea. On the way, we had a sudden stop because a huge flock of sheep had appeared in front of the bus. It was a beautiful sight and, according to Lebanese legend, a good omen. It took some time before the road was cleared and we could move on, but the tinkling of the sheep's bells remained with us for some time afterwards. We drove through another stretch of desert. This time we saw a few tents erected on red sand that looked smooth and velvety. I asked the driver to stop so I could take a picture. A Bedouin came out of his tent, followed by his family, and they insisted that we have tea with them.

On the road again, in the tremendous midday heat, we had to stop to buy some bottled water. Children of all ages crowded round our bus and started talking to us and posing for photographs. As the bus moved on they continued waving until they were lost on the horizon.

When we reached Apamea, our knowledgeable Syrian guide, Gina Zobian, gave us a vivid account of its history. We followed her in the blazing summer heat and did not regret our heroic determination for a second. Hardly any building from the Greek period remains, for in AD 115, a severe earthquake almost completely destroyed Apamea, which was then razed to the ground and rebuilt by order of the Roman emperor, Trajan. The ruins that we visited are from that period and subsequent periods. We stopped briefly at Hama to look at the giant water-wheels, which raise water from the river into the irrigation ditches. They have been in operation since the fourth century AD.

From Hama, we were driven to the north-west of Aleppo, to the ruins of the monastery of St Simeon, close to the Turkish border. St Simeon was a monk whose extreme asceticism made him retire into a mountain cave. Annoyed by the number of interfering visitors, he took refuge on a small platform at the top of a high pillar, where he spent 42 years preaching twice a day, until his death in AD 459. A few years after St Simeon's death, a monastery and four basilicas were built on the scene of his devoted life.

The site of the monastery is mystical and inspiring. It is not only the remarkable architecture of the remains that is superb, but also the breeze and the smell of the pine and oak trees. We were overcome in turn by bewilderment and admiration, spiritual exaltation and earthly enchantment. In the summer, St Simeon is best visited during the late afternoon, when the sun is low.

In Aleppo that evening, we went for a drink at the bar of the Hotel le Baron where Lawrence of Arabia, Agatha Christie and many other famous visitors have stayed. From the hotel we went to Sisi House, an old house that has been converted into a restaurant, where we had a delicious dinner. We talked passionately about food while simple yet interesting dishes appeared on our table, such as *muhammara*, and olive and red pepper salads.

The following day we visited the citadel and admired the massive structural design of the fortress, which has taken on multiple additions of towers and gates over more than 2,000 years. From there we headed towards the souk, a real market-place that caters for the local inhabitants and is far from being a fake performance for tourists. When entering the souk, I soon realized that here it is the laden donkeys that have right of way.

We saw row after row of small shops, displaying sacks filled with aromatic spices and dried herbs, colourful dried vegetables hanging on ropes, small bottles filled with perfume, fabrics, shoes, soap, and silk scarves. Unobtrusive mosques have been built within easy reach so that shopkeepers can pray several times a day.

I made my way into the central area of the souk to buy some *zaatar* (thyme), pomegranate syrup, sumac, cumin, bay-leaf soaps and hot pepper paste. Two local ladies were also buying spices and tempted me into buying more. They told me that they always purchased their provisions from the same shop and that the owner was trustworthy. I did not regret their advice one bit; on the contrary, I wish I had bought more, particularly of the *zaatar*, which had a very special flavour.

The shops are tiny and every single centimetre is crammed with goods. The front of many of these shops is occupied by a fixed counter, where a variety of goods is on display. There is no room left for a door, so the shopkeepers have found an ingenious way of going in and out of their shops without having to remove the goods from the counter: they swing over on a rope fixed to the ceiling.

My unforgettable visit to Aleppo ended with an informal dinner with Gina Zobian and her family. Among many dishes was a particularly original one, *kibbeh krassieh* and Maguy Zobian (Gina's mother) kindly gave me the recipe for it. These are small balls of burghol, flour and onion, kneaded with a little water and stuffed with sugar and blackcurrants or blueberries. They are simmered in salted, boiling water for 2–3 minutes and served with a sauce made from onions, dried coriander and the juice of half a lemon, a teaspoon of tomato purée and a touch of cayenne. This is a traditional dish from Aleppo, prepared during Lent. (See also *Kibbeh massalik* on page 39.)

Starters

Mabroumeh bi-zaitoun

OLIVE ROULADE

A delicious olive mixture encased in lovely oily pastry that can be served either with drinks or as a starter, with *houmous* and *tabbouleh*. It is simple to make although pitting the olives can be time consuming. If you prefer less oily pastry, the oil can be omitted and a little brushed over the dough, once it is rolled out. An attractive and tasty starter.

For the dough
500g (1lb 2oz) flour
200ml (7fl oz) vegetable oil
200ml (7fl oz) juice of one orange
3 teaspoons baking powder
1 teaspoon salt
1 egg yolk

For the filling
500g (1lb 2oz) green olives, pitted
500g (1lb 2oz) black olives, pitted
2 teaspoons cumin
1–2 teaspoons cayenne pepper
1½ teaspoons oregano

Mix all ingredients for the dough, except the egg yolk, in a basin, until a smooth dough is formed. Cover and leave to rest for half an hour.

Prepare the filling by mixing all the ingredients together, then divide the mixture into 4.

Divide the dough into 4 equal parts also, then roll each portion out to a rectangular shape of 24cm (9½in) by 18cm (7in). Cover each strip with the olive mixture and roll up into a 'log'.

Brush each roulade with egg yolk and bake in a preheated oven 180°C (350°F/gas mark 4) for 40 minutes, or until golden brown.

Allow to cool before slicing and serving.

Ejjet arnabit

CAULIFLOWER FRITTERS

These cauliflower fritters are both healthy and tasty. They are made from simple ingredients and will be enjoyed by everyone. They can be prepared in advance and eaten cold, which makes them an excellent addition to a buffet. Serve it with *Kibbeh al-hammam* (see page 96) and finish with the irresistible Lebanese dessert, *Kanafeh* (see page 79).

Ingredients
1 cauliflower (about 620g / 1lb 6oz)
3 eggs, separated
1 teaspoon salt
¼ teaspoon black pepper
115g (4oz) flour
200ml (7fl oz) water
1 onion (100g / 3½oz), finely chopped
5 garlic cloves, finely chopped
1 teaspoon ground cumin
45g (1½oz) chopped parsley
extra virgin olive oil for frying

Separate the cauliflower into florets and boil in salted water for 2 minutes, or until just tender. Drain and allow to cool. Carefully slice each floret into medium-sized slices. Set aside.

Whisk the egg yolks and sprinkle with salt and pepper. Add the flour, a little at a time, alternating with the water and whisking constantly until it is thoroughly incorporated. Add the onions, garlic, cumin and parsley, stir well and set the yolk mixture to one side.

Beat the egg whites until stiff. Gently fold into the egg yolk mixture. Heat enough oil in a frying pan to shallow fry. You may need to add more oil as you cook the fritters. Place a slice of cauliflower in a tablespoon, dip into the egg mixture, and coat well. Drop the cauliflower in the hot oil. Do not crowd the frying pan with too many fritters. Allow to brown, then turn over to brown on the other side. Remove and drain on kitchen paper. Arrange on a round serving plate. Serve hot or cold.

If you have cauliflower florets left over, make a salad with olive oil, a hint of lemon juice, a pinch of garlic, steamed carrots and a little chopped parsley.

Richetaya shorba

LENTIL SOUP

This is a modest and economical peasant dish, warming and comforting in winter, and rich in iron, carbohydrates and protein. Traditionally, square or rope-shaped dumplings would be added to the soup. Today, a more convenient addition is that of a handful of pasta shells. If you wish, you could also add tiny squares of baked pitta bread (see page 60).

In Aleppo, the Christians prepare this soup on the first day of Lent. It is simple to make, and can be prepared in advance and reheated when needed. It keeps in the fridge for up to 3 days. Eaten with wholemeal bread, olives, radishes and white cheese, it makes a complete meal.

Ingredients
225g (8oz) brown or green lentils
1 medium size potato (200g / 7oz), scrubbed and quartered
1 large onion, quartered
1.7 litres (3 pints) water
2 teaspoons salt, or to taste
¼ teaspoon black pepper
5 tablespoons extra virgin olive oil
2 medium onions, finely sliced
55g (2oz) pasta shells (optional)

Put the lentils in a pan with the potato, the onion quarters and water, and bring to the boil over high heat. Reduce heat to medium and sprinkle with salt and pepper. Cover and simmer over low-medium heat for 30–40 minutes or until the lentils are tender.

In the meantime, add the oil to a frying pan, and heat until hot but not smoking. Add the sliced onions and sauté for 5 minutes until golden brown, stirring frequently. Set to one side.

When the lentils are soft, place them with the other ingredients in the pan in a food processor and blend until creamy (you might need to do it in two batches) or pass through a vegetable mill. Return to the same pan. Bring to the boil, stir in the pasta, if using, and allow to simmer over medium heat until the pasta shells are soft. Add the fried onions and serve hot as a starter.

Chawki Istanbuli

ISTANBUL ARTICHOKES

This dish looks and tastes delightful. Nothing can beat this as a light starter. As a bonus, artichokes contain substances that protect the liver and the kidneys, and lower the level of cholesterol in the blood.

I prefer fresh artichokes, although frozen ones will do. Snap off all the leaves from the fresh artichoke, one by one, until you reach the base. Then, using a sharp knife gently scoop out the choke and discard. Trim the tough skin around the base and quickly rub with a lemon to prevent discoloration. I often boil the leaves separately and eat the base as a snack.

Ingredients
8 artichoke hearts
12 baby onions
1 large carrot, peeled and cut into 1cm (½ inch) sticks
150ml (5fl oz) hot water
3 tablespoons lemon juice
4 tablespoons extra virgin olive oil
1 teaspoon salt

Place the artichoke hearts in a pan with the baby onions, carrot, water, lemon juice, oil and salt. Bring to the boil over a high heat, then quickly reduce the heat to low, cover and simmer for 30 minutes. Reserving 4 baby onions and 4 carrot sticks for the garnish, place the rest of the onions and carrot in a blender and blend, adding about 5 tablespoons of the cooking liquid to reach a thick, creamy consistency.

Serve the artichoke hearts by spooning the vegetable cream into the hollows and placing one of the remaining onions on top. Drizzle with a little of the artichoke liquid and serve 2 artichoke hearts per person, one with an onion and one without, and with a carrot stick in between.

Muhammara

WALNUTS WITH POMEGRANATE SYRUP

This spiced walnut dish is the crowning glory of Aleppo's *mezzé*. It is also enjoyed in other parts of the Levant, with slight variations. The Damascene version, for example, uses *Debs al-flaifleh* (sweet pepper paste), to which fresh chilli may be added to give extra colour. *Muhammara* means 'made red' because of the quantity of cayenne that's used in this recipe. While in Turkey, Vedat Basaran served me a delicious version. He told me that he also adds a very little thick yogurt.

Walnuts are one of Aleppo's major products. They are rich in omega-3 oils and magnesium.

Muhammara can be served with one or two other starters, such as Olive salad (page 105) and *Kibbeh al-hammam* (page 96), or to accompany Lentil soup (page 93), which would make a complete and nutritious dinner.

Ingredients
3 tablespoons breadcrumbs
1 teaspoon cayenne pepper
150ml (¼ pint) hot water
170g (6oz) walnuts
1–1½ tablespoons pomegranate syrup
1 teaspoon cumin
½ teaspoon salt, or to taste

To garnish
2 tablespoons pine nuts

Put the breadcrumbs in a small bowl and sprinkle with the cayenne. Add the hot water and give the mixture a good stir. Put the walnuts, the pomegranate syrup, cumin and salt in a blender. Add the breadcrumb mixture and blend until the ingredients reach a creamy texture – if necessary, add a little hot water. If a blender is not available, grind the walnuts with a mortar and pestle then mix thoroughly with the other ingredients. Spread into a serving dish, garnish with pine nuts. Serve with lettuce or crackers.

Kibbeh al-hammam

BURGHOL AND TOMATO KIBBEH

Hammam literally means bath and this dish was traditionally prepared for the special journey when men and women would set out to have their bodies cleansed and purified. They would also spend hours gossiping and discussing the topics of the day. Baths were particularly important to the Romans and the Byzantines, and remained so for the Arabs and the Turks.

This dish is delicious and makes an excellent starter for 5 or a hungry 4. It also presents beautifully in a buffet. It has become one of my favourites.

Ingredients
140g (5oz) onion, finely chopped
4 tablespoons extra virgin olive oil
1 heaped teaspoon tomato purée
170g (6oz) fine burghol
4 large ripe tomatoes (675g / 1½lb), peeled and finely chopped
1½ teaspoons salt, or to taste
1–2 tablespoons pomegranate syrup
a large handful of parsley, chopped
2 spring onions (55g / 2oz), finely sliced
the seeds of one whole sour or semi-sour pomegranate

Combine the onions, olive oil and tomato purée in a small bowl and set to one side. Place the burghol in a mixing bowl, sprinkle with 3 tablespoons of water, cover with the tomatoes and sprinkle with salt. Add the onion mixture to the burghol, along with the pomegranate syrup. Knead and mix with your fingers and palm until all the ingredients come together.

To serve, place on a serving dish and smooth, garnish with parsley, spring onion and pomegranate seeds. Serve with lettuce.

Ejjet al-bakdouness

PARSLEY OMELETTE

In Aleppo, this dish is prepared on the Fridays during Lent and is eaten with lentil soup. The flavour of the eggs is enhanced by the aromatic herbs and spices. It is a perfect meal for all ages, and an excellent source of protein and vitamin B12, which is important for building red blood and nerve cells.

Serve as a starter or main course. If prepared as fritters, it makes an excellent addition to cocktails.

Ingredients
8 eggs
1¼ teaspoons salt
¼ teaspoon black pepper
3 garlic cloves, finely crushed
2–3 teaspoons ground dried mint
225g (8oz) onions, finely chopped
170g (6oz) parsley, finely chopped
2–3 tablespoons olive oil

In a bowl, lightly beat the eggs, sprinkle with salt and pepper and add the garlic and mint. Stir well and add the onions and parsley. Heat the oil in a large frying pan and when it is hot pour in the egg mixture. Leave to cook over medium heat for 3–4 minutes. Turn over to brown the other side. If you wish, you can fry in 2 batches.

If making fritters, heat the oil, spoon a heaped tablespoon of the egg mixture and drop it gently into the pan. Allow to brown for 1 minute, then turn on to the other side. Cook 3 or 4 of these at a time, adding more oil if necessary.

Serve hot, warm or at room temperature with Oriental salad (see page 35), a bowl of green olives and crusty bread.

Kibbeh naye

LAMB WITH BURGHOL

This raw *kibbeh* uses fresh parsley. It is easy to make and all you need is good, lean lamb, preferably organic.

This dish is generally served as part of the *mezzé* to accompany other dishes. Nevertheless, it makes an excellent starter on its own. When you add water to burghol, it doubles in size. This reminds me of a story about a man from the west who ate raw *kibbeh* and became so fond of it that he kept on eating it and drinking water until he became bloated with stomach pains. One day, he was walking to work when he saw some builders trying to blow up a rock with explosives. He ran towards them shouting, 'Don't use explosives, trust me, raw *kibbeh* and water will do the work.'

Ingredients
1 onion (about 140g / 5oz), chopped
a large handful of parsley
½ teaspoon cayenne pepper
170g (6oz) burghol
iced water
450g (1lb) lean lamb mince
1½ teaspoons salt, or to taste

To garnish
1 sweet red pepper, seeded and finely sliced
extra virgin olive oil

Place the onion in a blender and blend for 1 minute. Add the parsley and blend for a few seconds. Sprinkle the cayenne pepper over the burghol and splash with 2–3 tablespoons cold water. Add to the onion in the blender, along with the meat and salt. Blend for 1 minute, or until smooth, then remove. If a blender is not available, grate the onion and very finely chop the parsley, mix with the burghol and the meat and knead well. Take a handful of this mixture and press gently between the forefingers and palm.

Arrange on a serving dish, and repeat with the remaining meat and burghol mixture. Garnish with the red pepper and drizzle with the olive oil and serve.

Batinjan bourek

STUFFED BABY AUBERGINES

There are so many different ways of preparing baby aubergines; this is a particularly delicious one.

In Aleppo, a white cheese is produced called *jibni khadra*, which means 'green cheese', so-called because of its freshness. It is similar in taste to ricotta or *Jibn baladi*, which you can purchase from any Lebanese, Cypriot or Arab delicatessen. If you are unable to buy either of these cheeses, use feta; its delicate piquancy goes perfectly well with the aubergines.

Ingredients
4 fat baby aubergines, halved lengthways
sea salt
extra virgin olive oil
55g (2oz) grated white cheese
¼ teaspoon salt
a pinch of white pepper
a pinch of nutmeg (optional)
2 tablespoons chopped parsley
flour
1 egg, or as necessary

Trim the green tops of the aubergines, leaving a part of the stem intact. Peel and slice lengthways. Sprinkle with salt and leave to stand for 1 hour in a colander so that the water is extracted, which lessens the absorption of the oil when they are sautéed. Rinse and pat dry with kitchen paper.

Heat the oil in a frying pan and sauté the aubergines over medium heat until both sides become golden brown. Remove and allow to cool. Mix the cheese, the salt, pepper, nutmeg, if using, and parsley in a small bowl. Make a slit along the centre of the aubergines and, using your finger or a spoon, push as much as possible of the cheese mixture inside the aubergines. Dredge in flour and place on a lightly floured dish. Repeat with the remaining aubergines.

In a bowl, beat the egg with a fork. Add oil to a deep, small-size frying pan and place over medium heat. When the oil is hot but not smoking, take an aubergine at a time, dip in the egg and gently drop it in the oil. When it is golden brown on one side, turn to lightly brown the other side. Repeat with all the other aubergines.

Serve hot as a starter, allowing 2 halves for each person.

Kassis mshattah

FRIED AUBERGINES WITH TOMATOES

The name of this dish literally means 'the resting monk'. According to legend, a monk was invited to have lunch at the house of the village chief, whose beautiful wife was a renowned cook. She made this dish and served it to the monk with fresh bread. He ate his first helping, praising the hostess. He had another serving, and another and another – dipping the bread in the delicious orange-red sauce. He couldn't control his greed, so there was nothing left for the other guests, then he leaned back on the sofa to have a long rest. As long as you don't invite a gourmet monk to lunch, this should be a perfect starter!

Ingredients
1 kg (2¼lb) aubergines, sliced lengthways into 2cm (¼in) slices
sea salt
75ml (3fl oz) extra virgin olive oil for frying
5 large red tomatoes, peeled and sliced into three

Sprinkle the aubergines with salt, place over a large colander and leave for an hour to draw out their water. This minimizes the absorption of oil during the cooking process. Then rinse and dry well between thick kitchen paper.

Heat the oil in a frying pan, but do not allow it to smoke. Fry the aubergine slices until golden brown on both sides. In a pan arrange alternate layers of tomatoes and aubergines, beginning with a layer of tomatoes. Cover and simmer over a medium-low heat for 30–40 minutes. Turn off the heat. It is important to keep the pan covered until the cooked vegetables reach room temperature so that the flavours blend together. Serve with Arabic (pitta) bread, olives and white cheese.

Moufaraket batinjan

AUBERGINES WITH EGGS

The aubergine, or eggplant, is native to India and was brought by Arab traders to Arabia and Spain during the Middle Ages. It comes in a variety of sizes, shapes and colours and is prepared in myriad ways all over the Levant.

There is a story about a groom who said to his bride during the wedding ceremony, 'My dear bride, I love you so much but never ask me what I want to eat when the aubergines are in season. If you do, you will go back to your family.'

This is just one of the Levant repertoire of aubergine dishes, all of which are quick, easy to prepare and full of flavour. A good vegetarian starter.

Ingredients
sea salt
735g (1lb 10oz) aubergines, peeled and sliced
extra virgin olive oil for frying
6 eggs
1 teaspoon salt
a pinch of black pepper
140g (5oz) ricotta cheese, grated
2 handfuls of parsley, finely chopped

Sprinkle sea salt all over the aubergines and allow to stand in a colander for an hour with a plate over them, under a heavy weight. This will prevent the absorption of too much oil during the cooking process. Rinse and pat the aubergines dry between sheets of kitchen paper. Fry in the hot oil until golden brown, then remove and drain on kitchen paper.

Arrange the slices of aubergine in a heavy, medium-sized, ovenproof pan. Beat the eggs, add 1 teaspoon of salt, the black pepper, ricotta and parsley, and stir well. Pour the egg mixture over the aubergines in the pan. Cook in a preheated oven at 350°C (180°F/gas mark 4) for 25–30 minutes, or until the top has set and browned. Serve hot with Oriental salad (see page 35).

Shorba makhlouta

MIXED GRAINS SOUP

This delicious peasant soup makes a satisfying and nutritious meal, being rich in B vitamins, fibre and protein. It is pleasingly light and a great favourite of mine – a perfect starter or even a main dish, if served with crusty bread, green olives, spring onions and mint, the aromatic digestive herb that is so commonly used in the Levant.

Ingredients
225g (8oz) split red lentils
85g (3oz) short grain rice, rinsed once
85g (3oz) coarse burghol
2 litres (3½ pints) water
2 teaspoons salt, or to taste
4 tablespoons extra virgin olive oil
2 medium-size onions, finely sliced
1 teaspoon ground cumin

Place the lentils, rice, burghol and water in a pan. Bring to the boil, reduce the heat to medium, sprinkle with salt, partly cover to prevent it from boiling over, and simmer for 15 minutes or until the ingredients are soft. In the meantime, heat the oil in a frying pan until hot but not smoking. Add the onions and sauté until golden brown. When the grains are ready, add the onions and sprinkle with cumin.

Serve hot.

Kibbeh batata halabieh

ALEPPO'S POTATO KIBBEH

This simple vegetarian dish is for everyday home cooking. Many countries in the Levant have their own way of preparing *kibbeh*. Like many other dishes, it is difficult to pinpoint where this first originated. This dish can be prepared in advance and can be eaten hot or warm. It makes an excellent starter for 8. Cut into medium-sized pieces, it also makes a perfect addition to a buffet.

For the kibbeh *dough*
900g (2lb) potatoes, pre-cooked and mashed
2 eggs
8 tablespoons breadcrumbs
1½ teaspoons salt
¼ teaspoon black pepper

For the filling
285g (10oz) onions, chopped
150ml (5fl oz) extra virgin olive oil
1 small green pepper, seeded and finely diced (optional)
2 large handfuls of coriander or parsley, finely chopped
115g (4oz) walnuts, coarsely chopped
½ teaspoon cayenne pepper, or to taste
1–1½ tablespoons pomegranate syrup

Place all the *kibbeh* dough ingredients in a bowl. Knead to the consistency of smooth dough, and set aside.

Next prepare the filling. Place the onions and 3 tablespoons of oil in a frying pan. Sauté over medium-high heat for 1–2 minutes, then lower the heat and continue to sauté until the onions are golden brown. Add the green pepper, if using, stir well and sauté for 1 minute. Add the coriander or parsley, walnuts, cayenne pepper and pomegranate syrup, and stir for a further few seconds. Then turn off the heat.

With a tablespoon of oil, grease a rectangular 30x20cm (12x8in) baking pan. Moisten the hands with water, take a small portion of *kibbeh* dough at a time and flatten it over the pan. Repeat until you have a uniform, medium-thin layer over the pan. Spread the filling evenly over the top. Cover with another layer of the remaining potato dough, moistening the hands as necessary because the dough can be sticky, and smooth the surface. Moisten a pointed knife with water and run it around the potato *kibbeh*. Then cut into lozenge shapes or squares. Drizzle with remaining oil and bake in a preheated oven at 180°C (350°F/gas mark 4) for 50 minutes, or until the top becomes golden brown.

Ejjet al-batata

POTATO OMELETTE

This is a delicious and comforting dish. In Aleppo it is prepared as a starter or even as a main course, accompanied by a salad.

It can also be served as fritters, to be enjoyed when friends are around. Serve with *Muhammara* (see page 95), *Kassis mshattah* (page 100) and *houmous* (page 16).

This potato omelette serves 5.

Ingredients
8 eggs
1½ teaspoons salt, or to taste
¼ teaspoon black pepper
1 pinch of grated nutmeg
450g (1lb) potatoes, boiled, peeled and finely mashed
2–3 tablespoons olive oil

In a bowl lightly beat the eggs. Add the salt, pepper, nutmeg and potatoes, and stir well. Heat the oil in a heavy frying pan and, when it is hot but not smoking, pour in the egg batter and allow 3–4 minutes to set and brown over medium heat. Turn over and brown the other side.

If making fritters, spoon 1 heaped tablespoon of the egg batter and drop it gently into the pan. Allow to set for 1 minute then turn to brown the other side. Cook as many as the frying pan can take, adding oil as necessary. Remove from the pan, drain over kitchen paper and repeat until all the fritters are cooked.

Serve the omelette hot with a salad, and the fritters either warm or cold with *Baba-ghanouj* (see page 23).

Salatet al-zaitoun

OLIVE SALAD

This unusual olive salad is a pleasure to make and will delight everyone. It is full of flavour, is simple to prepare and goes very well with drinks. I first sampled it in a restaurant in Aleppo and fell for it immediately.

In Aleppo, olive salad is a part of the *mezzé*, which includes a selection of appetizing dishes that feast the eye and whet the appetite.

Ingredients
200g (7oz) green olives, pitted and halved
1 small onion, finely chopped
½ teaspoon cayenne pepper, or 1 hot chilli, finely sliced
½ teaspoon cumin (optional)
1 small carrot, finely shredded
a large handful of parsley, finely chopped
1 tablespoon extra virgin olive oil
1½ tablespoons pomegranate syrup

Combine the olives, onion, cayenne pepper or chilli in a serving bowl. Add the cumin, if using, the carrots and parsley. Toss in oil and pomegranate syrup and leave to marinate for 10 minutes.

Eat on its own or serve as part of a *mezzé* with Arabic (pitta) bread. Red peppers go well with this dish and so does *baba-ghanouj* (see page 23).

Mortadella

GARLIC LAMB WITH PISTACHIOS

This dish does not bear any similarity to the Italian sausage of the same name, except in shape. It is simple to prepare and freezes well (it can be sliced before freezing to speed up defrosting). In Aleppo, when guests arrive unannounced and need to be fed (and this happens all the time in the Levant), people take the *mortadella* out of the freezer and serve it with drinks. Other accompaniments could be quickly prepared, such as *Muhammara* (see page 95) and *Olive salad* (see page 105). *Mortadella* makes a good starter and is ideal for a buffet. Today, some people prefer to use chicken or turkey. Why not see for yourself?

Ingredients
1kg (2¼lb) lamb
2 teaspoons black pepper
2½ teaspoons salt
55g (2oz) fine breadcrumbs
1 head of garlic, crushed
24 shelled pistachios, split in two
1 chicken breast, cut into thin strips
the white of an egg
120ml (4½ fl oz) hot water
200ml (7fl oz) cider vinegar
bouquet garni, consisting of celery stick, bay leaf, cinnamon stick, cardamom, black
    peppercorns, 4 cloves and onion

Put the lamb in a mixing bowl. Add the pepper, 2 teaspoons of salt and breadcrumbs. Knead and mix well. Divide into 3 portions, and taking each portion, flatten in a round shape, using the palm and forefingers, to a thickness of 5mm (¼in). Scatter the garlic and the pistachios evenly over the top.

Sprinkle the remaining salt over the chicken strips and mix. In the centre of each round of meat place 3 (or more) strips of chicken. Roll up the meat, enclosing the garlic, pistachio and chicken. Pack it gently, forming a log-shaped roll. Moisten your hands with egg white and dab the top of the roll to prevent it bursting as it cooks. Repeat with the other 2 rolls.

Place the lamb rolls on a plate which has been moistened with a little water so that the meat logs do not stick. Place in the freezer for 15 minutes. Remove and put the rolls in a pan. Cover with water and vinegar, and add the bouquet garni. Bring to the boil, cover and simmer over high heat for 5 minutes. Then reduce the heat to medium and continue cooking for a further 40 minutes. Remove and allow to cool to reach room temperature. Cut in slices. Serve cold.

Salatet flifleh hamra

SWEET RED PEPPER SALAD

Although grown locally, sweet peppers originally travelled from South America to Spain, and from there to the Levant. I discovered this salad when I was in northern Syria and fell for it. It is normally served as part of a *mezzé* and its consistency and texture make it perfectly suitable for a dip to eat with crackers or French fries. It is dressed with a small quantity of pomegranate syrup, which adds an extraordinary tang.

This is a simple recipe to prepare, so practical when entertaining and looks beautiful. It is an excellent addition to a buffet and can be served as a starter. The sweet peppers are traditionally blended until smooth, but they are just as good if left a little lumpy.

Ingredients
8 large red peppers
1½–2 tablespoons pomegranate syrup
1 teaspoon salt, or to taste
10 black or green olives, halved or quartered
55g (2oz) walnuts, coarsely crushed
extra virgin olive oil

To garnish
a handful of fresh mint leaves or basil

Preheat the grill. Place the peppers in an oven pan 10cm/4in below the grill. Grill for 18–20 minutes or until charred on all sides. Remove the peppers and allow to cool slightly.

Using a small pointed knife, remove the skin, cap and seeds, and discard. Place the flesh in a blender and run the motor for a few seconds or until nearly smooth but not watery. If it is too watery, strain, and keep the liquid to use in salads. If a blender is not available chop the peppers very thinly lengthways (or pass through a vegetable mill). Transfer the puréed pepper to a bowl and toss lightly in the pomegranate syrup and salt.

Place in a serving dish, scatter with olives and walnuts, drizzle over the oil and garnish with mint or basil. Eat with cos lettuce leaves and potato salad.

Burghol bi shaariyeh

CRACKED WHEAT WITH VERMICELLI

The combination of burghol and vermicelli in this pilaff provides nourishment and flavour. It is filling and greatly comforting. This version is also prepared in Lebanon, especially in the mountains. A variation uses rice instead of burghol and is as delicious as this pilaff but, of course, it tastes different.

In this recipe, the vermicelli is sautéed in extra virgin olive oil until it reaches a deep golden colour. If you wish to follow the traditional method, use *samneh* (clarified butter).

Serving it hot with a bowl of chilled yogurt offers a delightful contrast.

Ingredients
1 tablespoon extra virgin olive oil
2 or 3 vermicelli nests (about 55g/2oz), crushed by hand into small pieces
225g (8oz) coarse burghol
400ml (14fl oz) water
1½ teaspoons salt, or to taste
¾ teaspoon cinnamon

Place a small to medium pan over medium-high heat. Add the oil and when it is hot but not smoking, add the broken vermicelli and stir continuously until it becomes golden brown. Be careful not to burn it. Add the burghol, stir once with the vermicelli and quickly add the water. Season with salt and bring to the boil. Cover and simmer over low heat for 5–7 minutes, or until the water has been absorbed. Turn off the heat and cover the pan with a thick towel for 5 minutes. Arrange on a warm serving dish. Sprinkle with cinnamon.

Serve on its own or with yogurt, or as an accompaniment to stews.

Main courses

Labanieh

CHICKEN AND LAMB IN YOGURT

This rich Aleppo dish is a gastronomical delicacy that is prepared to celebrate special occasions such as the New Year. It is believed that seeing in the New Year with white dishes brings good luck.

An appetizing and comforting dish, its only drawback is its lengthy preparation. First, you need to make a chicken stock. The next step is to prepare the *kibbeh* dough shells, stuff them, roll them into balls and cook them in the stock. You can prepare the yogurt while *Labanieh* is cooking. Finally, assemble the dish.

This unusual and filling *Labanieh* is particularly good for Sunday lunch in winter. Despite its long preparation time, it can be cooked in advance and assembled with the yogurt before serving.

This recipe serves 6.

For the chicken
½ chicken, rubbed with salt and lemon
1.10 litres (2 pints) water
bouquet garni, consisting of cardamom, 1 cinnamon stick, small onion, 5 cloves, celery
*   stick, bay leaf, black peppercorns*
½ teaspoon salt

For the kibbeh *balls*
225g (8oz) lean minced lamb
115g (4oz) fine burghol
85g (3oz) onion, finely grated
½ teaspoon salt
¼ teaspoon black pepper
¼ teaspoon cayenne pepper
3 teaspoons ground cinnamon
85–100g (3–3½oz) butter

For the yogurt
600ml (1 pint) yogurt
1 egg
1 teaspoon cornflour
1 teaspoon water
1 teaspoon salt
4 garlic cloves, finely crushed
1 teaspoon dried mint

Rinse the chicken and place with the water in a pan. Bring to the boil, skim, then reduce the heat. Add the bouquet garni and cook for 50–60 minutes until tender.

While the chicken is cooking, prepare the *kibbeh* balls. In a bowl, mix and knead the minced lamb with the burghol, onion, salt and the black and cayenne peppers to form a smooth and manageable consistency (you might need to add 1–2 tablespoons of ice-cold water). Mix the cinnamon with the butter, divide into 16 equal portions and leave in a cool place.

Divide the dough into 16 portions. Moisten your hands with water as necessary, then take each portion and roll between the palms of your hands to form a ball. Holding the meat ball with one hand, poke a hole in the centre with the index finger of the other and work around the inside until you have a medium thin shell. Fill with a portion of cinnamon and butter and gently reshape and smooth to enclose the filling into a round shape. When all the *kibbeh* balls are finished, set to one side.

Combine the yogurt with the egg. Mix the cornflour with the water and stir into the yogurt until well-blended. Stir through a sieve into another bowl and set aside.

Remove the chicken from the pan, cut into tiny pieces and discard the skin and bones. Put to one side. Measure 450ml (15fl oz) of the chicken stock, place in a medium-size pan and bring to a boil. Drop the prepared *kibbeh* balls into the stock, return to a boil, then reduce the heat to medium. Cover and simmer for 2 minutes. Remove the kibbeh balls with a slotted spoon and place on a dish. Add the strained yogurt to the broth, stirring with a wooden spoon, always in the same direction, until it boils. At this point, return the *kibbeh* balls to the pan, add the chicken pieces and bring back to the boil. Reduce the heat to low. Now sprinkle with the salt, garlic and mint. Leave to simmer, uncovered, for 3–4 minutes. Serve hot on its own or with plain cooked rice.

If you wish, prepare the garlic and mint in the authentic Aleppo and Lebanese way. Sauté them in butter for a few seconds, then stir into the yogurt.

Sheikh al-mihshi koussa

STUFFED COURGETTES

This recipe is often served at home in Aleppo. Pomegranate trees grow in abundance in Syria, and the juice is used in many Syrian dishes. A most delectable syrup is made from sour pomegranates, giving a unique flavour and zest to a dish. In this recipe, it brings out the delicate sweetness of the courgettes.

For the courgettes
8 baby courgettes
1 tablespoon butter
85g (3oz) onion, finely chopped
170g (6oz) minced lamb
¾ teaspoon salt
¼ teaspoon black pepper
1 egg
a large handful of parsley, finely chopped
½–1 tablespoon breadcrumbs

For the sauce
150ml (5fl oz) pomegranate juice
60ml (2½fl oz) lemon juice
1 teaspoon sugar
1 heaped tablespoon tomato purée

Slice off the top of the courgettes. Using a corer, gently hollow out the inside until you have a uniformly thin shell. (You can use the discarded flesh to make an omelette. Add some finely chopped, sautéed onions and a tablespoon of pine nuts and beat with 3–4 eggs. Season with cinnamon, black pepper and salt. Prepare as on page 97.)

Heat half the butter in a frying pan and add the onion and lamb. Stir for 2–3 minutes or until the meat loses its blood colour. Sprinkle with salt and pepper. Turn off the heat. When the mixture reaches room temperature, stir in the egg, parsley and breadcrumbs. Fill the hollowed courgettes with this mixture.

Heat the remaining butter in a pan, add the courgettes and sauté lightly on both sides. Add all the sauce ingredients and bring to the boil. Cover and simmer over medium heat for 20–30 minutes. Serve hot with rice or cracked wheat with vermicelli (page 108).

Kibbeh ala-sikh

SKEWERED LAMB AND BURGHOL

This is similar to Aleppo's raw *kibbeh*, except that it uses dried mint instead of fresh parsley, more burghol and less meat. Although the name suggests that the mixture is cooked on skewers, actually the skewers are only used to make the hole in the *kibbeh* ball. A good deal of fat is added to moisten the meat and enhance the flavour. Don't let the quantity of fat deter you because, while the *kibbeh* bakes, the fat melts out and is easily discarded.

This dish is easy to make and can be served as a part of a *mezzé*. It is delicious with Oriental salad (see page 35), *Baba-ghanouj* (page 23) and Sweet red pepper salad (page 107).

Makes about 28 *kibbeh* balls.

Ingredients
1 onion (about 325g / 11oz) cut in half
225g (8oz) burghol
2 teaspoons dried mint
½ teaspoon cayenne pepper
3 tablespoons cold water, or as necessary
400g (14oz) minced lamb
115 (4oz) lamb fat (ask your butcher for a fat that melts)
2 teaspoons salt, or to taste
56 pine nuts
¼ tablespoon butter

Put the onion in a blender and run the motor until it reaches a creamy texture. Grate if a blender is not available. Mix the burghol with the mint, cayenne pepper and water, then add this mixture to the onion. Add the lamb, fat and salt. Blend to reach a smooth consistency (if you don't have a blender ask your butcher to twice mince the fat together with the lamb meat). Take a little of the mixture and form into a ball, moistening hands with water if necessary. Repeat until all the mixture is used up.

Pierce each ball with a thick skewer, then remove the skewer. Stick 2 pine nuts into each meat ball and place in a lightly buttered pan. Heat the oven to 180°C (350°F/gas mark 4). Cook for 20 minutes or until the meat balls are nicely browned and the fat has melted out of the meat. Remove and discard the excess fat.

Serve hot as part of a *mezzé*, or as a main dish.

Habra el samak

CHICKEN PATTIES WITH CORIANDER

Although actually prepared with chicken, this Aleppino dish is known by the locals as 'lean of fish', which sums up its delicacy and finesse. It takes time to make but the result is very rewarding.

These patties make an excellent starter and, if prepared in a smaller size, can be served as canapés to eat with cocktails. However, that would take a lot of patience and someone to help, but they can be prepared ahead of time, frozen and used when required.

Serve hot together with *Baba-ghanouj* (page 23), *Salatet flifleh-hamra* (page 107), *Kibbeh al-hammam* (page 96), or eat on their own with a salad of your choice. This dish, if made with fish, would be equally delicious.

Makes 26 patties.

Ingredients
450g (1lb) potatoes
480g (1lb 1oz) chicken breasts, minced
1 tablespoon ground coriander
4 garlic cloves, finely crushed
1½ teaspoons salt
fine breadcrumbs
85ml (3fl oz) olive or peanut oil or as necessary

Put the unpeeled potatoes into a pan and cover with boiling water. Cover the pan and simmer over medium heat until tender. Remove the potatoes, leave to cool, then peel and press through a vegetable mill or mash (*not* in a blender) until you have a smooth texture. Place in a mixing bowl with the minced chicken, coriander, garlic and salt, and knead to form a soft paste.

Moisten your hands with water and divide the mixture into 26 portions. Take a portion, flatten between the palms of your hands to form a patty, and dredge in the breadcrumbs (turn the patty over with a fork or palette knife to dredge the other side). If you have time, you can place the chicken mixture in the freezer for a few minutes to firm up – but do not forget them! Using your hands lightly, flatten the chicken patty until it is relatively thin and round. Place on a side plate and repeat with the other portions.

Heat the oil in a large frying pan. When it is hot but not smoking, add as many chicken patties as your pan can hold. Sauté over medium-high heat for 2–3 minutes, or until golden brown. Check the heat and reduce if necessary. Turn the patties over to brown the other side. Remove, drain over double kitchen paper and serve hot, warm or at room temperature.

Maldoum al-batinjan

AUBERGINES AND MEATBALLS

This Aleppino dish is simple, presents well and is very tasty. It makes an excellent main dish for the family and an unusual lunch on Sundays with friends.

You can cook it in advance, then reheat before serving. It tastes even better the next day. Makes about 30 meatballs.

Ingredients
1.5 kg (3¼ lbs) 3 medium size aubergines, peeled and cut into 30 slices
sea salt
extra virgin olive oil
450g (1lb) minced lamb
½ teaspoon salt
¼ teaspoon black pepper
6 medium red tomatoes, peeled and cut into 30 slices

Sprinkle the aubergine slices with salt and leave in a colander for an hour to draw out the water. Rinse, gently squeeze out the extra water and dry between kitchen paper. Brush with oil on both sides and grill or fry until golden brown on both sides. Set aside.

In a bowl, mix thoroughly the lamb, salt and pepper. Take a small portion at a time and shape into a small, flattish ball. Repeat until the mixture is used up. Place the tomato slices in a large, round pan. Top each piece of tomato with a meatball and then a slice of aubergine. Repeat, arranging them in a spiral. Cover and cook over medium or medium-low heat for 40–50 minutes, then turn the heat off and leave covered for 5 minutes. Serve hot with bread.

Hib el-ib

HIDDEN LOVE

When I first saw this recipe, I was surprised that the stuffed courgettes were cooked together with the beans. In the Lebanon, where I come from, I have always enjoyed eating them separately. I was intrigued by this sentimentally wild title and asked how it got its name. Here is the story I was told.

A long time ago two young people used to meet in a field that was their only refuge. It was their favourite place for there they found their freedom. Whenever somebody from the village passed by, they would pretend to be picking courgettes and green beans. They kept meeting for years but never married. Nobody knows why they never married, but for some reason they were not even allowed to meet. One day they vanished and their clothes were found. They had been made into a bundle, in which was a huge amount of courgettes and beans. The lovers were never to be found. It is a mystery to the present day, so these two vegetables became a symbol of their love and disappearance. The good villagers were saddened by the mysterious lovers so they prepared these two vegetables in one dish and called it *Hib el-ib* (hidden love) in their honour.

The story touched me and I came home eager to prepare this dish, hoping to find an answer to this enigma. The dish took some time to prepare but it was delicious. I am sure a good spell lay over the courgettes and beans.

This dish serves 5 as a main course.

Ingredients
8 baby courgettes
1 small onion (about 55g / 2oz), finely chopped
115g (4oz) minced lamb
55g (2oz) round-grain rice, rinsed once
1 teaspoon tomato purée
½ teaspoon salt
¼ teaspoon black pepper
30g (1oz) clarified butter
1 large onion about 350g (12oz) finely sliced
3–4 garlic cloves
285g (10oz) lamb, diced
450g (1lb) flat green beans rinsed, topped, tailed and strings removed, thickly sliced
1 tablespoon tomato purée
1 teaspoon salt, or to taste
¼ teaspoon black pepper
225g (8oz) tomatoes, each cut into 5 pieces
250ml (8½fl oz) hot water

With a knife, cut across the top of each courgette and trim the other end. Using a corer, gently scoop out the inside of each, leaving a shell with equal thickness all around. In a bowl, thoroughly combine the onion, minced lamb, rice, tomato purée, salt and the black pepper. Fill the courgette shells with this mixture and put to one side.

Put a pan over medium heat, add the butter, onions, garlic and diced lamb, and sauté for 5 minutes. Add the beans, cover and leave to cook in the steam for 4 minutes. Add the tomato purée, salt and pepper, the stuffed courgettes and finally the tomatoes and water. Bring to the boil, cover and simmer over medium heat for 30–40 minutes. Turn off the heat and leave covered for about 5 minutes to allow the flavours to develop.

Serve hot as a main dish with pitta bread, which you can dip into the delicious juices.

Yakhnet al-kabar

RAGOÛT DU CAPRES

A 10th-century caliph held a banquet. The distinguished guests included philosophers, poets and physicians. At the caliph's request, poetry was recited in praise of food. The caper was one of these foods: 'Here capers, whose fragrant odours to the soul are blown, grace sauce vermilion.' (From Baghdad cookery book, *Kitab al-tabikh*, translated from the Arabic by Arthur J Arberry p.2). Their strong, aromatic taste bestows a unique and distinctive flavour to this dish.

In Aleppo, capers are picked fresh and steeped in water overnight to rid them of their bitterness. I have never seen fresh capers in London but those that have been preserved in salt or vinegar are just as acceptable. Preserved capers need rinsing before use. The best way to get rid of the sharp taste of preserved capers is to soak them in boiling water and then strain.

The French-speaking bourgeoisie of Aleppo call this stew *Ragoût du capres*. It is usually prepared on special occasions, for a guest or as a Sunday lunch.

For the stew
450g (1lb) lamb, diced, with 3–4 bones
700ml (1¼ pints) water
bouquet garni consisting of celery stick, cardamom, a piece of lemon, 1 onion studded
    with cloves, cinnamon bark, black peppercorns and bay leaf
255g (9oz) salted capers, rinsed

For the roux
45g (1½oz) butter
2 tablespoons flour
6–8 tablespoons meat stock
3–4 tablespoons lemon juice

In a pan, combine the meat, bones and water, and place over medium-high heat. Bring to the boil and skim. Add the bouquet garni, cover and simmer over medium-low heat for 1 hour, or until the meat is tender. Remove the bones and discard.

Put the capers in a small pan with water to cover. Bring to the boil, cover and simmer over low heat for 20 minutes. Drain and discard the water.

To make the roux, put the butter in a frying pan. When it melts, add the flour and stir until it turns golden. Gradually add the stock, whisking constantly. The sauce will have a yellowish colour at this point. Add the lemon juice.

Add this sauce to the meat and to the stock that has already been cooked. Add the capers. Bring to the boil, cover and simmer for a few minutes, allowing just enough time for the flavours to blend. Serve hot with rice.

Kibbeh hamis

VEGETARIAN KIBBEH

On our way to Aleppo, we stopped to eat in Hama, an ancient city of Syria. In a local restaurant, we were served by a waiter called Ibrahim, a big man with a tanned complexion. He took our order and we were quickly served with the usual *mezzé*, including these delicious *kibbeh*. I asked Ibrahim how they were prepared because, from the texture of the shell, I was sure they were meatless. However, he insisted that there was just enough meat to make the dough malleable. After a long discussion, he was reassured that my interest in the dough of the *kibbeh* was purely culinary and that I was not suspiciously investigating the absence of meat.

The *kibbeh* below are completely vegetarian and are quite crunchy. To make the dough softer, you may add about 55g (2oz) of minced meat or 2 tablespoons of mashed potato. This recipe serves 4–5, and it is perfect as part of a *mezzé*.

Makes 16–18 *kibbeh* balls.

For the stuffing
1 tablespoon extra virgin olive oil
1 tablespoon butter
170g (6oz) onions, finely chopped
1 teaspoon cumin
115g (4oz) pistachio nuts, coarsely chopped
¼ teaspoon salt

For the dough
140g (5oz) fine burghol
45g (1½oz) fine semolina
85g (3oz) flour
1 teaspoon salt
a pinch of white pepper
¼ teaspoon turmeric
1 teaspoon osfour threads
115ml (4fl oz) warm water, or as necessary
olive oil for frying

Heat the olive oil and butter in a medium-size pan. When hot, add the onions and sauté until translucent. Add the cumin and stir for a few seconds to bring out the flavour. Stir in the pistachio nuts and salt. Turn off the heat.

Rinse the burghol, squeeze out the water and place in a medium-size mixing bowl. Add the semolina, flour, salt, pepper and turmeric. Dilute the *osfour* in 90ml (3½fl oz) water. Gradually add this to the burghol mixture in the bowl. Mix and knead, adding more water, if necessary, to form a medium-soft dough. Cover with a towel and leave to stand for 10 minutes.

Divide the dough into 16–18 portions. Take each portion and roll it between the palms of the hands to form an elongated oval shape the size of a small egg. Hold this in one hand and poke a hole in the top side of the *kibbeh* ball with the index finger of the other hand. Work around the inside to form a thin shell, moistening your hands as necessary.

Fill the *kibbeh* shells with the pistachio mixture. With moist hands, reshape and smooth the kibbeh to enclose the filling. Repeat until all the mixture is used up.

Heat the oil in a medium-size frying pan. When hot, fry the *kibbeh* until they are golden all over. Serve hot or warm.

Lahmeh bil-forn

MINCED LAMB IN THE OVEN

Lahmeh bil-forn is uncomplicated. In Aleppo people use the freshest of vegetables available in the enticing souk (market), and combine them with succulent mutton. This produces a savoury stew whose delicacy equals all their other dishes. Using *samneh* (clarified butter) is the authentic way for all meat or chicken preparations, but you can substitute olive oil instead. This dish is a perfect addition to our daily eating. It serves a family of five. Do give it a try.

Ingredients
45g (1½oz) clarified butter*
620g (1lb 6oz) onions, finely chopped
450g (1lb) minced lamb
1 tablespoon tomato purée
2 teaspoons salt, or to taste
¼ teaspoon black pepper
450g (1lb) medium size potatoes scrubbed, halved, cut into 3cm (1in) thick pieces
450g (1lb) courgettes, halved, sliced into 1cm / ½inch pieces
450g (1lb) aubergines, halved and sliced into 1cm / ½inch pieces
5 large red tomatoes peeled and quartered

In a pan heat the butter, then add the onion and the meat. Sauté, stirring occasionally for 5 minutes or until the meat is lightly browned. Stir in the tomato purée, and sprinkle with salt and black pepper. Add the potatoes, courgettes, aubergines and tomatoes. Cover and simmer over medium-low heat for 30–40 minutes. Remove and transfer into a serving oven dish. Place under a hot grill for 5 minutes or until the top is lightly browned and the sauce thickened. Watch closely that the strong heat does not burn the top of the dish. Serve immediately with radishes, green onions and pickles as well as bread.

   * Cut 450g of unsalted butter into ½ inch cubes. Place the cubes in a medium-size heavy-bottomed pan and melt over a low temperature. When the butter has melted, increase the heat slightly and leave to bubble for 2 minutes. Switch off the heat and skim the foam that has formed on the surface of the melted butter, then pour the remaining liquid into a glass container. Alternatively pour through muslin or a fine sieve. Refrigerate and use as necessary.

Warak enab bi-lahmeh

STUFFED VINE LEAVES WITH LAMB

A book about the cuisine of the Levant wouldn't be complete without stuffed vine leaves. Food has been wrapped in edible envelopes since ancient times and this is referred to in the writings of the Persians and Greeks. This Aleppino dish is not only delicious but also unusual because it includes artichoke slices, which give the dish an elegant taste. It takes time to prepare but it's worth the effort. I specially like to make it when fresh leaves are in season which can be bought from Lebanese shops.

This recipe makes a perfect main dish for 6–8. It would also adorn any buffet and is best accompanied by a bowl of yogurt on the side.

When I was at a friend's house in Aleppo, my attention was drawn to a plate full of peeled raw garlic cloves. When I wondered about it, I was told that this is how they eat their *Warak-enab bi-lahmeh* – accompanied by raw garlic. I am afraid this is one healthy practice I could not follow.

Ingredients
approximately 44–50 fresh vine leaves (about 225g / 8oz)
620g (1lb 6oz) minced lamb
350g (12oz) ground-grain rice, rinsed
1¾ teaspoons salt
¼ teaspoon freshly ground black pepper
2 heads of garlic (about 26 garlic cloves)
3–4 fresh artichoke hearts, sliced into 2 or 3 slices
4 slices of lamb from the neck
700ml (1¼ pints) hot water
150ml (5fl oz) lemon juice

Place the vine leaves in boiling water and simmer for 1–2 minutes. Remove and place in a colander. Thoroughly combine the minced lamb with the rice, 1 teaspoon salt and the black pepper. Take each leaf and if large, cut in half using a small, sharp knife, making sure to remove the thick stem and its vein.

Place each leaf lengthways, with the shiny side facing down. Depending on the size of the leaf, place a sausage-shaped portion of the lamb mixture at the cut end. Fold both sides of the leaf over the lamb mixture, hold firmly and roll to form a sausage shape. Repeat with the remaining vine leaves until they are all completed. Place one layer of stuffed leaves in a medium-size pan. Put about 8 garlic cloves over the top, followed by 2–3 slices of artichoke and 2 slices of lamb. Repeat by spreading another layer of stuffed vine leaves over the top, then the garlic, then the artichokes and then the lamb, until the pan is filled. Sprinkle on the remaining salt and pour over the water. Place over a medium-high heat, bring to the boil, cover the pan, then reduce the heat to medium and leave to simmer for 30 minutes.

Add the lemon juice, cover again and reduce the heat to low. Leave to simmer over low heat for 2 hours. Turn off the heat, cover with a thick towel and leave for 8 minutes.

Uncover the pan and pour the reduced cooking liquid into a bowl. Place a large deep serving dish over the pan and carefully invert. Wait for 2 minutes and gently remove the pan. Spoon over the cooking liquid.

Serve hot with pitta bread and a little yogurt, if desired.

Kebab karaz

MEATBALLS WITH CHERRY SAUCE

This mouthwatering seasonal dish, which uses fresh cherries, is typical of the village of Ariha, which is located south-west of Aleppo in a region of cherry orchards. It is said that this dish was first prepared by Muslims, who used to fry the lamb in mutton fat. Nowadays in Aleppo, in June, in the cherry season, a sauce is prepared and frozen so that it can also be enjoyed in winter. *Kebab karaz* is one among many other dishes that the Aleppinos are proud of.

During one of my visits to Aleppo, Maguy Zobian gave me some frozen cherry sauce, which I happily carried back all the way to London. This sophisticated sweet and sour dish is simple to prepare and is interesting to share with friends. For a fuller flavour you can add ½ tablespoon of pomegranate syrup.

Ingredients
300g (10½oz) fresh dark red cherries or dried sour cherries (found in supermarkets)
200ml (7fl oz) water
2 teaspoons sugar
juice of 1–1½ lemon
500g (1lb 2oz) minced lamb
1 teaspoon salt
¼ teaspoon black pepper
3 tablespoons butter
2 pitta breads, cut into triangles

To garnish
2–3 tablespoons pine nuts, toasted

Wash the cherries, cut in half and remove stones. Place the stones in a small pan with the water, and remove any remaining pulp with your fingers (in Aleppo nothing is wasted). Remove and discard the stones. Add the cherries to this water with the sugar and lemon juice. Bring to the boil and simmer over medium-low heat for 1 hour, or until the liquor reduces and thickens slightly.

In the meantime, mix the lamb with the salt and black pepper and form into balls the size of cherry tomatoes. Fry the lamb balls in the butter over medium heat until cooked through and browned. Add them to the cherry sauce.

To serve, place a few of the triangles of bread in a dish, spread all over with some cherries and sauce. Make another layer of bread and repeat as before. Finally, cover with the meatballs and the remains of the sauce. Garnish with pine nuts and serve immediately.

Kibbeh sobah

PUMPKIN STEW

In Aleppo there are four typical local recipes. On Sunday, one of these four dishes appears on the menu of the exclusive club of Aleppo as a *plât du jour*. All are succulent and worth trying. Basically they are prepared in the same way but use different vegetables. They also require lamb and its stock, a bouquet garni, and fresh juice or syrup of pomegranate. When the stock is too sour, a teaspoon of sugar is added; when it is too sweet, lemon juice is added.

All four recipes include *kibbeh* shells. However, for two of them you can choose to omit the *kibbeh* shells and serve with rice instead. Pumpkin stew and quince stew (page 127) can be eaten without *kibbeh* shells. The two that should contain *kibbeh* shells are: *Kibbeh jazarieh* (carrots), which substitutes carrots for pumpkin, and *Kibbeh rumanieh* (pomegranate), which has courgettes and peeled aubergines. To make the *kibbeh* shells see *Labanieh* (page 111) and for both follow the recipe below. Authentic *kibbeh* shells are filled with melted lamb fat.

For *Kibbeh sobah*, pomegranate juice can be substituted for lemon.

Ingredients
500g (1lb 2oz) lamb, diced
700ml (1¼ pints) water
bouquet garni consisting of 1 onion studded with 4 cloves, 2 bay leaves, 1 celery stick,
*   a few peppercorns and 1 cinnamon stick*
1½ teaspoons salt
1.5kg (3¼lb) pumpkin, peeled and cubed
55–75ml (2–3fl oz) lemon juice

Place the diced lamb and water in a pan over high heat. Skim, then add the bouquet garni and salt. Reduce the heat to low, cover and leave to simmer for 1 hour. When the hour is up add the pumpkin pieces and lemon juice, and simmer over medium-low heat for 20 minutes. Turn the heat off and, still covered, leave for 5 minutes before serving to allow a little time for the flavours to blend. Serve hot with rice.

Safarjalieh

QUINCE STEW

This famous Aleppino dish is deliciously succulent and has become a great favourite of mine, particularly because I can omit the *kibbeh* shells, which saves time. Instead, a plain cooked rice is eaten with the stew.

If prepared with *kibbeh* shells (see page 39), this recipe serves 6 people. In Aleppo, a dish such as this is preceded by a light starter and followed by fruit.

Ingredients
1kg (2¼lb) quinces, rinsed
1–2 teaspoons sugar
700ml (1¼ pints) water
500g (1lb 1oz) diced lamb
bouquet garni, consisting of 1 onion studded with 4 cloves, 2 bay leaves, a few
peppercorns and 1 cinnamon stick
1½ teaspoons salt, or to taste
150ml (5fl oz) pomegranate juice
2 tablespoons lemon juice

The night before, peel the quinces and save the peel. Place the quartered quinces in a bowl with their peel, sugar and water.

The following day, place the lamb in a medium-size pan, strain the quince water over the lamb, keeping the quinces to use later. Bring to the boil and skim. Add the bouquet garni and salt, reduce the heat to medium-low, cover and simmer for 30 minutes. Add the quinces, bring to the boil again, cover and simmer over medium-low heat for a further 30–40 minutes or until the meat and quinces are soft. Add the pomegranate and lemon juice when only 10 minutes of cooking time remains. Serve hot with rice.

Kibbeh sajieh

KIBBEH WITH WALNUT STUFFING

This is a classic of Aleppo cuisine, deliciously spicy and fragrant. The sweet shops in Aleppo have side-stalls filled with savoury delicacies, and this is one of them. No visitor should leave Aleppo without buying a portion over the counter and eating it straight away.

This dish is not very difficult to prepare but you need to practise making the shells. *Kibbeh sajieh* looks like a flying saucer. Traditionally they are made large but medium–small or small are ideal for parties.

This recipe serves 8 as a main dish, with Oriental salad (see page 35) and *Baba-ghanouj* (page 23).

Makes 16–20 *kibbeh* patties.

For the filling
140g (5oz) onion, finely grated
85g (3oz) softened butter
170g (6oz) medium-fine ground walnuts
1½ teaspoons cumin
¾ teaspoon cayenne pepper
½ teaspoon of salt

For the dough
225g (8oz) burghol, rinsed, drained and squeezed of excess water
85g (3oz) onion, finely grated
¼ teaspoon cayenne pepper
¼ teaspoon black pepper
1¼ teaspoons salt, or to taste
450g (1lb) minced lamb meat

For frying
clarified butter or oil

Mix thoroughly all the filling ingredients. Set aside. Place the burghol in a mixing bowl. To make the dough, combine the onion with the cayenne, black pepper and salt and rub with the burghol. Add the lamb and knead for a few minutes, or place in a blender and blend until smooth. Divide into 16 or 20 equal portions.

An easy way to prepare the circles of *kibbeh* is to turn a medium-size plate upside down and cover it with clingfilm. Take a portion of *kibbeh* dough and flatten over the part of the back of the plate. Shape into a thin patty. Repeat with the remaining dough until you have 16–20 patties.

Divide the walnut filling into 8–10 portions and place in the middle of 8–10 patties of *kibbeh*. Cover with another *kibbeh* patty, then pinch the two layers securely together to enclose the filling. To make a dome shape, place a sheet of cling film in a bowl the same size or slightly smaller than your patty. Gently press over the patty until the *kibbeh* takes the form of the bowl. Repeat with the rest of the mixture. Deep fry the *kibbeh* in butter or oil until nicely brown on both sides. Remove and place on kitchen paper to drain. Serve hot.

Syria: Aleppo

Desserts

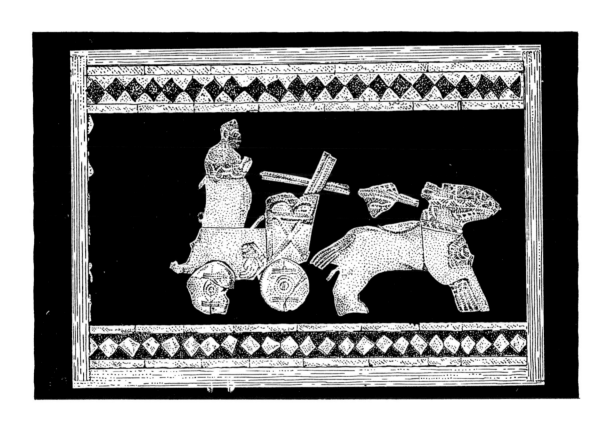

—

Baklawa al-halib

MILK BAKLAWA

This an unusual dessert, very different from those famous and irresistible sweets of the same name made from paper-thin filo filled with nuts and soaked with a sugary, honey syrup. Milk *baklawa* is a light dessert with a soft texture and easy to digest. It is rich in calcium and so is ideal for young children, older people or invalids.

For the dessert
850ml (1½ pints) milk
100g (3½oz) fine semolina

To garnish
icing sugar
¾ teaspoon cinnamon (optional)
55g (2oz) pistachio nuts, crushed medium fine

Put the milk in a pan and place over medium heat. When it is warm, add the semolina, stirring constantly with a wooden spoon until it boils and clings to the spoon. Remove and pour into a medium size buttered oven tray and leave to cool. Cut into small lozenges or squares and put in a preheated oven at 180°C (350°F/gas mark 4) for 15–20 minutes. Remove and immediately sprinkle generously with icing sugar, cinnamon (if using) and pistachio nuts.

Mrabba zahr al-ward

ROSE PETAL JAM

Rose jam is made with the fragrant roses of Aleppo. A recipe I have been given has been used for 40 years by my Syrian friend, Maguy Zobian. She told me that her grandmother's generation used to call it *gulseker*, a Turkish word meaning 'roses in sugar'. She thinks this may be because the rose bushes were originally brought from Turkey to be planted in Aleppo. However, she asserts that this recipe is very much from Aleppo.

Orchards of special fragrant roses known as *Ward al-jouri* bloom for a short period in Aleppo, Lebanon and Turkey, and from them rose water is distilled. *Ward al-jouri* are thought to have originated from India and are called Bengal roses. I have included this recipe under the dessert section because it can be used to flavour and garnish milk puddings, sponge cake, ice cream or even white cheese such as ricotta.

Ingredients
500g (1lb 2oz) pink rose petals
200ml (7fl oz) lemon juice
450ml (¾ pints) water
1.5kg (3¼ lb) sugar
¼ teaspoon citric acid (optional)

Rinse the rose petals, drain well, place in a colander and shake so that they are clear of any pollen. In a deep bowl, combine the rose petals and lemon juice. Knead them until they reduce in size, squeeze the petals and put in a pan. Save the lemon juice, which will have a deep pinkish colour.

To the petals in the pan, add the water and cover to keep their smell. On low heat, cook for 1 hour or until the petals have nearly melted (check them during cooking). Uncover the pan, and add the lemon juice. Boil for 5 more minutes uncovered. Stir in the sugar, bring to the boil and simmer for 20 minutes over medium heat, then turn off the heat and leave to cool completely. As it cools the consistency will become thicker. Finally, add the citric acid, if using.

Nammoura

SEMOLINA SQUARES STUFFED WITH WALNUTS

Nammoura is prepared with semolina, butter and yogurt, stuffed with walnuts and a touch of cinnamon, and it's absolutely divine. The thick syrup is made from sugar, water and a hint of lemon and is smothered all over the semolina cake which absorbs it, leaving a shine that embellishes the cake and entices you to devour more of it. A Baghdad cookery book, *Kitab al-tabikh*, translated by Arthur J Arberry, describes a dessert made with butter as

A lozenge, soaked in butter,
Buried deep in sugar sweet
And a sakis clover dimples,
Promise joy when lovers meet. . .

For the cake
500g (1lb 2oz) fine semolina
250ml (8fl oz) yogurt
3 tablespoons sugar
200ml (7fl oz) hot melted butter
2 teaspoons baking powder
2 teaspoons rose water

For the stuffing
200g (7oz) walnuts, crushed medium fine
½ teaspoon cinnamon

For the syrup
400g (14oz) sugar
175ml (6fl oz) water
¾ tablespoon lemon juice

The night before combine thoroughly all the cake ingredients, cover and refrigerate overnight. The following day, remove it from the fridge. It might be as hard as a rock to work with so allow it time to reach room temperature. In the meantime, mix the walnuts with the cinnamon and set to one side.

To prepare the syrup, combine the sugar with water in a pan and place over high heat. Stir until the sugar is completely dissolved. When it boils, add the lemon, reduce to medium heat and leave to simmer for 4–5 minutes or until it slightly thickens. Turn off the heat.

When the dough has softened, knead well and divide in half. Lightly moisten your hands with water, and, taking small lumps of the dough at a time, pat and press against the bottom of a buttered baking dish. Repeat until the base of the dish is covered to a uniform medium thickness.

Spread with an even layer of walnuts and cover with a layer of the remaining semolina dough. Cut into small squares. Bake in a preheated oven at 180°C (350°F/gas mark 4) for 40 minutes, or until the top is browned. Remove from the oven and pour the cooled syrup all over the top. Allow to cool completely and serve.

Karabije Halab

ALEPPO'S PISTACHIO FINGERS

Pistachio trees are one of Aleppo's major products. They also grow in other countries of the Mediterranean, such as Turkey. In the Levant, pistachio nuts garnish almost all desserts. In some, such as this one, they are also used as a filling. In Aleppo in the summer, it's possible to go to the pistachio orchards and buy the nuts as the men pick them fresh off the trees.

This dessert comes from Halab – as the name indicates. It is also prepared elsewhere in the Lebanon under the same name and is on sale at specialized patisseries. As a general rule, *Natef*, a thick dipping sauce, comes with it. A recipe for *Natef* follows on page 138. In Damascus *Karabije* are also known as *Twaitat*. This is a good recipe for a big party.

For stuffing
285g (10oz) coarsely crushed pistachio nuts, or walnuts
6 tablespoons sugar
2–2 ½ tablespoons rose water
½ teaspoon cinnamon (optional)

For the dough
750g (1lb 10oz) fine semolina
225g (8oz) butter
700ml (1¼ pints) water
½ teaspoon quick yeast (optional)

In a medium-size bowl, mix together the pistachios or walnuts, sugar, rose water and cinnamon, if using. To make the dough, put the semolina in a large bowl. In a pan, combine the butter and water, and place over a medium-high heat. Bring to the boil, making sure the butter has melted. Pour this over the semolina and leave to stand for 30 minutes.

Knead for 5 minutes but be careful as it might still be very hot. Add the yeast, if using, and knead. Spread a medium-thin layer of dough over the base of a buttered, 36 x 30cm (14 x 12in) baking dish. To do this, moisten your hands with water, take small portions of the dough at a time, and flatten them on to the dish, using the palm and heel of your hand, and your fingers. Spread the stuffing over the top. Cover with another layer of the remaining dough, and, using a pointed knife, gently cut into small squares. Bake in a preheated 180°C (350°F/gas mark 4) oven for 50 minutes. Then remove from the oven and while still hot sprinkle with icing sugar, or allow to cool. Smooth the *natef* over it or serve separately.

Natef

DIPPING SAUCE

This sauce is served with *Karabije Halab*. There are two ways of making the sauce, one of which takes time and is made with *chirch al-halaweh (soapwort)*. The sticks are available in Lebanese shops. It would be a good idea to have a friend around to help, because making it for the first time might be a bit messy, especially if you make a large quantity.

The other version, made mainly with egg white, is quicker to make. It lasts up to 2–3 days in the fridge. It is really delicious and the quantity is enough to serve with the *Karabije* (see page 137).

Version 1
The quantity below is a large one, so use what is needed and freeze the remainder in 2–3 small containers.

Ingredients
2 sticks chirch al halaweh *(about 75g / 2½oz)*
600ml (1 pint) water

For the syrup
1kg (2¼ lb) sugar
300ml (10fl oz) water
2 teaspoons lemon juice
3 egg whites
2 tablespoons acacia honey

Wash the sticks of *chirch al-halaweh*, breaking them if need be, then place in a pan and cover with the water. Leave to stand for 2 hours. Meanwhile, prepare the syrup. Stir the sugar with the water in a medium-small pan until it dissolves completely, bring to the boil, add the lemon juice and leave to simmer over medium-low heat for 5 minutes until it thickens. Turn off the heat and leave for 5 minutes before using. If it is left for longer, the syrup will become very stiff and difficult to pour, so make it just before you need it.

Strain the water from the *chirch al-halaweh* and place in a pan over the heat. Bring to the boil and simmer until the water reduces to a little under 200ml (7fl oz). In the meantime, beat the egg whites until fluffy. Then pour the reduced water of *chirch al-halaweh* into a bowl and whisk until it becomes a thick white foam. While still beating, gradually incorporate the syrup into the foam, then add the egg whites and then the honey. You should achieve a thick, shiny consistency.

Version 2

Ingredients
200g (7oz) sugar
60ml (2½fl oz) water
½ teaspoon lemon juice
1 egg white
½ teaspoon acacia honey

Combine the sugar and water in a small saucepan. Stir until the sugar dissolves then bring to the boil. Add the lemon juice and simmer over medium-low heat for 5 minutes. Meanwhile, beat the egg white in a small bowl until it is fluffy and stiff. Gradually add the syrup that you have prepared to the egg white while still beating. Add the honey and continue to beat to reach a thick and shiny consistency.

Serve immediately, or chill until required.

Mamounieh

SEMOLINA IN BUTTER

I urge you to try this delicious dessert. When I first heard what the dish included, I did not think that the basic ingredients would produce something so delicate, with such an unusual flavour.

Mahlab is a spice obtained from the kernel of the black cherry tree. Both Syria and Turkey produce it, and it is also known to be native to Europe and Southern Asia. Its flavour is not as strong as cumin, coriander or nutmeg, and it is sometimes used in sweets. Its mild nuttiness tones down the sugar and rounds up the flavour of the dessert, giving it greater depth. The recipe is so easy. It is economical and can be prepared in advance. The flavour improves with keeping, which makes it ideal for parties. *Mamounieh* is eaten by some in Aleppo for breakfast.

For the dessert
100g (3½oz) butter
200g (7oz) fine semolina
2 pints (40fl oz) water
225g (8oz) sugar
½ teaspoon freshly ground mahlab
1 tablespoon orange flower water

To garnish
1 teaspoon cinnamon, or to taste
85g (3oz) pistachios, coarsely crushed

Put the butter in a frying pan over medium heat. When the butter melts, add the semolina. Sauté until it reaches a slightly red-brownish colour, then turn off the heat. In another pan, combine the water and the sugar, and keep stirring until it boils. Stir in the fried semolina and keep stirring until it becomes thick and clings to the spoon. Stir in the *mahlab* and orange flower water. Remove and pour over a deep serving dish. Garnish with cinnamon and pistachio nuts. Allow to cool and set, then carefully cut into small squares.

A variation which is served hot traditionally uses a white cheese that is produced in Aleppo. When the semolina thickens and clings to the spoon, add thin slices of mozzarella cheese, stir and add the *mahlab* and flower water. Serve.

Khoshaf al-rumman

POMEGRANATE WITH PISTACHIO, ALMOND AND PINE NUTS

Pomegranate, the symbol of love and fertility, was the fruit that was given by Venus to Paris, according to mythology, and was eulogised in the *Thousand and One Nights*.

During the reign of Louix XIV, sauces and soups were prepared with the juice of pomegranates. The fruit was also used as a medicine until the end of the Renaissance – not surprisingly, for pomegranate supplies fibre, plenty of Vitamin C and iron.

In Aleppo, several recipes are based on this juice, and this particular dish was the dessert that was traditionally served at engagement parties. It is light and nutritious and is the perfect end to a vegetarian meal, as well as being an excellent addition to a buffet.

Ingredients
5 medium pomegranates

For the syrup
400g (14oz) sugar
100ml (4fl oz) water
1–1½ tablespoons of orange flower water
55g (2oz) pistachios, soaked for 1 hour
55g (2oz) almonds, soaked for 1 hour
55g (2oz) pine nuts, soaked for 1 hour
30g (1oz) walnuts, chopped medium-fine and soaked

Split the pomegranates, then break open. Scoop out the seeds and place in a serving bowl.

To prepare the syrup, combine the sugar and water in a pan, stir until sugar is completely dissolved and bring to the boil. Allow to simmer over medium heat for 4 minutes. Add the orange flower water, remove from the heat and allow to cool for a few minutes.

Pour over the pomegranate seeds in the bowl. Add the nuts and stir well. Chill and serve.

Syria: DAMASCUS

PART 3

Syria: Damascus

During World War I, the Ottoman Empire allied itself with Germany. In 1918, when Germany lost the war, the Empire collapsed, and two of its provinces, Lebanon and Syria, were mandated to the French for over 20 years until they gained their independence. After the Arabs had wrested Damascus from Byzantine rule, Muawiya, founder of the Umayyads, chose Damascus (in AD 661), rather than Mecca, as the capital of the Islamic Empire. The Umayyads were followed by local Muslim dynasties, the Ayyubids and the Mamelukes and, finally, the Turks.

In the first century AD, Saul, later known as St Paul, converted to Christianity on the road to Damascus. When he reached the city, he showed such a missionary zeal that he set the Jewish community against him and had to flee, lowered from the city wall in a basket.

I travelled from Lebanon to Damascus with my sister and we had to go on narrow roads and mountain passes. Going uphill, we passed through mountain villages which, before Lebanon's war, were the summer retreats of the well-to-do. In no time at all, we were going downhill towards a most beautiful landscape, the rich farmland of the Bekaa Valley.

We reached Chtoura, a small town where travellers stop to have a snack, usually a sandwich made with a paper-thin bread called *markouk* filled with a thick yogurt known as *labneh*, mint and a drizzle of the finest olive oil. We were also offered *sahlab*, which is a hot milky drink with cinnamon that is particularly good in the early hours of the day. A long time ago, newlyweds used to go to Chtoura for their honeymoon. Asthmatics were often advised to spend some time there, too, because of the dry climate.

In Syria, about 15 minutes from Damascus, our driver stopped at a grocery shop to buy some cold drinks. The name of the shop was Istirahat Abou-Ayad, which means 'the rest house of the father of Ayad'. Seeing us admire his range of fruit preserves and pickles, the shop owner, Abou-Ayad – a wonderful man – offered us samples of his apricot jam. His hospitality triggered a long chat about food customs and, as I sat taking notes, I was enchanted by his generosity and by what he could tell me about traditional customs.

He explained to me the importance of consuming apricots during the holy month of Ramadan. He said that dried apricots are diluted with water and drunk to break the fast, in the authentic tradition of Damascus. He told me about another drink, made from the roots of the liquorice plant, which is believed to purify the blood. It would quench the thirst of travellers who used to cross the desert in search of trade. Liquorice roots are ground and put in special bags of rough material for sale in the souk.

Always, according to Abou-Ayad, during Ramadan, when the *muezzin* call the faithful to break their fast at dusk, the customs of all Muslims – grown-ups and children alike – is to say a prayer thanking Allah for making them able to fast and for giving them their daily bread. After drinking *kamar el din* or liquorice, they eat a vermicelli or lentil soup. He even gave me the recipe: 'Minced meat fried in butter with finely chopped onion, add water, and when it boils for 5 minutes, throw in a handful of broken vermicelli with 2 tablespoons of thick tomato purée. Leave it to simmer for 15 minutes and that's it, you have a delicious soup.'

The shopkeeper showed me how to prepare a famous dish, *badweh*, which consists of cooked chick peas, houmous, toasted bread and yogurt. To make it, put a layer of toasted bread on a dish and sprinkle with a little of the liquid that the chick peas have been cooked in. Spread with houmous, then chick peas, and cover with yogurt that has been mixed with a tablespoon of tahini, drops of lemon juice and a hint of garlic. Garnish with fried pine nuts and melted butter. In Damascus you can buy this snack from street-sellers and in the many specialist restaurants, such as *Al janani* café in *bab Msallah*, which is one of the city gates.

After we left, we visited the city of the Umayyad, where we were enchanted by the many historical places, including the magnificent and vast Umayyad Mosque. I was naturally drawn to the souks and the food they had to offer. There are two other souks that I never fail to visit when I am in Damascus: the *Bzourieh* bazaar and the *souk-al-Tanabel*. These are very different from the 'tourist' souk *al-Hamidiyeh*, with its many coloured fabrics and souvenirs.

The *Bzourieh* bazaar (grains bazaar) has spices, grains, nuts in sacks or tins, and dried herbs of all kinds. The shop owners are ready to explain the medicinal benefits of each one of them at length.

The name of the souk *al-Tanabel* means 'the Fainéants market'. It's a fascinating place, with all kinds of fresh vegetables from courgettes that are hollowed out and ready to be stuffed, shelled peas, chopped parsley, to the famous *moulou khieh* (Jews' mallow) and okra that is topped and tailed. All these are prepared on a daily basis for the housewife to come and buy for the meal of the day. If only we had this facility in London. However, some Arabic shops in London have, in fact, started selling hollowed-out courgettes and aubergines but, of course, the prices are ten times higher than those in Damascus.

In the city of the Umayyad, the hungry traveller has a vast choice of eating places. There are the modern restaurants of the city palaces, where 'international food' is served with the occasional plate of *houmous* (see page 16) and chicken kebab. Alternatively, there are the many small and popular restaurants, where *fatteh*, for which Damascus is renowned, a delicious lamb kebab and *Lahm bi ajeen* (page 162) can be eaten for a very modest sum of money.

Writing about *fatteh* reminds me of a story about Geha, the character in Arab folklore who is both foolish and wise. Having heard about a banquet held by a local dignitary for the marriage of his daughter, Geha presented himself at the door where the banquet was taking place. Due to his miserable appearance, he was turned away by the caretakers. Undaunted, he went back home, changed into his best clothes, borrowed his neighbour's mule and went back to the dinner party to be welcomed by those who had turned him away earlier. Geha seated himself next to a cauldron of inviting-looking *fatteh*. He took a spoon and plunged it into the pot. Unaccustomed to wearing fine clothes, he did not pay attention to his large sleeve, which fell into the pot and became soaked with *fatteh*. The man sitting beside him whispered to him, 'Pull back your sleeve.' Geha replied, 'I'll not do that. It is because of my clothes that I was allowed in here, so it is only fair that they eat their fill as well.'

If the hungry visitor is lucky, he will be able to sample some home cooking, which is by far the best and the most sophisticated of Syrian food. I was lucky to be invited for dinner by friends whose family have been in Damascus for generations. Damascenes are very family orientated, but when a guest is invited he is honoured like a king. I was presented with a display of all delicious dishes: *Fattet al makdouss*, Okra stew, *Lahm bi ajeen*, *Kama bi-lahm*, *Sabanekh bi-zeit*. For dessert we had a large tray of seasonal fruits and *kataif* (crêpes). No wine was offered on this occasion, but whether this was for religious reasons or because my hosts had heard the 17th-century French traveller Jean Thévenot's assertion that 'Syrian wines are potent and treacherous', I never discovered.

While enjoying my dinner, I was given a recipe for *kama*. The *kama* (Damascene truffle) is sliced and added to fried onions in a pan to cook for a few minutes. Meanwhile, in another frying pan, chopped coriander and crushed garlic are sautéed in butter, then stirred into the *kama* mixture, and it is ready to eat after squeezing over a few drops of lemon juice.

The Damascenes love their vegetables, in particular broad beans. When they are in season, they are often frozen to be used the whole year round in lots of different recipes. They also have a condiment known as *debs al-flaifleh* which is made from sweet or chilli peppers. They would add a teaspoon of the sweet pepper paste to Okra stew and, as a general rule, to all tomato sauces. This gives more flavour and rounds off the dish.

The following day, after a most enjoyable dinner, I suggested a stroll to my sister to burn off some of the calories. Instead, we ended up at Dadoush's, at *bab al-Jabieh*, one of the city gates, which is renowned for being the best and most popular eating place.

Heading back to our car, my attention was drawn to a shop making *kataif* (crêpes). I couldn't resist the temptation to ask about their preparation because they looked so beautiful. The owner very kindly offered us *kataif* filled with *kahsta* (clotted cream), which were extremely good and well worth the stop.

Returning to our hotel, we dined in the slowly rotating roof restaurant that overlooks a huge area of Damascus and listened to the rhythms of Arabic music played with the *oud*, ancestor of the guitar. One of the waiters came over and chatted with us about a yogurt recipe called *Malahiat al Suweida*, which is made by the people of Suweida. To make this, mix 1kg (2¼lb) yogurt with 1 egg and 1 teaspoon of cornflour. Then strain the mixture over a pan, stirring in one direction until it boils. Stir in ½–1 teaspoon of turmeric, and eat the yogurt with burghol or *Burghol bi shaariyeh* (page 108). I left Damascus charged with so many touching memories that I am eager to return.

Palmyra

About 200km (125 miles) from Damascus, are the magnificent ruins of Palmyra. This oasis in the middle of the Syrian desert lies exactly halfway between Mesopotamia and the Mediterranean.

During the Roman Empire, Palmyra became an important trading post for goods on their way to Rome. It reached its peak with Zenobia, the erudite and beautiful queen who claimed descent from Cleopatra. She was also enormously ambitious and took advantage of a temporary weakness of the Roman Empire to occupy lands of the Nile in AD 270 and declare herself Augusta. Emperor Aurelian restored order in the Empire and marched against Zenobia, defeating her in AD 272 at Antioch. She fled but was captured and died in captivity. The descent of Palmyra into political and commercial decline started from that time. Its past greatness is evident from the colossal ruins, which make it one of the most interesting archaeological sites in the world.

My visit to Palmyra was motivated by more than the desire to see glorious remains of Queen Zenobia's seat of power. I also wanted to steep myself in the right atmosphere in the hope that the spirit of the unfortunate queen would inspire me to find out more about Syrian recipes.

Starters

Fattouche al-batinjan

BREAD SALAD WITH AUBERGINES

This is a bountiful mixture of marvellous flavours and aromas. Fresh, fragrant herbs are combined with juicy, red tomatoes and tasty, fried aubergines to be tossed in pomegranate syrup, extra virgin olive oil and lemon juice.

It is different from the famous Lebanese *Fattouche* (see page 18), which uses a variety of vegetables, including purslane, and dressed them with lemon juice, olive oil and sumac. Both versions are delicious. This is perfect to serve for friends as a starter.

Ingredients
extra virgin olive oil for frying
325g (11oz) aubergines, cubed into 1cm (½in) pieces
115g (4oz) parsley, coarsely chopped
140g (5oz) green pepper, finely diced
350g (12oz) tomatoes, cubed into 1cm (½in) pieces
2–3 spring onions, 140g (5oz), thinly sliced
1 medium-sized pitta bread, cut into small squares and fried
1 teaspoon salt, or to taste
a pinch of black pepper
1 tablespoon lemon juice, or to taste
1–1½ tablespoons of pomegranate syrup

Put a generous amount of oil in a frying pan and when hot, add the aubergines and fry over medium-high until golden brown, stirring occasionally. (At first the oil will be absorbed by the aubergines, then after 1–2 minutes the oil will be released.) Remove from the pan and drain on triple kitchen paper.

Place the rest of the ingredients in a bowl and add 2–3 tablespoons of oil. Add the fried aubergine, toss and serve.

Warak enab bi-zeit

DAMASCENE STUFFED VINE LEAVES

It is said that stuffed vine leaves featured on the Byzantine table. They were adopted by the Byzantine provinces of Lebanon and Syria and later by the Ottomans. No wonder they have lasted so long, since those artfully rolled vine leaves look impressive. Without them a *mezzé* is considered incomplete.

This dish is ideal for special occasions. It makes an excellent starter for 10.

Ingredients
375g (13oz) about 37–40 large vine leaves
juice of 1½ lemons
6½ tablespoons extra virgin olive oil
1 large potato, rinsed, scrubbed and sliced
535g (1lb 3oz) onion, finely chopped
225g (8oz) round-grain rice
300ml (10fl oz) water
1 tablespoon dried mint
¾ tablespoon cinnamon
1 tablespoon sugar
1½ teaspoons salt
1 tablespoon pomegranate syrup (optional)

Trim off the stem of each vine leaf and blanch in boiling water to which half the lemon juice has been added, and then leave for a few seconds. Remove gently and drain.

Put ½ tablespoon oil in a medium-size pan, cover with a layer of sliced potato and set to one side.

Heat the remaining oil in a pan, add the onions and sauté for 2 minutes, or until translucent and pale in colour. Add the rice to the onions, reduce the heat, and continue to sauté for 2–3 more minutes. Stir in the water, cover and simmer for two minutes or until the water has been absorbed and the rice is slightly tender. Turn the heat off and add the mint, cinnamon, sugar and salt. Give the mixture a good stir.

On a clean surface, place one vine leaf at a time, stem towards you and the shiny side facing down (cut large leaves in half). Spread some of the filling near the stem end. Roll once, fold in both sides of the leaf over the filling and continue to roll into a cigar shape. Place the finished vine leaf over the potato slices in the pan. Repeat with the remaining vine leaves, packing them close to one another over the potato.

Add water to cover and secure with a lid. Bring to the boil, cover and simmer over a low heat for 1½ hours, or until the leaves are soft and water has reduced. Thirty minutes before the end of cooking, add the pomegranate syrup, if using, and the rest of the lemon juice. Turn off the heat and leave covered to cool. Invert over a serving dish and serve cold with bread.

Fattet al-makdouss

STUFFED AUBERGINES IN YOGURT

It is acknowledged that Damascus (*al-Sham*) is where the best *fatteh* come from. The name *fatteh* is derived from the Arabic world *youfatfet*, meaning cut up in tiny pieces. *Fatteh* can be made with a grain, a vegetable and meat or chicken, to which are added yogurt, nuts and pieces of bread.

It is customary for a dish of *fatteh* to adorn the table during the holy month of Ramadan. It is so popular that street-sellers in the bustling markets sell many varieties, including the popular *taskieh badweh* and *taskieh bi-zeit*. The mingled aromas of spices and butter steam out of the large copper pots to seduce the sense of smell and encourage shoppers to buy. Prices vary from very cheap to very expensive. *Taskieh* comes from the word *taski* meaning 'give a drink'. *Fattet al-makdouss* is a favourite of mine and a gastronomical feast worthy of royalty. If you do not have the time or inclination to hollow the aubergines, fry them for a few minutes on both sides until soft, then split and stuff them. In Damascus, aubergines are fried in butter, which gives them a wonderful flavour.

This dish makes an excellent starter for 8 or a main dish for 4.

For the stuffing
1½ tablespoons extra virgin olive oil
1 onion (about 115g / 4oz), finely chopped
170g (6oz) minced lamb
½ teaspoon salt
pinch of black pepper
pinch of white pepper

For the stew
8 baby aubergines, about 8cm (3in) long
75ml (2½fl oz) extra virgin olive oil
450g (1lb) onions, finely sliced
600ml (1 pint) boiling water
2 tablespoons tomato purée
1 teaspoon salt, or to taste
1 tablespoon pomegranate syrup
pinch of black pepper
pinch of white pepper

For the yogurt
1 large garlic clove, finely crushed
½ teaspoon salt, or to taste

1 teaspoon lemon juice (optional)
2 tablespoons tahini (optional)
450–600ml (¾–1 pint) yogurt

To garnish
30g (1oz) pine nuts, toasted (optional)
1 medium pitta bread, cut into small squares, fried in oil and drained on kitchen
*   paper*

To make the stuffing, heat the oil in a frying pan. When it is hot but not smoking, add the onion and sauté until translucent. Add the meat and cook for 3–4 minutes until just turning brown. Sprinkle with the salt and black and white peppers, and stir.

For the stew, place the aubergines on a hard surface, press each one and roll under the palm of your hand until soft. This makes them easier to hollow out. Cut across the top of each aubergine and, using a corer, hollow the inside, leaving a thin shell. Stuff with the meat mixture.

Heat the oil in a medium-size pan, add the onions and sauté over medium-high heat until nicely browned. Add the water, tomato purée, salt and stuffed aubergines. Bring to the boil. Cover and allow to simmer over medium heat for 20–25 minutes. Ten minutes before the end of the cooking time, add the pomegranate syrup and the black and white peppers. Check the heat and lower if necessary, so that the sauce does not burn.

In the meantime, place the garlic and salt in a bowl and add the lemon and tahini, if using. Stir in the yogurt and whisk well.

To serve, arrange the aubergines in an oblong dish with some of the onion. Smooth over the yogurt and add the sauce and the remaining onion in the pan to the yogurt in a swirl. To garnish, sprinkle with pine nuts, if using, and top evenly with bread, or serve the bread separately in a bowl. Serve immediately.

Sabanekh bi-zeit

SPINACH IN OLIVE OIL

This unpretentious dish is a typically rural meal. In the country, the concept of food is not so much what goes on the plate as what the economy allows. For this meal, a substantial quantity of onions and garlic are browned in olive oil, then the dark green leafy spinach is added. Sometimes the skinned inner bean of the broad beans is added, which makes the dish more nutritious and looks even more appetizing. The family sits on the floor around a small round wooden table. Before eating, every meal is started with the sentence, *Bismillah al-ruhman al-rahim* which means 'in the name of God'. At the end of a meal they say, *Al-hamdo Lil-Lah rab al-Alamin*, which means 'thanks to God for the whole of creation'.

Spinach is not just full of flavour. It is also nutritious, low in fat and rich in iron, and its high levels of carotenoids help to strengthen the immune system. Squeezing over some lemon juice will enhance the absorption of the iron.

This dish serves 4–6 as a starter, or as part of a *mezzé*, accompanied by crusty bread, olives and yogurt or cheese.

Ingredients
100ml (4fl oz) extra virgin olive oil
450g (1lb) onions, finely sliced
1 whole head of garlic, slivered
1 teaspoon ground coriander
1kg (2¼lb) spinach, rinsed several times and roughly sliced
1½ teaspoon salt, or to taste
pinch of white pepper
140g (5oz) broad beans, frozen or freshly skinned (optional)
60–90ml (2½–3½fl oz) lemon juice
1 teaspoon pomegranate syrup (optional)

To garnish
a large handful of pomegranate seeds

Heat the oil in a large, deep frying pan. Do not allow to smoke. Add the onions and sauté over medium heat for 5–7 minutes or until golden, then add the garlic and sauté for a further 3 minutes. Remove a little under half the amount of the onion mixture and reserve for the garnish.

Add the coriander to the remaining onion in the pan, stir and add the spinach in batches, adding more as the spinach reduces in size, until a little liquid appears. Sprinkle with the salt and pepper, add the beans, if using, cover and simmer over low heat for 10–12 minutes. Check the liquid content after 7 minutes and, if there is too much, turn the heat up to medium.

Turn off the heat, stir in the lemon juice with the pomegranate syrup if using, cover and allow enough time for the flavours to blend before serving. Garnish with the remaining onions and garlic, and the pomegranate seeds. Eat warm or at room temperature with bread.

Salatet batata

POTATO SALAD

Damascene villagers have learned how to get the best out of the vegetables that grow in the fields.

This dish is typical comfort food and can be made from the most basic ingredients. A similar dish is prepared in the Lebanon, except that it calls for parsley instead of mint, and is tossed in a tahini sauce instead of lemon and oil.

Potato salad is a good starter and it is perfect when accompanied with other dishes such as grilled meat and aubergines.

Ingredients
675g (1½lb) potatoes
1 small garlic clove
1 teaspoon salt, or to taste
¼ teaspoon black pepper
2½ tablespoons lemon juice
a handful of fresh mint leaves, finely chopped, or 1 teaspoon dried mint
2½ tablespoons extra virgin olive oil
a pinch of cayenne pepper

Put the potatoes in a pan with sufficient boiling water to cover. Return to a boil, cover and simmer over moderate heat until they are tender.

In a salad bowl, crush the garlic with the salt until smooth. Sprinkle with pepper, add the lemon juice, the fresh or dried mint and the olive oil. Stir well.

When the potatoes are tender, drain, allow to cool slightly then peel and cut in 1cm (½in) cubes, and toss with the dressing in the bowl. Sprinkle with the cayenne pepper and serve with bread.

Salatet al-hindbeh

WILD CHICORY SALAD

This comforting and satisfying dish, which uses the wild chicory that grows in Syria, is typical of the frugal yet healthy food of the country people.

It makes a simple and nourishing starter, or can accompany other dishes in a buffet. Wild chicory is on sale in Lebanese, Syrian or Cypriot grocers.

Ingredients
salt
2 bunches of wild chicory (1kg / 2¼lb)
1 large garlic clove
½–1 tablespoon pomegranate syrup
½ tablespoon lemon juice, or to taste
1½–2 tablespoons extra virgin olive oil

To garnish
3 tablespoons pomegranate seeds

Heat plenty of water in a large pan with ½ tablespoon salt. Bring to the boil, add the wild chicory and boil rapidly for a minute or two. Remove, drain and allow to cool.

Crush the garlic until creamy and add the pomegranate syrup, lemon juice and oil. Coarsely chop the chicory, add it to the dressing, toss and adjust the salt to taste. Garnish with pomegranate seeds. Serve and eat with bread.

Tabakh rouhou

VEGETABLE STEW

The traditional version of this homely Damascene dish is made with meat and does not include carrots or courgettes, but I like this vegetarian version, for the vegetables add colour, flavour and texture which are pleasing to the palate.

Tabakh rouhou is an uncomplicated starter for 4–5. You can also add this to a buffet or serve it with a barbecue, since it can be prepared ahead of time and is eaten cool.

Ingredients
4 tablespoons extra virgin olive oil
775g (1lb 11oz) onions, finely sliced
1 teaspoon tomato purée
450g (1lb) aubergines sliced in 2.5cm (1in) rounds
255g (9oz) courgettes, sliced in rounds
115g (4oz) carrots, peeled and cut in 1cm (½in) rounds
900g (2lb) tomatoes, peeled and cut in 1cm (½in) pieces
1½ teaspoons salt, or to taste
4 garlic cloves, finely crushed
1 teaspoon dried mint

Heat the oil in a pan and sauté the onions for 5 minutes or until translucent and pale in colour. Stir in the tomato purée. Place a layer of aubergines on top of the onions, and then a layer of courgettes, carrots and finally tomatoes. Sprinkle with salt. Cover and simmer over medium-low heat for 30–40 minutes.

About 10 minutes before the end of the cooking time, add the garlic and mint. Leave the pan covered until it reaches room temperature. Eat with bread, or serve hot with cracked wheat with vermicelli (see page 108).

Harak isbao

GREEN LENTILS WITH TAMARIND AND POMEGRANATE

The name of this dish literally means 'burner of its finger', possibly because the lengthy process of producing it results in a 'burned' (or 'tired') finger.

Despite the effort required, this famous Damascene dish is served throughout the country and captivates the palate of those who taste it. The tamarind, an important addition for this dish, blends perfectly with the pomegranate syrup, lemon juice and sugar, giving a well-balanced flavour of sweet and sour. Traditionally, the raw dough is cut into shapes like spaghetti and added to the lentils. Nowadays, many people find it saves time to add a handful of pasta instead. In the version below the dough is fried and used as a garnish instead of adding it to the dish. The courgettes release their juices and give a texture that is slightly similar to the dough.

This dish is prepared for special occasions and is ideal for parties. It is also a dish that is given as a gift to friends and neighbours. It is eaten warm or at room temperature, and lasts for about 4–5 days in the fridge.

Serves 6 generously as a starter.

Ingredients
30g (1oz) tamarind, coarsely sliced

For the dough
55g (2oz) flour
¼ teaspoon salt
30ml (1fl oz) water, or as necessary

For the vegetables
200g (7oz) green lentils
850ml (1½ pints) water
1½ teaspoons salt, or to taste
extra virgin olive oil
8 garlic cloves, finely crushed
225g (8oz) coriander, finely chopped
170g (6oz) courgettes, finely diced
1 tablespoon pomegranate syrup
2 tablespoons lemon juice
½ tablespoon sugar
450g (1lb) onions sliced

Maldoum al-batinjan (Aubergines and meatballs)

Kibbeh sajieh (Kibbeh with walnut stuffing)

Nammoura (Semolina squares stuffed with walnuts)

Khoshaf al-rumman (Pomegranate with pistachio, almond and pine nuts)

Sabanekh bi-zeit (Spinach in olive oil)

Lahm bi-ajeen (Lamb and pine nut pastries)

Bamieh (Okra stew)

Balouza (Milk and orange pudding)

Soak the pieces of tamarind in 300ml (½ pint) boiling water and leave to stand for 30 minutes.

To make the dough, combine the flour with the salt, add the water and knead to a smooth dough. Cover with a towel and set to one side.

In a pan combine the lentils with the water. Bring to the boil, reduce the heat to medium-low, sprinkle with salt, cover and simmer for 25 minutes.

Heat 4 tablespoons oil in a frying pan, add the garlic, sauté for a few seconds, then stir in the coriander. Sauté over medium-low heat and leave without stirring for 2–3 minutes. Turn off the heat.

To the cooked lentils, add half the amount of the sautéed garlic and coriander, and the courgettes. Squeeze the tamarind until the seeds come out and strain the liquid over the lentils. Add the pomegranate syrup, lemon juice and sugar. Cover and simmer over medium-low heat for a further 15 minutes, or until the lentils are tender. Turn off the heat and leave covered until it reaches room temperature.

Roll out the dough, cut into small lozenges and fry in 50ml (2fl oz) hot oil. Remove and drain over kitchen paper. Add the onions to the remaining oil in the pan, adding more oil if necessary, and stir occasionally for 5–7 minutes, or until golden brown. Remove and drain on kitchen paper.

To serve, spread the cooled lentil mixture over a large dish, cover with the remaining garlic and coriander, top evenly with onions and then with the fried lozenges.

Lahm bi-ajeen

LAMB AND PINE NUT PASTRIES

This is a Damascene speciality. Although there are several versions of these tasty pastries in the Levant, this is one of the best. They make an excellent starter and, as this quantity makes about 20 pastries, these will fill a memorable corner of your buffet table. They take time to prepare but they are not at all difficult to make and the result is a great joy. Some add pomegranate syrup to the *Lahm bi-ajeen* stuffing, but only a teaspoon; any more will make the colour of the stuffing very dark.

I serve the pastries with yogurt. Just spoon a little over the meat so that it does not mask the subtleties of either the topping or the dough. Alternatively, serve with lemon wedges and squeeze a few drops of juice over the meat. Both work well with the pastries.

For the dough
55ml (2fl oz) warm water
1 teaspoon yeast
½ teaspoon sugar
5 tablespoons yogurt
3 tablespoons olive oil
250g (8½oz) flour, sifted
½ teaspoon salt

For the stuffing
1½ tablespoons extra virgin olive oil
225g (8oz) onion, finely chopped
225g (8oz) minced lamb
285g (10oz) tomatoes, peeled and finely chopped
½ teaspoon cinnamon
¼ teaspoon black pepper
1½ teaspoons salt
2 tablespoons tahini
3 tablespoons yogurt
½ tablespoon organic cider vinegar
1½ tablespoons pine nuts

In a small cup, combine the water, yeast and sugar, stir, cover with cling film and leave in a warm place for 10 minutes.

Mix together the yogurt and oil until well blended. In a bowl, combine the flour and salt, add the yeasted water and the yogurt mixture, mix and knead to form a soft, shiny dough. Cover with a cloth and leave to rest for 1–2 hours.

To prepare the stuffing, put the oil in a frying pan and add the onions, stirring occasionally. After a minute, add the lamb to the onions and cook over medium heat for 2–3 minutes, stirring and breaking up any lumps of meat with the back of a wooden spoon. Add the tomatoes, cinnamon, black pepper, salt, tahini, yogurt, vinegar and pine nuts, stir well and allow to simmer for 5 minutes, or until the water evaporates. Turn off the heat and allow to cool.

By now, the dough should be ready. Sprinkle some flour over a work surface and take some of the dough. Using a rolling pin, roll out to about 3mm (⅛ in) thick. Cut out with a 10cm (4in) oval pastry cutter. Repeat with the remaining dough. Transfer the dough ovals to a buttered oven tray. Spoon about 1 tablespoon of the filling and spread over each dough oval. Bake in a preheated oven at 180°C (350°F/gas mark 4) for 15 minutes or until the top is lightly browned.

Serve hot or warm with a bowl of yogurt or lemon wedges.

Main courses

Burghol ma-koussa

CRACKED WHEAT WITH COURGETTES

A wonderful vegetarian dish that belongs to the delicious cuisine of Damascus. I make it with the pale green variety of courgettes that are on sale at Lebanese and Cypriot shops. They are nearly seedless and have a delicate flavour. However, the courgettes that are found all year round in supermarkets will do fine. Healthy and extremely simple, it is a satisfying dish, especially when eaten hot with cold yogurt. Quinoa, which is high in protein, and rich in B and E vitamins, calcium, iron and phosphorus, would be an excellent substitute for burghol but needs more time to cook. Some people add a chicken stock cube to enhance the flavour.

Ingredients
extra virgin olive oil
2 onions, about 285g (10oz), finely chopped
450g (1lb) courgettes, topped, tailed and cubed in small pieces
600ml (1 pint) hot water
225g (8oz) coarse burghol
7 cloves of garlic, minced
1 bunch coriander, about 140g (5oz), finely chopped
1¼ teaspoons salt, or to taste

In a pan heat 2 tablespoons of oil, add the onions and sauté for about 3–4 minutes or until translucent. Add the cubed courgettes and sauté with the onions for about 5–8 minutes, stirring occasionally. Add the water and the burghol. Bring to the boil, cover and simmer over low heat for 8–10 minutes or until the water is absorbed by the burghol.

In a small frying pan add about 1–2 tablespoons of oil. Over medium heat, sauté the garlic and coriander for a few minutes or until the coriander reduces in size. Add this to the courgettes and burghol in the pan, sprinkle with salt, stir and finish cooking. Turn the heat off, cover with a thick towel and leave for 5 minutes. Serve hot with a bowl of yogurt.

Kama

DAMASCENE TRUFFLES WITH LAMB

Kama is the Arab version of French or Italian truffle. Whenever somebody invites you to eat *kama*, you are greatly honoured. Although expensive, *kama* is used in a variety of Damascene dishes. This one is flavourful and simple to make, and allows the flavour of the truffle to dominate the dish. This recipe uses a leg of lamb and makes an interesting dish to serve 4–5. The bouquet garni makes the stock even richer. Fresh *kama* is difficult to find in England, so you may use the tinned or frozen variety.

Ingredients
½ leg of lamb (about 1.5 kg / 3¼ lb)
2 litres (3½ pints) water
bouquet garni consisting of 1 celery stick, 6 cloves, 1 onion, 5 cardamoms, 1 large
      cinnamon stick, 6 black peppercorns and 3 bay leaves
sea salt
extra virgin olive oil, or butter
225g (8oz) onion, finely chopped
1 tin of **kama** *(about 500g / 1lb 2oz), halved*
1 tablespoon flour
½ teaspoon black pepper
a pinch of grated nutmeg

Place the meat and water in a pan. Bring to the boil and skim. Add the bouquet garni, cover and simmer over low heat for 2–2½ hours or until the lamb is tender. About 30 minutes before the end of cooking, sprinkle on 1 teaspoon of salt.

Heat 2–3 tablespoons of oil or butter. Add the onions, sauté for 2 minutes, add the *kama* and sauté over medium heat for nearly 15 minutes more. At this point, ladle out about 200ml (7fl oz) of the meat stock and add this to the *kama* and leave to simmer, covered, over low heat for 30 minutes.

Heat 1 tablespoon of oil or butter and add the flour. When it begins to change to golden brown, stir and gradually add a little stock, whisking until it reaches the consistency of single cream. Season with black pepper and nutmeg, then add this mixture to the *kama* in the pan and continue cooking. Arrange the lamb in a serving dish and place the *kama* and stock in a serving bowl. If you like, make a dish of plain rice.

To serve, place a piece of meat on a plate, arrange a little rice on the side and ladle some of the *kama* over the top.

Mishmishiya

LAMB AND BROAD BEANS IN YOGURT

Mishmishiya is the name of a dish mentioned in a Medieval Arabic cookbook about the caliphs' cuisine at Baghdad's court. The book has been translated into English by the great Orientalist, Arthur J Arberry. The Baghdad recipe includes apricots, mastic, cumin, ginger, coriander and almonds. It sounds great but it is different from the Damascene one, which is a more homely, everyday concoction, and very enjoyable. When the recipe was given to me, it reminded me of the many yogurt-based Lebanese mountain dishes that I have eaten in such wonderful atmospheric surroundings.

In the recipe below, the most time-consuming part is in the preparation of the *kibbeh*. It makes an exciting and exotic dish for entertaining friends. It has such a wonderful flavour that it has been included in my winter menu. It can be prepared in advance and assembled before serving. If any is left over and you find that it has coagulated, just add 1–2 tablespoons water, stir and put on low to reheat. This recipe serves 5 as a main course.

For the kibbeh
85g (3oz) onion, finely grated
¾ teaspoon salt
¼ teaspoon pepper
115g (4oz) fine burghol
225g (8oz) minced lamb
115g (4oz) butter
3 teaspoons of ground cinnamon

For the yogurt
1 teaspoon cornflour
1 teaspoon water
600ml (1 pint) plain yogurt
1 egg

For the stock
450ml (15fl oz) chicken or meat stock
140g (5oz) canned broad beans, skinned if possible
85–115g (3–4oz) Swiss chard ribs, sliced in 1cm (½in) pieces
1 heaped tablespoon round-grain rice, soaked in hot water for 15 minutes and drained
1 tablespoon olive oil, or butter
3–4 garlic cloves, finely crushed
¾ bunch of fresh coriander (about 140g / 5oz), finely chopped

Put the onion in a mixing bowl and rub with salt and pepper. Rinse the burghol, drain and squeeze out the extra water before it is absorbed. Mix with the onion in the bowl. Add the lamb and knead with the other ingredients for 4–5 minutes or until you obtain a soft dough. Divide the dough into 15 *kibbeh* portions. Next, mix the butter and cinnamon thoroughly, divide into 15 portions and place in the fridge for 5–10 minutes to solidify and ease handling. Take a portion of *kibbeh* dough and roll it between the palms of the hands to form a ball. Hold firmly with one hand and with the index finger of the other hand poke a hole in the centre of the *kibbeh* ball. Work around the inside until you have a medium shell. Fill the shell with a portion of the cinnamon butter. Gently reshape to enclose the filling into an oval or round ball, moistening hands with water as necessary. Repeat with the other portions of *kibbeh* dough.

Put the chicken or meat stock in a medium-size pan and bring to the boil. If unsalted sprinkle with ½ teaspoon salt. Drop the *kibbeh* balls into the stock, cover and simmer over low heat for 2 minutes. Turn off the heat and remove the *kibbeh* with a slotted spoon to a side dish. Set aside the stock.

Stir the cornflour into the water then combine well with the yogurt and egg. Strain into a medium jug and set aside.

Place the stock in a pan over medium-high heat. Bring to the boil, add the broad beans (do not worry if you can't skin them, I never do), the Swiss chard ribs and the rice. Reduce the heat to low, cover and simmer for 5–6 minutes or until both vegetables and rice are tender. At this point, turn up the heat to medium and, using a wooden spoon, stir in the yogurt mixture and keep stirring in the same direction until it boils. Drop in the *kibbeh* balls, bring back to the boil, reduce the heat to low and leave to simmer, uncovered, for 3–4 minutes.

While they simmer, place a medium-size frying pan over medium heat. Add the oil or butter. When hot, sauté the garlic and coriander. Stir to coat them with the oil or butter and leave to cook for 30 seconds. Add to the yogurt in the pan and bubble for a minute or two.

Serve hot.

Mansaf el-badou

LAMB WITH FRESHLY BURNED WHEAT AND PINE NUTS

This is a traditional Bedouin meal, prepared with rice or *freekeh*, a fresh green wheat that is picked and flamed to give an exceptional burned flavour. This is mixed with the delicious meat stock, so there is no need to use any seasoning other than salt. You can buy the *freekeh* from speciality Lebanese or Arabic shops. If you cook this dish with rice, season it with a touch of allspice, cardamom powder, black pepper, cinnamon and ground coriander. Almonds go better with the rice than the *freekeh*, while pine nuts are acceptable with both.

If you are worried about the amount of fat that is released from the leg of lamb into the stock, sieve it into another pan and refrigerate until the fat solidifies on top. Then gently remove the layer of fat, reheat the stock and add the *freekeh*. This dish makes an excellent Sunday lunch for family or with friends, especially on cold, wintry days.

Ingredients
1.35–1.5kg (3–3½lb) leg of lamb
3 litres (5 pints) water
bouquet garni consisting of celery stick, 2–3 cardamoms, bay leaf, onion studded with
*   cloves, 2 large sticks of cinnamon and black peppercorns*
1¼ teaspoons salt, or to taste
5 tablespoons thick yogurt
285g (10oz) **freekeh**
450ml (15fl oz) meat stock

To garnish
½ tablespoon olive oil
30g (1oz) almond flakes (optional)
30g (1oz) pine nuts (optional)

Put the leg of lamb in a large pan, add the water and place over medium-high heat. Bring to the boil and skim. Add the bouquet garni, cover and simmer over medium-low heat for about 2½–3 hours or until the meat is tender, sprinkling with salt towards the end of the cooking time. Remove the leg of lamb and put in an oven pan, smooth all over with the yogurt and cook for 30–40 minutes, or until brown in colour.

Place the *freekeh* with the meat stock in a medium pan. Bring to the boil, salt to taste, cover and simmer over low heat for 12–15 minutes, or until the *freekeh* is tender and the liquid has been fully absorbed. Turn off the heat, cover the pan with a thick towel and leave for 5–10 minutes, to allow the flavours to mingle.

If using the nuts for garnish, heat the oil in a small frying pan and sauté the almonds for 30 seconds, then add the pine nuts and continue sautéing until golden brown.

Place the *freekeh* on a serving dish. Remove the leg of lamb from the oven and carve large or medium-size pieces of meat. Place on top of the *freekeh* and garnish with almonds and pine nuts, if using both.

Ouzi

PASTRY WITH RICE AND NUTS

Ouzi is a typical Damascene savoury pastry, enhanced by a delicious mixture of minced lamb, rice, nuts and spices. The first time I came across this wonderful food was when I visited Damascus with my parents. My mother and two sisters went on a shopping spree, while my father took care of me. For lunch, he took me to a rustic restaurant in a busy street. The waiter took our order and in no time we had two plates with an attractive pastry bundle, translucent gold in colour, placed in the centre of each plate and accompanied by a bowl of plain yogurt. As I ruptured the dough with my fork, the smell of the *samn asli* (Syrian butter) wafted out, as if imprisoned and happy to be free. The taste of this marvellous dish stayed with me until this day and I am happy to share it with you.

Ouzi is satisfying and filling. The traditional dough takes time to prepare but nowadays things have been made easier for us. A good quality, ready-made puff pastry will do just as well.

The recipe makes 5 good portions to serve as a main course. It can be prepared beforehand and a bowl of yogurt gives it a refreshing taste. You can even use it for big parties by making small parcels using filo instead of puff pastry, which can be baked, frozen and reheated when needed.

Ingredients
1–2 tablespoons extra virgin olive oil
15g (½oz) almonds
15g (½oz) pine nuts
15g (½oz) pistachio
115g (4oz) minced lamb
115g (4oz) rice, rinsed
1 cardamom, freshly crushed
a pinch of cinnamon
a pinch of black pepper
a pinch of coriander
a pinch of allspice
a pinch of cumin
1 teaspoon salt, or to taste
55g (2oz) peas, or skinned broad beans
240ml (8fl oz) meat stock, or water
310g (11oz) ready-made puff pastry
55g (2oz) butter, melted

Heat the oil in a small pan, add the almonds and stir continuously until a deep golden colour. Remove with a slotted spoon. Add the pine nuts to the same oil and repeat as before. Add the pistachios and sauté for a few seconds, then remove. Set the nuts aside.

Add the lamb to the same oil in the pan, and sauté, stirring occasionally, until it loses its red colour. Leave the meat to cook in its juices until they evaporate. Stir in the rice and sprinkle with cardamom, cinnamon, black pepper, coriander, allspice, cumin and salt. Add the peas or broad beans and the meat stock or water. Bring to the boil, reduce the heat to low, cover and simmer for 5 minutes or until the liquid evaporates. Allow the meat mixture to cool to room temperature, then stir the nuts.

Take a piece of the puff pastry. Roll out one large rectangle, or as many as needed, as thinly as possible. From each rectangle cut 10 even rectangles 7.5 x 20cm (3 x 8in). Arrange 5 pairs in the shape of the letter X. Divide the meat mixture into 5 portions, placing one portion in the centre of each letter X. Fold the pastry layers one after the other over the meat mixture to cover. With your hands, arrange into a round parcel to secure. Place on to a baking sheet and pour butter over each one. Bake in a preheated oven at 180°C (350°F/gas mark 4) for 25 minutes or until lightly golden. Serve immediately with a bowl of yogurt to accompany.

Mjadra el-rif

COUNTRYSIDE LENTILS

It may be a simple meal but it is definitely a dish that I am happy to eat, particularly in winter. Lentils give warmth, comfort and nourishment. A similar dish is prepared in the Lebanese mountains, using rice instead of burghol.

This dish can be served as a starter or a main course to eat with the delicious Lebanese *Fattouche* (see page 18).

Ingredients
5 tablespoons extra virgin olive oil
575g (1lb 5oz) sliced onions
1 teaspoon sugar
225g (8oz) brown lentils
1–1.1 litres (1¾–2 pints) water
225g (8oz) coarse burghol
1¼ teaspoons salt, or to taste

Heat the oil in a pan, add the onions and sauté over medium heat. After 2 minutes, sprinkle with sugar and continue to cook for a further 4 minutes or until brown in colour. Remove just under half, drain over double kitchen paper and reserve for garnish.

Add the lentils and water to the remaining onions in the pan and bring to the boil. Add the burghol, sprinkle with salt, cover and simmer over medium-low heat for 30–35 minutes or until the lentils are soft and the water has been absorbed by the burghol.

Serve hot garnished with the reserved onions.

Kwaj

FINGERS OF MINCED LAMB

This is a classic dish to suit all tastes. It is a traditional dish, which will be well received when friends visit. The recipe is simple to follow and the result is delicious. Adding diced carrots is not authentic but I have included some as they add to the flavour. Eat with rice or bread.

Ingredients
450g (1lb) minced lamb
¼ teaspoon salt
60 pine nuts
285g (10oz) onions, finely chopped
6 tablespoons olive oil or butter
225g (8oz) green pepper, diced
480g (1lb 1oz) tomatoes, peeled and chopped
1 heaped teaspoon tomato purée
¾ teaspoon salt, or to taste
¼ teaspoon black pepper
285g (10oz) potatoes, scrubbed and cut into 5mm (¼in) cubes

Season the lamb with salt and divide into 12 equal patties. In each pattie place 5 pine nuts and roll into the shape of a thick sausage. Place on a hot baking dish and grill until nicely browned, then remove and set to one side.

Sauté the onions in 2 tablespoons of hot oil or butter in a medium-size pan for 3–4 minutes or until golden brown, then add the green pepper, tomatoes, tomato purée, salt and pepper. Add the meat fingers, cover and simmer over medium-low or low heat for 8 minutes.

Heat the remaining oil or butter in a frying pan and, when it is hot, add the potatoes and sauté until golden brown, adding more oil or butter if necessary. Remove and add to the lamb and the tomato sauce. Simmer for 8 more minutes. Serve hot.

Makloubet al-batinjan

UPSIDE-DOWN AUBERGINES

'Damascus is the home of *Makloubet al-batinjan*,' said Abd al kader Shbat, a top Damascene chef. 'For this authentic, traditional dish you fry the aubergine slices. You also fry the meat and leave it to simmer in the liquid until tender. At that point you add the aubergines, then the rice. You leave it again to simmer then you serve upside down, garnished with nuts. It's simple, it looks beautiful like a cake, and it's delicious.'

'What about the seasoning?' I asked.

'Ah, no, no, no,' he replied. 'You don't want to meddle with the exquisite aroma of the aubergines and meat that enrich the rice and give it a deep flavour.'

So, I followed his advice and the result was exactly as predicted. My neighbours and tasters, David Hutchins and Bonnie Green said it was fabulous.

Makloubet al-batinjan is an excellent main dish for 4–5 if you have a starter. It is also ideal to have as a centrepiece in a buffet. It presents well, especially if garnished with golden pine nuts and almonds, but remember to double or triple the quantity.

Ingredients
1.1kg (2½lb) aubergines cut into 2cm (¾in) slices
75ml (3fl oz) extra virgin olive oil for frying
½ teaspoon butter
30g (1oz) almonds
30g (1oz) pine nuts
5–6 thin slices of leg of lamb (500g / 1lb 2oz)
600ml (1 pint) hot water
1 teaspoon salt
285g (10oz) rice

Sprinkle the aubergine slices with salt. Place in a large sieve, put a plate on top and weigh them down. Leave to stand for one hour. This will get rid of the liquid and cuts down the absorption of oil when the aubergines are fried.

Place a pan over medium heat for a few seconds. Add 1 tablespoon of oil and the butter. When hot, add the almonds. When they start to change to a pale golden colour, add the pine nuts and sauté until both are deep golden in colour. Remove with a slotted spoon and set to one side. Add the lamb to the same oil and butter in the pan, and sauté on both sides for 1–2 minutes until browned. The lamb might produce some liquid, in which case leave it to cook in its juices until they evaporate. Then add the water, bring to the boil, sprinkle with ½ teaspoon salt, reduce the heat to medium-low, cover and simmer for 30 minutes or until the meat is tender.

Soak the rice in hot water for 15 minutes. Remove the aubergines from the sieve, rinse off the salt and dry well between sheets of kitchen paper. Heat the remaining oil in a frying pan and when it is hot, fry the aubergine slices until golden brown on both sides (or grill). Add more oil if necessary. Remove and drain on kitchen paper. By this time, the meat will have softened. Carefully pour the stock into a bowl, measure out 350ml (12fl oz) and put to one side.

To assemble the dish, layer the meat evenly over the base and sides of the pan, then cover with aubergine slices. You will end up with a sort of nest. Drain the rice, mix with the remaining salt and place over the aubergines. Add half the measured amount of stock, making sure it covers the meat. Then cover the rice with the remaining aubergines, and add the remaining stock. Place over a medium heat, bring to the boil and reduce the heat to medium-low. Cook for 10 minutes or until the stock has been fully absorbed.

Turn off the heat, cover with a thick towel and leave to stand for 5–8 minutes, allowing enough time for all the flavours to mingle. Uncover, invert over a serving dish, count to 10, then gently remove the pan. Serve hot with a bowl of yogurt.

Riz bi-tasseh

UPSIDE-DOWN LAMB WITH RICE AND NUTS

This combination of rice, minced lamb and nuts is a straightforward, honest dish that is inexpensive yet still delicious. It is quick to prepare and can be transformed into a party dish which will please your friends. For a party, be generous with the nuts and meat. If you have any left-over stock, use this instead of water as it enriches the flavour. Another tip for parties is to grill slices of aubergines as a side dish to be served with a bowl of yogurt to which you have added some dried mint.

This recipe will serve 3–4 as a main course, accompanied by Oriental salad (see page 35).

Ingredients
30g (1oz) butter
1 tablespoon extra virgin olive oil
15g (½oz) whole or flaked almonds
15g (½oz) shelled pistachio nuts
15g (½oz) pine nuts
225g (½lb) minced lamb
285g (10oz) rice
¼–½ teaspoon cinnamon
¼ teaspoon allspice
a pinch of black pepper
450ml (¾ pint) water
1¼ teaspoons salt, or to taste

Put the butter and oil in a small pan. Sauté the almonds for a few seconds or until they are about to change in colour, then add the pistachio and pine nuts and sauté until they are all golden brown. Using a slotted spoon, transfer all the nuts to a side dish. Add the lamb to the same pan and sauté over medium heat, stirring occasionally, until it loses its red colour. As the liquid emerges from the meat, leave it to cook until it evaporates.

Mix the rice with the cinnamon, allspice and black pepper. Add the rice and the water to the meat, bring to the boil and sprinkle with salt. Reduce the heat to low, cover and simmer for 8–10 minutes or until all the water has been absorbed. Turn off the heat, cover with a thick towel and leave to stand for 10 minutes. Invert over a serving dish, garnish with the nuts and serve.

Bamieh

OKRA STEW

Okra, also known as ladies' fingers, is native to Africa. Popular in the Middle East, it is prepared as a stew with shanks of lamb or cooked with olive oil without meat. Dishes made with oil are known as oil dishes, such as the Damascene *Sabanekh bi-zeit* (page 155), and are eaten at room temperature. This recipe is made with lamb and makes a delicious, homely meal. The best way to achieve a rich flavour is to fry the okra, onions and pepper in butter.

If you prefer to cut down on frying, cook the meat as described then add the okra, onions, green pepper, tomato purée and seasonings. Leave to simmer over low heat for 15 minutes. Then add the garlic, coriander, tomatoes and ½–1 tablespoon olive oil and continue the cooking for a further 10–15 minutes.

Traditionally, a plate full of raw sliced green pepper adorns the Damascene table to accompany many dishes, including this Okra stew.

Ingredients
450g (1lb) diced lamb
600ml (1 pint) water
1½–2 teaspoons salt, or to taste
450g (1lb) okra, rinsed
10–12 baby onions
3 teaspoons olive oil
3 teaspoons butter
1 green pepper (225g / 8oz), diced
1 tablespoon tomato purée
1 teaspoon sweet red pepper paste (optional)
1 teaspoon pomegranate syrup (optional)
¼ teaspoon black pepper
1 teaspoon sugar
55g (2oz) fresh coriander, finely chopped
4 garlic cloves, crushed
5–6 tomatoes, peeled, seeded and quartered

Put the lamb and water in a pan over medium-high heat. Bring to the boil, skim, sprinkle with salt, reduce the heat to medium-low, cover and simmer for 30 minutes.

Peel the pointed tops of the okra but do not cut them off. Add to the lamb.

Sauté the onions in half the oil and butter until golden brown. Add the pepper and sauté for a further 1–2 minutes. Add this to the lamb in the pan at the same time as you add the okra. Add the tomato purée, red pepper paste, pomegranate syrup, if using, black pepper and sugar, and simmer for a further 20 minutes.

Sauté the coriander and garlic in the remaining oil and butter for 2 minutes, stir occasionally, and add to the ingredients in the pan along with the tomatoes 10–12 minutes before the end of cooking. Cover the pan and continue the cooking. Serve with rice and Arabic bread (pitta bread).

Sharhat al-kadi

THE JUDGE'S LAMB SLICES

The name of this recipe comes from a story about a city butcher who, at the annual feast of *Id al Fitr*, annoyed his customers by telling them that he was too busy to serve them because he was slicing 20kg (45lb) of lamb for the judge. Disgruntled customers cursed the judge, asking one another what on earth this huge quantity of meat was for. His servant could not keep her tongue when she heard how they belittled her noble master for depriving them of their meat at this important celebration. When the secret was revealed – that the dish was to be sent for the orphans to enjoy – they named it after him.

An uncomplicated and tasty Damascene dish to enjoy eating with tomato and cucumber salad that has some fresh mint.

Ingredients
4–5 tablespoons extra virgin olive oil
550g (1lb 4oz) onions, finely sliced
620g (1lb 6oz) slices of lamb
¼ teaspoon black pepper
a pinch of white pepper
a pinch of freshly grated nutmeg
450g (1lb) potatoes, sliced medium-thick
700ml (1¼ pints) boiling water

Heat the oil in a pan and sauté the onions until translucent and pale in colour. Using a slotted spoon, transfer them to a side dish. Add the lamb slices to the remaining oil in the pan and sauté over medium-high heat until lightly browned on both sides. Return the onions to the pan, sprinkle with the black and white peppers and the nutmeg. Add the potatoes and give them a gentle stir.

Leave to cook for about 2 minutes, then add the water and bring to the boil. Reduce the heat to medium, cover and simmer for 40–50 minutes or until the meat and potatoes are tender.

Serve hot with bread, which you can dip into the delicious sauce.

Basmishkat

STUFFED FILLET OF LAMB

There are extensive areas of pasture in Syria, where flocks of sheep and goats graze in a perfect climate. This contributes to tender meat that is tasty and moist. Despite its superior quality, the meat is also sold at affordable prices, and this has resulted in the wide range of meat recipes on offer in the Damascene cuisine.

Basmishkat is a classic that belongs to the city of the Umayyads. It is a princely dish, suitable for dinner parties. An advantage of this dish is that it can be prepared in advance. To do this, you need pieces of meat which have been pounded until they are large enough to encase the filling. Most butchers will be prepared to do this for you. Lamb is my choice of meat for this recipe, but beef or veal will do just as well, if you prefer, and might actually be easier to pound and stuff.

For the stuffing
1 teaspoon extra virgin olive oil
1 teaspoon butter
15g (½oz) pine nuts
55g (2oz) minced lamb meat
85g (3oz) rice
¼ teaspoon black pepper
¼ teaspoon freshly grated nutmeg
½ teaspoon salt
150ml (5fl oz) chicken stock or water

For the meat
4 slices of meat fillet (about 140g / 5oz) each thinly pounded
¼ teaspoon black pepper
¼ teaspoon allspice (optional)
2 teaspoons butter, or olive oil
¾ teaspoon salt, or to taste
200ml (7fl oz) chicken stock, or water
bouquet garni consisting of celery stick, bay leaf, cardamom, black peppercorns, stem
   of parsley and a tiny, skinned piece of lemon

Heat the oil and butter in a small pan. When it is hot, add the pine nuts, stirring continuously until golden. Remove and set aside. Add the minced lamb to the remaining oil in the pan and sauté until it loses its red colour. Leave the meat to cook in its juices until they evaporate, then add the rice, black pepper, nutmeg and salt. Stir for 1 minute, add the chicken stock or water. Bring to the boil, cover and simmer over a low heat for 4 minutes, or until the water has been absorbed. Turn the heat off and allow to cool to room temperature.

Lay the meat slices over a dish. Sprinkle all over with black pepper and allspice, if using. Divide the rice mixture among the 4 slices of meat. Fold the meat slices to enclose the rice mixture, and sew or secure well with toothpicks. In a medium-small pan, heat the butter or oil. Sauté the stuffed fillets, turning to brown all over. Sprinkle with salt. Add the water, or the chicken stock for a better flavour, and the bouquet garni. Bring to the boil, reduce the heat, cover and simmer on medium-low heat for about 10 minutes, or until the meat is tender. Serve hot.

Kizartma

LAMB WITH ONIONS

You are in for a big surprise if you prepare this delicious recipe, which was given to me by Mrs al Adem Yafi, of Syrian origin and wife of a former Prime Minister of Lebanon. It was her favourite dish, prepared with real *samn Arabi* (Arabic butter) and the succulent meat of Syria. (I have used olive oil.) However, this dish may be of Turkish origin. *Kizartma* is Turkish meaning 'to fry'. During my research work on Turkish food I found the same recipe with the same name in an old Turkish cookery book.

Whatever its origins, a velvety texture and a depth of flavour come through magnificently in this dish. Give it a try; you won't regret it.

As a main course, it serves 4 to 5.

Ingredients
150ml (5fl oz) extra virgin olive oil
675g (1½lb) onions, finely sliced
675g (1½lb) lean diced lamb
1 teaspoon salt, or to taste
a pinch of white pepper
a pinch of black pepper
850ml (1½ pints) boiling water

Set a medium-size pan over a fairly high heat, add the oil and, when hot but not smoking, add the onions and sauté for 5 minutes, or until nicely browned, stirring occasionally. You should watch the heat, turning it down to medium after the first 2 minutes. Remove the onions with a slotted spoon, and set aside.

Add the lamb to the remaining oil in the pan and sauté over a high-medium heat, stirring occasionally. The lamb will produce a liquid, so leave the meat to cook in its juices until they evaporate. Sprinkle with salt, stir for a minute, and sprinkle with the white and black peppers. Stir again, then add the browned onions and water. Bring to the boil, cover and allow to simmer over a medium-high heat for about 10 minutes (check that the water does not evaporate too quickly). Reduce the heat to medium and continue cooking for a further 20 minutes or until the meat is tender.

Serve hot with rice or preferably fried or roasted potatoes.

Kastaletta khodar wa naanaa

LAMB CUTLETS WITH VEGETABLES AND MINT

This dish is flavoured with fresh mint and garlic, whose wonderful aromas will fill the kitchen, soothe the spirit, calm the nerves and stimulate the palate. This large quantity of fresh mint not only adds to the taste but also helps the digestion. Traditionally, slices of fat are added to the cutlets to enrich the sauce, but I have omitted them for this recipe.

This dish makes a good family Sunday lunch which can be prepared in advance and reheated when required.

Ingredients
1–2 tablespoons extra virgin olive oil
4–8 lamb cutlets
1½ teaspoons salt, or to taste
¼ teaspoon black pepper
a pinch of white pepper
85g (3oz) chick peas, soaked overnight and precooked
450g (1lb) aubergines, rinsed and cut into 2cm (¾in) squares
450g (1lb) courgettes, rinsed and cut into 2cm (¾in) squares
450g (1lb) tomatoes, rinsed and cut into 2cm (¾in) pieces
6 garlic cloves finely crushed
55g (2oz) mint leaves, finely chopped

Heat the oil in a medium-size pan and sauté the cutlets on both sides until sealed and lightly browned, leaning the sides of the cutlets against the sides of the pan to brown as well. Sprinkle with salt, black and white pepper, then add the chick peas, aubergines, courgettes and tomatoes. Cover and allow to simmer over medium heat for 30–40 minutes. About 5 minutes before the end of cooking, add the garlic and mint.

Serve hot with bread and yogurt.

Mnazaleh ahmar

TOMATOES, LAMB AND CORIANDER

Tomatoes, originally called 'love apples', were once thought to be poisonous then later believed to be an aphrodisiac – hence the name! Today, this versatile fruit is an indispensable ingredient in the cuisines of many countries, including Lebanon, Syria and Turkey. Not only do they taste delicious, they also contain antioxidants which are important for health. *Mnazaleh ahmar* is a homely Damascene dish, well balanced, easy to make and full of flavour. For those who are vegetarian, tofu from soya beans, rich in protein, may be used as a substitute for meat.

Ingredients
½ tablespoon olive oil
450g (1lb) minced lamb meat
3 garlic cloves, crushed
45g (1½oz) coriander, finely chopped
900g (2lb) tomatoes, finely chopped
1¼ teaspoons salt, or to taste
30g (1oz) pine nuts (optional)

Heat the oil in a medium-size pan, add the lamb and sauté until nicely browned. Stir in the garlic and coriander, add the tomatoes and sprinkle with salt. Add the pine nuts, if using. Cover and simmer over low heat for 30 minutes. Serve hot with rice or cracked wheat with vermicelli (see page 108).

Syria: Damascus

Desserts

Houboubieh

BEANS, GRAINS AND NUTS

Houboubieh is a modest reminder of the Turkish dessert *Asure*, a substantial dessert made of beans, chick peas and grain. I discovered it during one of my visits to Damascus, when my sister, Rafat, and I decided to take a stroll along *al-shaalan* street. It was six o'clock and it was getting dark. The street was lit by strings of bulbs and lined with shops on both sides, each one specializing in various delicacies, sweet or savoury, that were seductive and inviting. We didn't hesitate and we were in and out of those shops with our mouths and hands filled with goodies!

As we reached a crossroads, a huge, unattended cauldron on a low flame burner drew my attention. Getting close, I found that most of it was covered with a transparent plastic wrap with a small part left open to ladle for customers. I peered into the cauldron, trying to identify the mysterious concoction inside.

Within moments, we were surrounded by a lot of men, wondering what we were doing. I asked what was in the cauldron. With one voice they answered: *Houboubieh*.

I was none the wiser but at that moment, the shop owner materialized, probably believing that there was a riot in front of his shop. Reassured, he went in and came out again with a bowl in his hand. He filled it with the mixture from the cauldron and handed it to me to share with my sister. His generosity did not surprise me, bearing in mind the legendary Arab hospitality. After tasting it, I had mixed feelings, only because I am not used to eating chick peas in a sweet preparation, but my sister, Rafat, loved it. An elderly man intervened to give me the exact recipe and told us that this dish is eaten in winter to give strength and warmth. It is also traditionally prepared when a child's first tooth appears. It is a meal in itself, interesting to serve for brunch or afternoon tea. Serve hot and (although not authentic) top with a little vanilla ice cream to make a refreshing end to a light meal.

Ingredients
115g (4oz) wholewheat, soaked overnight, rinsed and drained
1.1 litres (2 pints) water
85g (3oz) haricot beans, soaked for 8 hours, drained, and pre-cooked
85g (3oz) chick peas, soaked overnight, drained, pre-cooked and drained again
1 tablespoon cornflour
½ tablespoon water
1 tablespoon anise powder
5 tablespoons sugar, or to taste
1 tablespoon orange flower water
1 tablespoon rose water

To garnish

4 tablespoons sultanas, soaked in water for 30 minutes, drained

45g (1½oz) pistachios, soaked for at least ½ hour, drained

45g (1½oz) pine nuts, soaked for at least ½ hour, drained

a handful of desiccated coconut

Put the wheat and water in a pan, bring to the boil, cover and simmer for 50 minutes or until tender. Add the haricot beans and chick peas. Stir the cornflour into ½ tablespoon water and sieve into the pan. Stir continuously until it returns to the boil. Stir in the anise powder and sugar to taste. Leave to simmer for a further 10 minutes over medium-low heat. Stir in the orange flower and rose waters, and turn the heat off.

Place in a large bowl and garnish with sultanas, pistachios, pine nuts and coconut. Serve warm.

Balouza

MILK AND ORANGE PUDDING

Balouza, given to me by my sister, Samira, is a very refreshing dessert that is simple, healthy, economical and quick to prepare. It soothes the palate in summer and brightens your table in winter. To make it richer, cover the top with sliced ripe bananas, ground almonds and a thin drizzle of honey. Its flavour is delicate, not sweet.

Serves 10–12.

For the milk pudding
1.1 litres (2 pints) milk
7 tablespoons cornflour
4 tablespoons sugar

For the orange pudding
450ml (¾ pint) orange juice
3 tablespoons cornflour
2 tablespoons water

Thoroughly mix the milk with the cornflour and sugar in a medium-size pan and place over medium-high heat. Stir constantly with a wooden spoon until it boils. Reduce the heat and keep stirring for 3–5 minutes until it thickens. Pour into a deep, medium-size serving dish. Leave to cool for at least 2–3 hours.

While the milk pudding cools, prepare the orange pudding. Place the orange juice in a saucepan. Mix the cornflour with the water in a small cup. Add to the orange juice, place over medium heat and stir constantly until it boils and thickens. Remove from the heat and wait for 1–2 minutes.

From one corner of the dish slowly pour the orange mixture over the cooled milk pudding to cover it. If it doesn't, just tilt the dish gently to one side until it runs all over the milk pudding. Chill and serve.

Hilatiyeh

MILK PUDDING

This is a heavenly dessert, which takes only a short time to prepare. The word *hilatiyeh* is thought to have come from the Arabic word *halata* which means 'to eat fiercely or in one go'. This delicious dish is, indeed, one to devour voraciously.

In the old days, people used to sit for hours, stirring the ingredients in order to obtain a thick, smooth and velvety texture. I was told by the wonderful lady who gave me the recipe that it is served without garnish because the syrup that is poured over the milk pudding is garnish enough. However, if you wish, you can sprinkle some ground pistachios over the top. The authentic syrup is usually thicker in texture and sweeter in taste.

If you're throwing a party, this dessert is enough for 10–12.

For the dessert
1½ teaspoons mastic pieces
1 teaspoon sugar
1.1 litres (2 pints) milk
75g (2½oz) cornflour

For the syrup
250ml (8fl oz) water
115g (4oz) sugar
¾ teaspoon lemon juice
1½–2 teaspoons rose water

Optional garnish
pistachio nuts

Place the mastic in a mortar and cover with sugar. With a pestle, grind in a clockwise motion until you have a powder.

Put 1 litre (1¾ pints) milk in a pan. Stir the cornflour into the remaining milk until it dissolves. Strain this over the milk in the pan and stir, then place the pan over medium heat, stirring with a wooden spoon continuously in the same direction until it starts to bubble. It will thicken and should coat the spoon. Reduce the heat to low and leave to bubble, uncovered, for 3 minutes. Continue to stir and gradually sprinkle in the mastic. Remove from the heat, pour straight away into a deep dish and leave to cool.

Meanwhile, combine the water with the sugar in a small pan and place over a high heat. Stir continuously until the sugar dissolves completely. Bring to the boil, add the lemon juice, and leave to simmer, uncovered, over medium heat for 5–7 minutes. Stir in the rose water and turn off the heat. Leave to cool.

When both the milk pudding and the syrup have reached room temperature pour the syrup to cover the surface of the milk pudding. If adding a garnish, grind a handful of pistachio nuts and sprinkle over the top, then serve or chill and serve.

Maamoul

CHEESE AND DATE PASTRIES

I was offered this pastry while I was visiting friends in Damascus with my sister, Samira. It was still warm and I very much enjoyed eating it with my coffee. This was the first time I had eaten this kind of pastry with white, unsalted cheese, because in my country, the Lebanon, *Maamoul* are filled with pistachio, walnuts or dates. However, as the date filling is my favourite, I have included it here.

Special wooden moulds for pastry making, which have various engravings, are on sale in Lebanese shops, although any kind of unpatterned moulds are also suitable. In Lebanon some households use tweezers to create their own pattern. An oblong mould is ideal for the cheese pastry, and a round one for the date. *Maamoul* are excellent to serve with morning coffee, at teatime, or even as part of a buffet. The cheese pastries freeze well and can be reheated when needed.

Makes 32 pastries.

For the dough
500g (1lb 2oz) fine or medium-coarse semolina
200g (7oz) melted butter
100ml (4fl oz) orange flower water
60ml (2½fl oz) warm water
½ teaspoon baking powder

For the cheese filling
140g (5oz) mozzarella
55g (2oz) halloumi
30g (1oz) feta cheese
3–4 tablespoons icing sugar, plus a little extra for dusting
1¼ tablespoons orange flower water

For the date filling
45g (1½oz) butter
400g (14oz) dates, pitted and chopped
1 teaspoon **mahlab**
1½ teaspoons rose water

To make the dough, place the semolina in a mixing bowl. Add the butter and mix thoroughly. Leave overnight. The next day, mix the orange flower water and water for a few seconds, then add to the semolina, along with the baking powder. Knead for 5–8 minutes or until dough is soft. Cover and leave to rest for 15 minutes.

In the meantime, make the cheese filling. Rinse the mozzarella and halloumi, making sure both are clear of salt, then pat dry with kitchen paper. Blend with the feta cheese for a few seconds. (In the absence of a blender shred them finely.) Stir in the icing sugar and orange flower water.

Divide the dough into 32 equal portions. Take each portion and roll between the palms of your hands to form a ball. Hold in one hand and, using the index finger of the other hand, poke a hole and work around the inside to form a medium-thin shell. Take some of the cheese mixture and push inside the pastry shell. Gently bring the edges together to enclose the filling. Smooth and press gently into the mould. Turn the mould upside-down and tap the top side against a hard edge so that the pastry drops on to the palm of your hand.

Preheat the oven to 180°C (350°F/gas mark 4). Bake for 20 minutes or until lightly golden on all sides. Remove, dust with icing sugar and serve.

To make the date filling, melt the butter in a pan over a medium heat, stir in the dates with a wooden spoon and mash until smooth. Sprinkle on the *mahlab* and add the rose water, mix thoroughly and assemble as above for the cheese filling. Bake until golden brown, remove and allow to cool. Serve or store in an airtight container.

Ghoraibeh

DAMASCENE SHORTBREAD

Damascus is the home of these biscuits; when well done using the real *samn-asli* (sheep's butter) they can be addictive. As a young girl, they were a favourite of mine; even today I try to keep away because I don't seem able to stop eating them once I start.

I have added a few drops of arak (a drink distilled from grapes and flavoured with aniseed) to the traditional recipe, as I found it gave it some 'oomph'. The biscuits have a velvety surface and a crunchy inner texture. Their flavour develops as they cool and they taste even better the next day.

Makes 12–14 biscuits.

Ingredients
85g (3oz) butter
a little under 85g (3oz) icing sugar
170g (6oz) flour, sifted
1 tablespoon arak (optional)
12–14 pistachio nuts

Cream together the butter and sugar. Mix in the flour, add the arak and knead thoroughly for a few minutes. Place the dough in a plastic bag and put in the fridge for 1 hour, then knead a little until it is manageable.

Preheat the oven to 160°C (350°F/gas mark 3). Divide the dough into 12–14 equal parts. Roll each one into a coil and bring both ends together, pinch lightly to seal and push 1 pistachio nut in the centre. Repeat with the remaining dough. Place the coils on a greased baking sheet, leaving a little space between them, and bake for 12–15 minutes. Remove from the oven and allow to cool for several hours before serving.

Barazek

SESAME AND PISTACHIO BISCUITS

No one visits Damascus without bringing back a box of *Barazek*. The secret of these delicious biscuits lies in the use of authentic Syrian butter. I make *Barazek* in advance and keep in an airtight tin to offer when friends come round for a coffee. They look and taste wonderful.

If you decide to try them, you will need to lightly toast the sesame seeds and pistachio nuts. Put the sesame seeds in a heavy-bottomed non-stick frying pan, set over medium heat, stir until they reach a deep golden colour and spread over a tray to cool. For the pistachio nuts, place whole nuts in a plastic bag, and crush gently with a rolling pin to flake, then toast in a preheated oven at 220°C (425°F/gas mark 7) for about 10–15 minutes or until lightly browned.

Ingredients
100g (3½oz) butter, melted and cooled
85g (3oz) icing sugar
1 egg
1 teaspoon vanilla essence
1 teaspoon cider vinegar
200g (7oz) flour, sifted
a pinch of salt
½ teaspoon baking powder
1 tablespoon egg white, lightly beaten
1 tablespoon iced water (optional)
¾ teaspoon cider vinegar
about 55g (2oz) flaked and toasted pistachio nuts, or as necessary
about 85g (3oz) toasted sesame seeds, or as necessary

Cream together the butter and sugar until smooth. Add the egg, vanilla and vinegar. Stir thoroughly. Add the flour, salt and baking powder. Mix well to form a soft dough, cover with a cloth and refrigerate for 30 minutes or until it becomes firm enough to work with. Divide the dough in half, and leave the half you are not working with in the fridge until you are ready to use it.

Preheat the oven to 180°C (350°F/gas mark 4) and grease a baking sheet. Mix the egg white, iced water, if using, and vinegar and set aside. Take small portions of dough and shape between the palms of your hands to form thin circles about 5cm (2in) in diameter. Cover one side of the circle with pistachio flakes and press lightly with 4 fingers. Turn over to the other side, brush lightly with egg white mixture and place this side over the sesame seeds, pressing lightly with 4 fingers. Remove gently and place on the baking sheet, pistachio side down. Repeat until all dough is used up. Bake for 15–18 minutes then remove from the oven. Lift the *barazek* off the baking sheets with a spatula while still hot. Allow at least 2–3 hours to cool before serving.

PART 4
Turkey

I sat on the floor, my notebook resting on my lap and my pen grasped between my fingers, in an attempt to share with you the feelings and memories that have caught my eye and spoken to my heart through my many visits to Turkey.

The Ottoman Empire has benefited from the legacy of the ancient Anatolian; the Roman and the Byzantine Empires, and their influence is reflected in the cuisine of the region. The Turkish tribes – both nomads and hunters – migrated from the east to settle in the steppes of central Asia. Their cuisine is the basis of the Anatolian kitchen as it was influenced by the earlier Anatolian civilization. Unlike the food of the Lebanon, Ottoman cuisine is a product of geography not religion, and there are striking regional variations.

Istanbul is an important crossroads of culture and gastronomy, between east and west, north and south. When I first visited the city, I was startled by the waters of the Bosphorus and Golden Horn on one side and the splendours of the mosques and historical monuments on the other. I was allured by a city that has a striking blend of old and new: Byzantine façades, wooden doors with religious motifs, Baroque architecture and modern, Western buildings.

That evening I dined on the roof terrace of a restaurant overlooking the luminous Bosphorus. My London friends and I tried to guess, from the smells wafting by, what the starter would be. After a short wait, the table was spread with a selection of small, inviting dishes, one of which I will never forget: fresh squid that had been made into a simple salad dressed with lemon juice and olive oil. There was also a dish of king prawns; so delicious that I am still dreaming of it.

The following day we visited Topkapi, the sultan's legendary palace, which played such an important role in shaping one of the world's great cuisines. Unlike the palaces built in Europe, Topkapi was not the project of a single individual whose aim was to show strength and inspire awe. It was, rather, the fruit of the determination of successive sultans to make additions to unimposing quarters to accommodate their increasing entourage. Consequently, the size of the rooms, in general, is rather small compared to what might be expected of royal palaces. Charming pavilions were built among small courtyards and gardens. The impression is not of an imposing royal house, but of a charming village that extends over a large area.

The frugality of most of the sultans is best illustrated by how their chefs were recruited: a simple meal of eggs with onions, flavoured with sugar, vinegar and cinnamon, would be prepared to the sultan's order. The cooks tried to outdo each other to produce the finest dish. The sultan would taste each one and the winner would be appointed as chief pantry keeper for the year.

It seems that the palace kitchen catered every day for some 5,000 people, including state employees and soldiers. The sultans made sure that there were regular supplies of food in Istanbul so that, at times, it was forbidden to take coffee and rice outside the city. The palace kitchens form a prominent part of the grounds, proof of the high regard in which cooking was held. At the time of Suleiman the Magnificent, the architect, Sinan, built a kitchen with six domes in order to have enough space to cater for large numbers. Utensils are on display, including giant kettles and cauldrons in which soups were stirred and *Asure*, a substantial dessert made of beans, chick peas and grains, simmered. Sometimes the sultan himself would watch over the preparation.

From the kitchen, we moved to the more sensual part of the palace, the harem – the place that excites women's curiosity and men's jealousy. Contrary to accepted belief, most of the women of the harem were there through choice. At least, that was the case when the Ottoman Empire became established and the time for conquest and taking prisoners had come to an end. When a woman expressed the desire to leave the harem, she was often provided with a husband to take care of her needs once she was outside. My mind was instantly transported to this era and those beautiful harem girls, perfumed and extravagantly dressed in purple, red, gold or green embroidered satin, which gave a glow to their striking white complexions and black hair as they waited in turn to please the sultan. Of course, today there is no longer a harem in Turkey, only a reminiscence of sensuous pleasure found in the many titles of food recipes such as 'Beauty's Lips', 'Lady's Thighs', 'Dainty Fingers' and 'Lady's Navel'.

A visit to Istanbul's Grand Bazaar is a must. As you enter the gate there are carpets, jewellery, fabrics, leather – an unbelievable variety of shops and items in an unbelievably huge market place which is an integral part of daily life. As I ambled through, my eyes caught a slender figure standing at the intersection with a side alley, a strategic point where passers-by could not miss seeing him. The man, in his sixties, was wearing an impeccably spotless white coat. I walked over to him wondering what this man was doing: was he a doctor or a health inspector? As I drew closer I saw a round pan covered with a thick white napkin by his side. He spoke only Turkish but I managed to convey my wish to see what was inside the pan and as he did I saw a most artistic display of *kibbeh*. I bought one which went straight to my mouth; it was warm, spicy and very tasty. So this impressively neat man was a street vendor.

Later on that day, while still ambling in Istiklal Street, a pedestrian street, I met him again. I hurried up to him hoping that we could communicate. It was a difficult endeavour until a young man came to buy one of the goodies. Luckily he spoke English and translated all I needed to know: the man sells what the wife prepares – a speciality of eastern Turkey called *Içli Köfte*, shells made of minced lamb, burghol and seasonings and stuffed with walnuts, many spices and herbs. I was told that the heart of the bazaar and Istiklal Street are the only vendor places where he could be seen. I bought more *Içli Köfte* and resumed my stroll, enjoying the view of food displayed behind windows of humble but very inviting eating places. There were dishes of *imam bayildi*, *sü borek*, *manti*, *musakka*, stuffed aubergines and courgettes and so on. There were also shops with mouth-watering spreads of *baklava*, *ekmek kadaifi*, *tulumba* and *firin sutlac*. Wow! I was so tempted that I couldn't resist and had to taste nearly everything. Such a pleasure should not be missed.

The next day, I also wandered in the streets of Istanbul. This time I indulged in buying and eating *simit*, a girdle bread sprinkled all over with sesame seeds. *Simit* is found on almost every corner for sale in small glass boxes.

Ayran, a popular yogurt drink diluted with water, as well as fresh cucumbers, peeled and cut ready to eat, attracted my attention next. *Ayran* and cucumbers are extremely popular in spring and summer. The vendor handed me a slice of cucumber to taste. It was juicy, refreshing and very tasty.

Talking about food sold in the street, *kakoreç* came to my mind – intestines filled from the very delicious part of the lamb found next to the neck and mixed with herbs such as oregano, red and black pepper – it was an extremely popular preparation before it was discarded for hygienic reasons. Another famous food is doner kebabs, lamb meat left to cook on a revolving vertical spit. This is seen all over Turkey. I was told that doner kebabs originated from Bursa.

Also, what one cannot miss seeing everywhere are the corn cobs and chestnuts grilled over charcoal, the latter being most popular in winter. *Pilav* with *nohut* (rice with chick peas) is sold near the bazaar and old shopping areas and only during Ramadan, the fasting month for Muslims.

But my main interest was in the spice market, also called the 'Egyptian bazaar', as most spices and other ingredients used to be imported from Egypt. I ambled through the *souk* and was hit by the aromas emanating from dozens of shops with their displays of all kinds of spices. These were kept in plastic containers or tins arranged to look like a vivid, colourful patchwork. It is difficult to imagine food being cooked without them: cinnamon for dusting over a bowl of *salep*; strong-smelling saffron for fish sauces. Whenever used the spices harmonize with the other ingredients to produce truly delectable dishes. My eye was also caught by the beautiful displays of seasonal fruit and vegetables, including aubergines, the crowning glory of the Ottoman kitchen which originated in India and are used in so many marvellous recipes.

Istanbul is also renowned for the freshness of its fish and for its preparation. Shops offering fish of all kinds are side by side. As I walked further, there were vendors of *Midyedolmassi* (stuffed mussels), clustered together in huge round pans with a cauldron of piping hot oil in front of them. There were also four or five men, one handing a sandwich to a customer and another frying squid. This reminded me of the *falafel* street sellers in the busy streets of Beirut.

Pastirma, which is also enjoyed today in Turkey, is a legacy of the way Turkish tribesmen used to cook their meat. These people spent their lives on horseback and they did not have time to build fires, so they used to spice pieces of meat and keep them between the back of their horse and the saddle. After a few days, the meat was ready to be eaten.

Smelling this multitude of aromas that were wafting all around us made me very hungry, so my friends and I entered a nearby restaurant where I had a tasty, simple meal of fish simmered with vegetables, followed by a Turkish coffee.

Later, we dined at the Divan restaurant, to the sound of an orchestra playing 1950s and 1960s music. We had remarkably large prawns from the south of Turkey, the like of which I have never tasted before. To follow was a soup of sheep's trotters, which had a very distinctive flavour. According to a tradition dating back to the Ottoman Empire, this soup was served to a gathering of women the day after a royal wedding.

The following day our visit started at the palace of Ibrahim Paça, Grand Vizir of Sultan Suleiman. Today the palace, a house built in the 16th century for the Grand Vizir, is the Turkish and Islamic Art Museum. Ibrahim Paça, who was Greek in origin, became extremely powerful and the Sultan began to feel threatened by his arrogance. When the Grand Vizir married the Sultan's daughter, the wedding feast was on such a scale that a contemporary poem compared the laden table to the heavens. Ibrahim was finally executed when he made a final mistake in addition to his many other outrages and displayed three bronze statues of Greek mythology in the garden of his palace, which caused great offence to the faithful.

Hospitality is a feature of Turkish life. The people, rich and poor alike, have great dignity. The sight of a child begging reminded me of a story that was told about Geha, the fool philosopher. He was asked, 'What is the proper time for taking meals?' He replied, 'It depends. For the man who has something to eat, the most convenient time to eat is when he feels hungry. But for the man who has nothing to eat, he has no choice: he eats when he finds food.'

Starters

Su böreği

DOUGH FILLED WITH CHEESE

Böreks are said to be of Balkan origin. *Su böreği* is one of them. It is delicious but needs time to prepare. When I was in Istanbul, this dish was prepared in front of me and I was told that the dough should have the texture of an earlobe. The dough is rolled very thinly into large circles and flour is used to prevent the rolling pin from sticking to the surface. Each circle is gently dropped into boiling water to simmer for up to a minute, then it is removed and immersed into cold water. Afterwards the circles are spread out over a buttered pan and brushed generously with melted butter. This is repeated until there are 8 layers. A filling of cheese is spread over them, which is covered by a further 10 layers of pastry. Experimenting is the key to success. *Su böreği* looks beautiful and is very presentable as a starter or as part of a buffet.

This recipe is enough for 12 people.

For the filling
400g (14oz) feta cheese
2 handfuls finely chopped parsley
2 tablespoons cream (optional)

For the dough
650g (1lb 7½oz) sifted flour
6 eggs
3 teaspoons salt
60ml (2½fl oz) water, or as necessary
250g (8½oz) melted butter

In a medium-size bowl mash down the cheese and mix thoroughly with the parsley and the cream, if using.

In another bowl, place the flour, make a well in the centre and add the eggs. Sprinkle over the salt, mix the egg and salt, and then mix with the flour. Add the water gradually, you might need a little less or more. Knead the dough until it reaches the consistency of an earlobe (sprinkle the surface with a little flour if necessary). Leave to rest for 30 minutes, covered with a wet towel so that the surface of the dough does not dry.

To make the dough sheets, have ready a large pan of slightly salted, boiling water and a largish bowl filled with cold water, a round pan a little larger than 30cm (12in), which you have greased with 2 tablespoons of butter and a rolling pin (or an *oklava*, a thin Turkish rolling pin, if possible).

When the dough is ready divide into 16–18 portions. Sprinkle the work surface with flour. Take one dough portion, place over the floured surface and press with four fingers to flatten. Roll out as thinly as you possibly can or to reach a diameter of 30cm (12in).

Drop gently into boiling water for a minute or until soft (like spaghetti), using a wooden spoon to spread out in the pan. Remove and immerse in the cold water. Remove from the water, spread over the buttered pan and brush all over with butter. Repeat the same, boiling, cooling and buttering until you have done 6 or 7 layers. Now spread over the filling and cover with the remaining layers of dough, following the same method as before. To cook, heat the pan slowly and leave for 10 minutes. Occasionally check the bottom by lifting one side of the layers of dough. When the bottom and sides are golden, turn over to brown the other side. To do so, lay a flat metal sheet over the top of the *su böreği* and invert. Again butter the pan and, with a lot of care, slide the uncooked side back into the buttered pan. Leave to cook until golden in colour as before. If you find this difficult, bake in the oven until it is golden brown. Serve warm or at room temperature.

Kilyos pilavi

RICE AND MUSHROOMS WITH DILL

This is a delicate, fragrant dish which makes an excellent starter, although in Turkey it is traditionally served as an accompaniment to other dishes. It originates in the Black Sea region in the west of Turkey, where they often add a little *kaimak* (clotted cream) towards the end of the cooking time to balance the flavours. With or without the cream, this wonderful dish has been added to my long list of Turkish favourites. If you have the patience, it is better to clean the mushrooms with a piece of kitchen towel and then rinse once rather than to soak them in water. This way, they will keep most of their B vitamins and their flavour.

This dish serves 5 as a starter. It also makes a good addition to a buffet. Serve either hot or cold.

Ingredients
75ml (3fl oz) extra virgin olive oil
250g (8½oz) mushrooms, finely sliced
2 garlic cloves, finely chopped
30g (1oz) dill, chopped
600ml (1 pint) water
1½ teaspoons salt, or to taste
350g (12oz) long-grain rice, preferably basmati

Heat the oil in a medium-size pan and when it is slightly hot, add the mushrooms. Sauté over medium heat for 30 seconds and add the garlic, stirring occasionally for 1 minute further or until a liquid appears. Allow the mushrooms to simmer in their juices for 1–2 minutes, but do not allow the liquid to evaporate completely. Stir in the dill, add the water and sprinkle with salt. Bring to the boil, add the rice and return to the boil. Cover and simmer over low heat for 10 minutes or until all the water has been absorbed. Turn off the heat, cover the pan with a thick towel and leave for 10 minutes, then serve.

Nohutlu pilav

CHICK PEAS WITH RICE

If you are looking for something simple, tasty, nutritious and economical, this delicious Turkish pilaff is the perfect answer. Served hot and eaten with yogurt, it makes a satisfying meal in itself. It can also be served, in the authentic Turkish way, to accompany main dishes of chicken, meat, fish stew or kebabs. It can be served as part of a buffet because it tastes good at room temperature. As a starter, a bowl of yogurt and a seasonal leaf salad are a good addition. A long time ago, *pilav* with *nohut* (chick peas) used to be sold in the streets of Istanbul. Nowadays, during the holy month of Ramadan it is found on sale next to the bazaars and in the old shopping area.

Ingredients
200g (7oz) rice soaked in hot water for 15 minutes
45g (1½oz) butter
½ teaspoon sugar
1 teaspoon salt
85g (3oz) chick peas, soaked overnight and cooked until tender
350ml (12fl oz) hot water, chicken or meat stock

In a small pan, sauté the rice in butter over low heat for about 6 minutes. Sprinkle with sugar and salt. Add the chick peas and water or stock. Bring to the boil, cover and simmer over low heat for 8 minutes or until water has been absorbed. Turn the heat off, place a thick towel over the covered pan and serve within 15–30 minutes.

Yoğurt çorbasi

YOGURT RICE SOUP

Yogurt has always been part of the Turkish diet. It became a staple during the Ottoman rule. This nourishing soup is prepared all over Turkey. It is made with handy and economical ingredients, reflecting the simplicity of Turkish cuisine. The yogurt amalgamates with the rice rendering the broth as smooth as velvet. Instead of rice, you could use whole wheatgrain which has been soaked overnight, drained the following day and cooked in water until tender.

This soup is a perfect starter all year round and you will have a meal which is kind to the stomach. Eat with olives, bread and a vegetable salad.

Serves 6.

Ingredients
225g (8oz) rice, rinsed in water several times
50fl oz (2 pints) water
2½ teaspoons salt, or to taste
1 egg
1 kg (2¼lb) thick yogurt

Put the rice, water and salt in a large pan and bring to the boil. Cover and simmer over medium-low heat for about 15 minutes, or until the rice is soft.

In the meantime, thoroughly combine the egg with the yogurt in a bowl, using a wooden spoon or electric mixer. Then sieve the yogurt mixture into another bowl.

When the rice is tender, turn off the heat. Immediately, gradually add the yogurt in the bowl to the rice while stirring with a wooden spoon until it blends. Serve at once.

Zeytinyağlı enginar dolması

ARTICHOKES STUFFED WITH RICE

Stuffed artichokes and other vegetables are a common feature of Turkish cuisine. Fillings can be made from either meat or herbs. The meat variety is generally eaten hot and may be accompanied by rice. Authentically, vegetable versions are cooked in olive oil and eaten cold.

Artichokes originally grew wild in north Africa and from there they travelled to Sicily. They were known to Ibn Batuta, the medieval Arab traveller, who describes a plant with branches like those of an artichoke. From Italy, it seems that it was taken to France in the 16th century, when Catherine de Medici travelled there to marry the heir to the French throne, later Henry II. In Turkey, artichokes are greatly valued. They are flavourful and have health-giving properties. They aid digestion, are diuretic and thought to help reduce blood cholesterol. Above all, a substance found in the artichoke is thought to protect the liver.

These stuffed artichokes make an unusual starter. For a richer flavour, sauté the onions and the remaining mixture for a minute or two before stuffing the artichokes.

Serves 5.

Ingredients
2 tablespoons flour
juice of 1 lemon
5 artichokes
30g (1oz) round-grain rice
3 tablespoons finely chopped parsley
3 tablespoons finely chopped mint
3 tablespoons finely chopped dill
55g (2oz) spring onions, finely chopped
2 teaspoons sugar
1 teaspoon salt
3 tablespoons extra virgin olive oil
170–200ml (6–7fl oz) hot water

Have ready a bowl of water mixed thoroughly with 2 tablespoons of flour and the lemon juice. Trim the artichokes using scissors or by pulling off the leaves until you reach the base. Using a sharp knife or a spoon, scoop out the choke and discard. Quickly rub with the lemon mixture to prevent discoloration. Slice off the stem, also rub with lemon and put in the bowl. Repeat with the other artichokes.

In a small bowl, combine the rice, parsley, mint, dill, spring onions, sugar, salt and 1 tablespoon of olive oil. Mix thoroughly. Drain the artichokes and fill them with the rice mixture. Place in the pan with the water and remaining oil. Bring to the boil, reduce the heat to low, cover and simmer for 30–40 minutes, or until artichokes are tender.

Allow to cool while covered and serve when they reach room temperature.

Düğün çorbasi

WEDDING SOUP

This is a sophisticated *velouté* soup that equals the top soups in the world. After tasting it, I understood why it is so famous and has taken Turkey by storm. In rural Turkey, soups are sometimes served for breakfast — they are strengthening and energizing, which makes them an excellent start to the day. This is a soup that, according to an 18th-century cookbook, was traditionally prepared on occasions of public rejoicing, such as weddings — hence its name.

I believe this soup to be a superstar which should be appreciated not only in Turkey but also the world over. Serve it for a special and memorable dinner, followed by another exotic dish, Artichokes stuffed with chicken (see page 252), and Pumpkin dessert (page 271).

It is a simple, inexpensive recipe, but it is important to use the best-quality ingredients and to prepare it with care.

Serves 6.

For the soup
2.25 litres (4 pints) water
450g (1lb) neck of a lamb, sliced into medium-thin slices
1 onion
1 large cinnamon stick
2–3 bay leaves
3–4 cardamoms
1 stem of celery, cut into 3
1 carrot, cut into 3
1 stem of parsley
1 teaspoon salt

To thicken
75g (2½oz) butter
1 tablespoon extra virgin olive oil
8 tablespoons flour
1.5 litres (2½ pints) meat stock (from cooking the lamb)
1 egg yolk
5–6 tablespoons lemon juice
2 tablespoons water
30g (1oz) pistachios, soaked in boiling water and peeled
½ teaspoon dried chilli flakes (optional)
a knob of butter (optional)

Put the water and slices of lamb in a large pan. Heat over medium-high heat, bring to the boil and skim. Add the onion, cinnamon, bay leaves, cardamom, celery, carrots and parsley. Sprinkle with salt and reduce heat to medium-low, cover and simmer for 1½ hours or until the meat is very soft. Remove the lamb and divide into very small pieces. Set this to one side and discard the bones. Strain the stock and measure out 1.5 litres (2½ pints).

Heat the butter and oil in a medium-size pan and add the flour. Allow it to reach a pale golden colour. Gradually whisk in the measured meat stock. Keep stirring until it boils. Simmer over medium heat for 10–15 minutes, stirring occasionally, until its consistency reaches that of double cream.

In the meantime, in a small bowl mix thoroughly the egg yolk, lemon juice and water. Using a wooden spoon, gradually stir the egg yolk mixture into the soup. Keep stirring until it boils. Add the pistachios and pieces of meat to the soup, and simmer for 2–3 minutes. Sauté the chilli flakes in the butter, if using, and add to the soup. Serve hot.

Kısır salatası

FRAGRANT HERBS WITH BURGHOL

This is a fragrant, succulent salad that is typical of south-eastern Turkey. It is a green mixture of mint, parsley, dill, green pepper and the green parts of spring onions, with a red contrast from the tomatoes. Traditionally, it is tossed only with pomegranate syrup and lemon juice. If olive oil is added, it interferes with its tangy character and its lightness, unlike two other burghol salads: the famous *Tabbouleh* (page 17), which is hungry for the olive oil; and the northern Syrian, *Kibbeh al-hammam* (page 96), in which oil contributes to its succulence.

Kisir, *Tabbouleh* and *Kibbeh al-hammam* are variations of salads with a dominant local staple, burghol. Which of these salads came first is debatable.

This salad makes a wonderful starter for 6 or otherwise 3 hungry people. Follow this with Istanbul lamb (page 62) or *Kalkan baligi Tavasi* (page 250). Finish the meal with *Apple muhallebi* (page 278).

Ingredients
170g (6oz) fine burghol
200g (7oz) dill, finely chopped
55g (2oz) mint leaves, finely chopped
200g (7oz) parsley, finely chopped
200g (7oz) spring onions, finely sliced
170g (6oz) green pepper, finely diced
450g (1lb) tomatoes, peeled and chopped
4 tablespoons pomegranate syrup, or to taste
3½ tablespoons lemon juice
2 teaspoons salt, or to taste

Rinse the burghol and place in a sieve for 15 minutes, allowing it to absorb the water and soften. Mix with all the other ingredients in a bowl. Using a fork, mix thoroughly, yet gently, without mashing. Taste, adjust the seasonings and serve.

Havuçlu haydari

CARROTS IN OIL AND YOGURT

This dish can be served as part of the *mezzé*. It is so simple to make and yet so delicious. The carrots are shredded and sautéed in oil, and then yogurt, mixed with garlic, is poured over them. As I was sautéing the carrots, I decided to experiment by adding spring onions and was pleased with the result, which I thought added depth and zest, so I have added them to the recipe as an optional ingredient. I hope that this addition will be welcomed by my Turkish friends.

A perfect starter and a great addition to a summer buffet, this colourful dish soothes the palate.

Ingredients
5–6 tablespoons extra virgin olive oil
285g (10oz) spring onions, finely sliced (optional)
675g (1½lb) carrots, shredded
450ml (¾ pint) yogurt
1 garlic clove, crushed
¾ teaspoon salt, or to taste
toasted or sautéed hazelnuts, chopped (optional)

Heat 4 tablespoons of oil in a large frying pan and, when hot, add the spring onions, if using. Sauté the onions for 1–2 minutes, or until their aroma comes out and their colour becomes pale. Stir once, then remove to a side dish.

Wipe the frying pan with kitchen paper and add more oil. Sauté the carrots for 4–5 minutes, stirring occasionally. Remove and place on a serving dish. Arrange the spring onions over the top.

Mix the yogurt with the garlic and salt, and pour to cover the carrots and spring onions. Garnish with chopped toasted or sautéed hazelnuts, if using, and serve – this is a real treat.

Zeytinyağlı semizotu

PURSLANE STEW

An unusual stew of fresh purslane topped with a little garlicky yogurt, this dish is eaten all over Turkey. It is traditionally cooked with meat, but I prefer the meatless version that allows the special peppery flavour to dominate. Purslane is a herb that has been grown for centuries in the Levant and was used in Roman times. It is rich in omega-3 oils, generally found in oily fish. A little rice is added to give substance.

This is a good starter; served with *Musakka* (see page 247) as a main dish and the Damascene *Hilatiyeh* (page 194) as a dessert, you will have an excellent meal.

Ingredients
5–6 tablespoons extra virgin olive oil
200g (7oz) onion, finely chopped
55g (2oz) round-grain rice, rinsed
1.1 kg (2½lb) purslane
1 teaspoon salt, or to taste
50ml (2fl oz) hot water
2 medium-size tomatoes, peeled and sliced
a handful of dill, chopped (optional)

Heat the oil in a medium-size pan and sauté the onions until translucent. Stir in the rice and sauté for 30 seconds. Strip off all the leaves from the purslane, reserving the tender stems, rinse and add to the pan. Sprinkle with salt, add the water and cover the pan, then simmer over a low heat for 10–15 minutes. Five minutes before the end of cooking, add the tomatoes. Turn the heat off and keep covered for 5 minutes.

Sprinkle with dill, if using, and serve hot. If it is eaten as a main course, serve with yogurt, bread and olives.

Yayla çorbası

RICE, CHICK PEAS AND YOGURT SOUP

This simple and very healthy soup comes from eastern Turkey. It has a velvety, smooth texture and takes surprisingly little time to prepare. Sometimes, instead of mint or dill, a little *tarhun* (tarragon) is sprinkled over towards the end. This lovely and unusual soup has a refined flavour. As a general rule, lemon juice is added when the yogurt is not sour.

This quantity serves 5–6 as a starter.

Ingredients
1.5 litres (2½ pints) water
100g (3½oz) short-grain rice
1¼ teaspoons salt, or to taste
55g (2oz) chick peas, soaked overnight and pre-cooked
500g (1lb 2oz) tub of yogurt
1¼ tablespoons flour
2–3 tablespoons lemon juice
15g (½oz) butter
1 teaspoon dried mint or 1 teaspoon chopped dill

Put the water and rice into a pan and bring to the boil. Add the chick peas and reduce the heat to low, sprinkle with salt, cover and simmer until the rice is soft.

In the meantime, thoroughly mix the yogurt with the flour and lemon juice. Add this to the pan after the rice and chick peas have softened, while stirring in the same direction with a wooden spoon over medium heat until the mixture boils. Reduce the heat to low and leave to simmer for 5 minutes. In a small frying pan, heat the butter, add the mint and sauté for few seconds or until you smell the mint (that shouldn't take long so take care not to burn). Add the sautéed mint or dill, to the yogurt and leave to bubble for a minute over a low heat. Serve hot.

Mercimek çorbası yoğurtlu

LENTIL AND YOGURT SOUP

In Turkey, during the holy month of fasting, a meal always begins with soup. This recipe has made its way into my family repertoire because it is delicious, economical and easy to prepare. I am reminded of a Turkish lady who told me that where she comes from in Gaziantep, a woman can spend 10 hours a day in the kitchen cooking for her family. Be assured that this recipe fits a busy lifestyle perfectly.

This soup goes wonderfully with another starter, Cheese and dill pie (see page 228). Spoil yourself and finish the meal with the Apricots stuffed with cream (page 272) for a real treat.

Ingredients
200g (7oz) red split lentils
225g (8oz) onions, finely chopped
1.7 litres (3 pints) water
1½ teaspoons salt, or to taste
1 tablespoon rice
2 tablespoons coarse burghol
115g (4oz) grated carrots
1 heaped tablespoon tomato purée
1 tablespoon flour
1 tub of thick yogurt (about 200g / 7oz)
1 teaspoon extra virgin olive oil
1 teaspoon dried mint

Combine the lentils with the onions, water and salt. Bring to the boil. Add the rice, burghol, grated carrots and tomato purée. Return to the boil, cover and simmer for 10 minutes, or until the lentils, rice and burghol are soft.

In the meantime, mix the flour thoroughly with the yogurt. When the lentils, rice and burghol have softened, stir in the yogurt using a wooden spoon. Stir in the same direction all the time until it reaches boiling point. Reduce the heat to low and simmer for 1–2 minutes. Heat the oil to sauté the mint for a few seconds without stirring then add this to the soup in the pan. Take off the heat and serve hot with a bowl of green olives, fresh mint and bread.

Domatesli mercimek çorbası

RED LENTIL AND TOMATO SOUP

It is said that lentils were the daily food of the witty poet Abi al-Alaa al Maari, who could answer any question that he was asked with poetry.

Be that as it may, this soup came as a pleasant surprise when I discovered how delicious and subtle it was. You could include a little lemon to lift the flavour, a common addition in Turkey, Syria and Lebanon.

Ingredients
2½ tablespoons extra virgin olive oil
250g (8½oz) onions, chopped
375g (13oz) tomatoes, peeled and quartered
285g (10oz) red split lentils
900ml (1¾ pints) water
1½ teaspoons salt, or to taste
lemon wedges (optional)

Heat the oil in a medium-size pan. Add the onions and sauté until pale gold in colour. Stir in the tomatoes, add the lentils and water, and sprinkle with salt. Bring to the boil. Cover and simmer over a low heat for 25–30 minutes, or until the lentils are tender.

Put everything in a food processor and blend until it reaches a creamy consistency, or pass through a vegetable mill. Return to the same pan, bring again to a boil and simmer for a few minutes. Serve hot with lemon wedges to squeeze over, if using.

Zeytinyağlı bakla

FAVA BEANS IN OIL

Dishes containing broad beans are popular and cherished in the Levant. A similar dish to this one is made in Lebanon and Syria. Both carry the same Arabic name but use coriander; dill is commonly used in Turkish cuisine. Fava beans in oil make a perfect starter and, like many dishes of the Levant, it can be a meal in itself. Dill and yogurt marry well; here the yogurt tames the strength of the dill, producing an elegant and memorable flavour.

Broad beans are one of the favourite vegetables of Annie Bell, journalist and food writer. In the invaluable *Annie Bell's Vegetable Book* (Michael Joseph) she gives many wonderful recipes. Besides their delicious taste, broad beans constitute a highly nutritious meal excellent for vegetarians.

Ingredients
water
1 tablespoon flour
juice of a lemon
500g (1lb 2oz) broad beans
4 tablespoons extra virgin olive oil
225g (8oz) onions, finely chopped
1¼ teaspoons salt
1 teaspoon sugar
75ml (3fl oz) hot water
20g (¾oz) dill, finely chopped
1 small garlic clove, finely crushed
200g (7oz) tub of thick yogurt

Mix the water, flour and lemon juice in a bowl. Top and tail the beans, removing the string from either side of the pod, and cut into 2.5cm (1in) long pieces. Rinse and place in the bowl of water, flour and lemon – this lifts their flavour – but do not leave them for long because you do not want to lose their rich B vitamins. Drain and do not rinse again.

Heat the oil in a medium-size pan, add the onions and sauté for a few minutes or until the onions are translucent. Add the beans, sprinkle with 1 teaspoon salt and the sugar and stir gently with a wooden spoon. Cover the pan and leave the beans to sweat over a low heat for about 8 minutes. Add the hot water, cover the pan and leave to simmer over a low heat for 40 minutes.

Sprinkle with dill, cover the pan and allow them to cool. Meanwhile, stir the garlic into the yogurt with the remaining salt. Serve the cooled beans with yogurt, bread and green olives.

Fasulye müjveri

LAMB AND BEAN FRITTERS

These fritters, combining French beans and a little minced lamb, were apparently prepared towards the end of the 16th century when French beans first reached Turkey from Europe.

This recipe is quick and simple, making it a perfect dish for busy schedules while being infinitely superior in both flavour and nutrition to any ready meal you can buy. These miniature omelettes are ideal as a starter or as a family main course to eat along with the Lebanese Aubergine dip (see page 23) or one of the many salad recipes in this book.

Serves 3.

Ingredients
1 heaped tablespoon flour
115g (4oz) French beans, sliced and blanched
extra virgin olive oil for frying
115g (4oz) minced lamb
3 eggs
¾ teaspoon salt, or to taste
a pinch of black pepper
a pinch of allspice
a pinch of cinnamon
15g (½oz) butter (optional)

In a bowl, mix the flour and beans thoroughly until all the beans are coated with flour. In a frying pan, heat 1 tablespoon of olive oil, and sauté the meat for 2–3 minutes or until it is lightly browned. Add the sautéed meat to the beans in the bowl, then add the eggs, salt, black pepper, allspice and cinnamon. Mix thoroughly.

In a large frying pan, heat enough olive oil to shallow fry and the butter, if using. When the oil and butter (if using) are hot, place 1 tablespoon of the bean mixture in the pan and repeat until you have about 6 fritters, or as many as the pan can hold. Leave each one to set, then gently turn it over, using a spatula and fork. Repeat until all are done. Serve hot.

Zeytinyağlı enginar

ARTICHOKES IN OIL

Istanbul and the Aegean coast of Turkey are famous for the delicious and various ways of preparing vegetable dishes with oil that are to be eaten at room temperature. In Istanbul, street vendors can be seen peeling the artichokes at high speed to sell to busy housewives. This dish is easy to make but it would be quicker if someone would clean the artichokes in advance. A famous chef in Istanbul told me that the flavour of the oily dishes improves if they are left to cool while still covered. He added that cooked vegetables are similar to red wine: the more they age the better they taste. They make an elegant and delicious starter.

Ingredients
4 artichokes
1 small carrot, diced
1 small potato, diced
8–10 pearl onions
200ml (7fl oz) water
4 tablespoons olive oil
1 teaspoon sugar
1 teaspoon salt
1–2 stems of dill
1 tablespoon lemon juice

Snap or trim the leaves off the artichokes using scissors until you reach the heart. Using a sharp knife or a spoon, scoop out the choke and discard. Every time you finish trimming an artichoke, rub it with lemon to prevent discoloration. Leave the stem but peel and trim the tough part around the artichoke heart. Place the artichokes in a medium-size pan. Add the carrot, potato, onions, water, oil, sugar and salt. Bring to the boil, then reduce the heat to low. Cover and simmer for 30–40 minutes or until tender. Turn off the heat, then add the dill stems and lemon juice. Cover again and allow to cool to room temperature, then serve.

İçbaklalı enginar

ARTICHOKES STUFFED WITH BROAD BEANS

In the past, on the Aegean coast, the artichokes for this recipe were served warm with a drizzle of olive oil, while in Ottoman palace style they were served a day after cooking drizzled with olive oil to give them enough time to cool and mellow. Nowadays, they are served cold as part of a *mezzé*. A similar dish is made in the Lebanon using Swiss chard as an extra ingredient. The broad beans used in this recipe have been shelled. You can either buy them fresh and shell them to use the inner part, or buy them frozen already shelled.

This makes an unusual and healthy starter.

Ingredients
4 artichokes
125g (4½oz) broad beans (fresh or frozen)
3 tablespoons extra virgin olive oil
1 bunch spring onions (about 140g / 5oz), finely chopped
2 teaspoons sugar
¾ teaspoon salt
200ml (7fl oz) hot water

Trim the artichokes as directed for *Zeytinyağli enginar dolmassı* (page 214). Place the broad beans (freshly shelled or frozen) in boiling water for a few seconds, remove and peel the skins unless you prefer to leave them on.

Heat 2 tablespoons of oil in a medium-size frying pan, add the onions and sprinkle with sugar. Sauté for 1 minute, then add the beans and sauté gently for a further 30 seconds. Sprinkle with salt. Remove and fill the artichoke hearts. Place the hearts in a pan large enough to accommodate all 4 in one layer, then add the water and remaining oil. Bring to the boil, cover and simmer over low heat for 30 minutes or until the artichokes are tender. Turn the heat off and leave them covered until they cool to room temperature. Serve with lemon wedges.

Patlican sote

AUBERGINES WITH TOMATOES

Immense pleasure is derived from eating this simple dish. The medley of flavours simmers over a low flame until it reaches an harmonious whole that satisfies the palate. Aubergines were popular during the Ottoman Empire and still are. Topkapi Palace is said to have had chefs from different parts of the Empire, bringing a wide variety of different aubergine recipes.

This is perfect as a starter for six, followed by the Lebanese Baked *kibbeh* (see page 66), or as an accompaniment to other dishes, such as Cheese and dill pie (see page 228).

Ingredients
750g (1lb 10oz) aubergines, cubed into 1cm (½in) cubes
2 tablespoons sea salt (approximately)
extra virgin olive oil
450g (1lb) onions, finely sliced
10 garlic cloves
½ tablespoon tomato purée
750g (1lb 10oz) tomatoes, peeled and cubed
1 teaspoon sugar
1 teaspoon salt, or to taste
4 green mild chillies

Sprinkle the aubergines in sea salt and leave in a sieve for at least 30 minutes. Rinse well and pat dry. Place some oil in a deep frying pan. When the oil is hot, sauté the aubergines over high heat. Alternatively, mix them with 3½ tablespoons of oil and bake them at 180°C (350°F/gas mark 4) in the oven until they are golden brown. If you choose to sauté, stir the aubergines occasionally until nicely browned. Remove with a slotted spoon, drain on kitchen paper and set aside.

Wipe the pan with kitchen paper and add 4 tablespoons of oil. When it is hot, add the onions and sauté over low heat for 5 minutes, or until translucent. Stir in the garlic and sauté with the onions for a minute or two, then stir in the tomato purée. Add the tomatoes and sprinkle with sugar and salt. When the liquid that is released from the tomatoes starts bubbling, add the reserved aubergines. Cover and simmer over low heat for 20 minutes.

Five minutes before the end of cooking, add the chillies, either whole or halved, if you prefer a hotter taste, cover again and continue with the remaining cooking time. Turn off the heat and leave the pan covered until the aubergine mixture has reached room temperature. Serve with bread and olives.

Tuzlu peynirli

CHEESE AND DILL PIE

This is a newcomer to Turkish home cooking and shows the influence of Western cuisine. The strong flavours of the feta cheese and the dill amalgamate harmoniously to produce a delicious savoury pie.

Serve it with a purslane salad, tossed in lemon juice and olive oil with a touch of crushed garlic. You could also add a few tiny cubes of tomato to the salad to introduce a splash of colour. The pie is best eaten when it has reached room temperature.

Serves 8 as a starter.

For the filling
170g (6oz) feta cheese, crumbled
45g (3½oz) dill, finely chopped
yolk of one small egg (optional)

For the dough
500g (1lb 2oz) flour, sifted
1 teaspoon salt
4 teaspoons baking powder
200g (7oz) softened butter
2 tablespoons olive oil
3 eggs
225g (8oz) yogurt
1 tablespoon lemon juice

Lightly butter a 25cm (10in) flan dish with a removable rim. Sprinkle with flour and shake off excess. Prepare the filling by combining the feta cheese and dill. Preheat the oven to 180°C (350°F/gas mark 4).

Put the flour in a bowl and blend in the salt and baking powder. Add the butter, the oil, and mix. Add one egg at a time, mixing after each one. Blend the yogurt with the lemon juice and combine well with the ingredients in the bowl. The dough will have a sticky consistency. Put three-quarters of the dough into the flan dish and level it out to fill the dish. Spread the cheese mixture into hte flan dish. Make strips with the remaining dough (moisten your hands to prevent sticking) and arrange them in a crisscross pattern over the filling.

Bake in a preheated oven for 50–60 minutes or until nicely browned. Remove and allow to cool completely before serving, otherwise the taste will be doughy. Slice and serve.

Istridye pilaki

OYSTERS IN PARSLEY SAUCE

Oysters were enjoyed by the early Greeks and Romans, who cherished them greatly. The French writer, Guy de Maupassant, describes one kind of oyster in his book, *Bel Ami*, in terms that are both lyrical and appetite-inducing.

This is a very pleasant oyster bouillon which needs little time to cook. The only time-consuming part is opening the oysters, which may be difficult when you do it for the first time. It is important to buy your oysters from a reputable place as they need to be fresh. Check that the shells are closed. This dish makes an elegant and impressive starter for 5. The recipe below includes an optional egg yolk sauce.

For the oysters
24 oysters
1½ tablespoons extra virgin olive oil
15g (½oz) finely chopped parsley
150ml (5fl oz) water

For the sauce (optional)
1 egg yolk
¼ teaspoon salt
2 tablespoons lemon juice
4 tablespoons oyster juice
1 teaspoon cream

Have ready a large plastic bowl filled with ice. Place a medium-size glass bowl on the ice. Using a clean tea towel, firmly grab an oyster shell with one hand and, with the other hand, insert an oyster knife into the hinge of the shell and carefully push it up and down to open. Take care not to spill the oyster's juice. Loosen the meat into the glass bowl with its juice. Repeat with all the others. Measure out 4 tablespoons of their juice and set aside.

In a small pan, heat the oil until very hot and sauté the parsley for half a minute. Add the oysters with their remaining juice. Add the water, bring to the boil then simmer over low heat for 6–8 minutes.

If making the optional egg yolk sauce, combine the egg yolk, salt, lemon and reserved oyster juice in a small pan. Stir the mixture constantly over very low heat until it boils and thickens. Reduce the heat even futher and stir in the cream. Strain the yolk sauce over the oysters, stir for 1–2 minutes then serve.

Patlican pilav

RICE WITH AUBERGINES

A meal in itself, this is one of the most delicious rice dishes and is another attractive way to use one of the most loved vegetables in Turkey. To illustrate how popular aubergine was (and still is), a story goes that one of Istanbul's residential quarters burned down because everyone was so busy frying aubergines in hot oil over a huge flame that several wooden houses actually caught fire.

A lovely dish to start with or to have as a main course. To follow, serve an apple pudding or have the Lebanese *Kanafeh* (see page 79).

Ingredients
75ml (3fl oz) extra virgin olive oil, or as necessary
675g (1½lb) aubergines cubed into 1cm (½in) cubes
2 tablespoons of butter
3 spring onions, finely chopped
1½ teaspoons sugar
285g (10oz) tomatoes, peeled and finely chopped
450ml (¾ pint) hot water
225g (8oz) rice
1 teaspoon salt or to taste
½ teaspoon black pepper or to taste

Heat some oil in a pan and sauté the aubergines over a high heat until browned. At first a lot of the oil will be absorbed by the aubergines, but it will then be released again. Remove and drain over kitchen paper.

To a medium-size pan, add the butter. Add the onions, sauté over medium heat for 2 minutes, sprinkle with sugar, add the tomatoes and leave to simmer until the water evaporates and the consistency becomes thick. Add the water and bring to the boil. Add the rice and the fried aubergines. Sprinkle with salt and pepper. Bring back to the boil, reduce the heat to low, cover and simmer for 8–10 minutes or until the water has been absorbed. Turn off the heat, then cover with a thick towel to keep warm. Leave for 10 minutes then serve.

Yalanci biber dolmasi

STUFFED PEPPERS

This dish is typical of the coastal Mediterranean region of Antalya. It was handed to me by a top chef at the Falez Hotel. In Turkey, they have delicious pale green peppers, known as *çarliston*, which have a thin skin and a sweet taste. They are perfect for stuffing. These peppers are on sale in Turkish, Lebanese and Cypriot shops.

A white Turkish cheese called *lor* is used for the filling, but it only lasts for 2 days in the fridge. If *lor* is not available, ricotta, feta or curd cheese are good substitutes.

Ingredients
5–6 small green peppers
85g (3oz) ricotta or feta cheese
2 tablespoons parsley, finely chopped
2 tablespoons mint leaves, chopped
2 tablespoons finely chopped dill (optional)
1 spring onion, finely sliced
1 small tomato, deseeded and finely cubed
½ teaspoon salt
extra virgin olive oil

Slice off the tops of the peppers and remove seeds. Mash the cheese with a fork. Mix the parsley, mint, dill, onion, tomatoes and salt in a bowl. Fill the peppers and stand them upright with the caps on to ensure that the stuffing does not fall out. Place under a preheated grill 10cm (4in) away from the heat and grill for about 10 minutes on each side, or until the peppers soften and change colour. Remove, drizzle the oil all over and serve.

Susamli kizarmis peynir

DEEP-FRIED CHEESE WITH SESAME SEEDS

During my visit to Istanbul in search of unusual and simple vegetarian dishes, my friends, Ali and Gülfem, introduced me to the famous chef, Vedat Basaran. He entertained us in his beautiful restaurant where we dined on the terrace overlooking the Bosphorous. Our table was covered with an amazing array of dishes.

The taste of these cheese fritters was outstanding, reminiscent of French cheese *beignets*. The outer covering of sesame seeds adds an Oriental touch, giving them a distinct nutty flavour and adding to the crustiness of the shell while the inside remains soft.

This recipe is not authentic to Turkish cuisine, rather an interpretation. It makes about 30 pieces – a perfect starter for 8 served with a green or, better still, purslane salad.

Ingredients
225g (8oz) strong-flavoured white cheese or goat's cheese
2–3 egg whites
flour, sifted
55–85g (2–3oz) sesame seeds, lightly toasted
peanut oil for deep frying

Cut the cheese into small cubes, about 1cm (½in). Take each cube of cheese, dip into the egg white and drench into the flour, shaking off excess. Again dip into the egg white, remove and cover with the sesame seeds. Once more dip into the flour and place on a plate. Follow the same procedure with each cheese cube.

Heat the oil in a small frying pan. Drop in the cheese pieces, a few at a time, and fry undisturbed for 1–2 minutes or until they rise to the surface of the oil. Remove with a slotted spoon and drain on kitchen paper. Serve immediately.

Maamoul (Cheese and date pastries)

Ghoraibeh (Damascene shortbread)

Mercimek çorbasi yoğurtlu (Lentil and yogurt soup)

Tuzlu peynirli (Cheese and dill pie)

Tonlu pilaki (Tuna in a fragrant parsley sauce)

Kabak tatlısı (Pumpkin dessert)

Kaymakli kuru kayısı (Apricots stuffed with cream)

Domatesli sebze

VEGETABLES WITH FRAGRANT TOMATO SAUCE

Many Turkish recipes include aubergines. In this dish it is simply prepared. It goes well with a more filling starter such as Circassian chicken (page 238). The fragrant herbs in the sauce combine well with the yogurt, aubergine and other vegetables. Like many other Levantine dishes, this can be prepared in advance. If you wish, the aubergines, green peppers and courgettes can be grilled instead of fried.

Ingredients

4 aubergines, cut lengthways in 1cm (½in) slices
extra virgin olive oil
4 slices of green pepper
4 courgettes, finely sliced (optional)

For the sauce

2 medium-size tomatoes, peeled and finely cubed
1 garlic clove, finely chopped
1 teaspoon sugar
1 tablespoon finely chopped green pepper
1 stem of parsley, finely chopped
a few green parts of celery, chopped
½ tablespoon finely chopped dill
salt to taste

To garnish
thick yogurt

Sprinkle the aubergines with salt and leave to sweat for 30 minutes. Rinse well and dry between kitchen paper. Heat the oil in a frying pan and sauté the slices of green pepper until they soften. Remove with a slotted spoon and drain on kitchen paper. Add the courgettes, if using, to the pan and sauté until they start to change colour, then remove with a slotted spoon and drain on kitchen paper. Do the same with the aubergines, making sure they reach a nice brown colour.

To make the sauce, heat 1 tablespoon oil in a small pan and sauté the tomatoes, garlic, sugar, green pepper, parsley stem and celery. Simmer over low heat for 5–7 minutes, then add the dill and salt to taste. Cook for 1 minute further then remove. Divide the vegetables between 4 plates. To serve cover the vegetables with a little of the sauce and place a heaped tablespoon of yogurt on the side.

Yalancı dolma

AUBERGINES IN POMEGRANATE SAUCE

This fragrant regional dish is very nutritious and perfect for vegetarians. It is excellent as a starter, although you could just as easily have it as a main course, accompanied by Mountain potato *kibbeh* (page 24). Finish the meal with a refreshing chilled Almond milk pudding (page 273).

Ingredients
8 baby aubergines (about 350g / 12oz)
1½ tablespoons extra virgin olive oil
85g (3oz) onion, finely chopped
85g (3oz) round-grain rice, rinsed
1 teaspoon tomato purée
1¼ teaspoons salt
1 teaspoon sugar
¼ teaspoon black pepper
1 teaspoon pomegranate syrup
15g (½oz) parsley, finely chopped
30g (1oz) walnuts
1 tablespoon currants, soaked for 20 minutes
1 tablespoon sultanas, soaked for 20 minutes
285g (10oz) tomatoes, peeled and sliced
2 tablespoons lemon juice
100ml (4fl oz) fresh pomegranate juice

Press each aubergine over a hard surface, rolling it under the palm of your hand. This will make them easier to hollow. Slice off the tops of the aubergines and hollow the inside. Set to one side.

Heat the oil in a frying pan and sauté the onions until translucent. Add the rice and sauté until it is also translucent. Remove from the heat and stir in the tomato purée, ¾ teaspoon of salt, sugar, black pepper, pomegranate syrup, parsley, walnuts, currants and sultanas. Stir well then fill the aubergines with this mixture.

Spread a layer of tomatoes in a medium-size pan, add the aubergines and cover with the remaining tomatoes. Add the lemon and pomegranate juices. (To make pomegranate juice, put the seeds in a food processor, blend and then strain.) Sprinkle with the remaining salt. Bring to the boil, cover, reduce the heat to low and simmer for 30 minutes. Leave covered until it reaches room temperature, then serve.

İmam bayıldı

AUBERGINES, TOMATOES, ONIONS AND GARLIC

You only need to taste this exquisite dish to understand the Turkish legend: 'the delicacy of *Imam bayıldı* made the Imam faint'. One variation on the legend claims that the frugal Imam fainted because he discovered his wife had used an entire bottle of oil for the dish. *Imam bayıldı* is very special and would make a good choice to start a meal. Although it is easy to make, for maximum flavour, prepare the day before serving. Baked *kibbeh* (page 66) or Chicken with olives (page 68) would complement this starter. Finish the meal with *Aish al-Saraya* (page 76) or, when in season, try the Quince dessert (page 276).

Ingredients
2 aubergines (about 350g / 12oz), halved lengthways
sea salt
150ml (5½ fl oz) extra virgin olive oil
2 onions (about 450g / 1lb), finely sliced
10 garlic cloves, sliced
4 tomatoes (about 400g / 14oz), sliced
a few strips of green pepper

Peel the aubergines in lengthways strips. Sprinkle with salt and leave for 30 minutes to sweat. Rinse and dry between kitchen paper. Heat the oil in a frying pan and sauté the aubergines until golden brown on both sides, then remove and drain over triple kitchen paper.

Add the onions and garlic to the same oil in the pan. Sauté until translucent. Transfer to a side dish with a slotted spoon. In a pan that can hold the aubergines in one layer next to one another, make a bed of tomatoes and put the aubergines on top. Arrange the onions and garlic to completely cover each piece of aubergine and then put on top the remaining tomato slices. Top lengthways with 1 or 2 strips of the green pepper. Sprinkle 1 teaspoon of salt all over. Cover the pan and simmer over medium-low heat for 20–30 minutes.

Turn the heat off. Leave covered until it reaches room temperature. Carefully transfer each portion to a plate and serve. A comforting pleasure is to eat while dipping the bread in the sauce.

Fasulye pilaki

BEANS IN OIL

This is a highly nutritious dish that is made with haricot beans. The haricot bean is said to have been given in the 16th century to Catherine de Medici by her uncle, Pope Clement VII. Haricot beans are also used in the preparation of the famous *cassoulet* of the Languedoc.

Ingredients
200g (7oz) white beans
1 litre (1¾ pints) boiling water
100ml (3½ fl oz) extra virgin olive oil
225g (8oz) onions
1 whole head of garlic (about 55g / 2oz), sliced
2 tablespoons tomato purée
1 carrot cut into 2.5cm (1in) pieces
1 teaspoon salt, or to taste
a large handful of parsley, chopped
cayenne pepper (optional)

Soak the beans overnight, drain, rinse and place in a pan with water just to cover. Bring to a boil and skim. Discard the water and cover with the fresh boiling water. Return to the heat, bring back to the boil, cover and simmer over medium heat for 5 minutes. Then reduce the heat to low and simmer for 50 minutes or until the beans are soft.

Heat the oil in another pan and sauté the onions for 2 minutes. Add the garlic and sauté for a further 5 minutes or until they are translucent. Using a slotted spoon, remove the softened beans from their pan, add to the onions and garlic and stir well. Stir in the tomato purée. Measure out about 175ml (6fl oz) of the bean cooking liquid and add to the beans in the pan along with the carrot. Bring to the boil. Cover and simmer over low heat for 30 minutes. Sprinkle with salt and parsley. Cover and leave to stand for 20–30 minutes. Sprinkle some cayenne pepper over the top, if using. Serve with wedges of lemon and some bread.

Zeytinyağlı pırasa

LEEKS WITH OIL

Leeks have been cultivated for thousands of years by the Egyptians and the Hebrews, and were introduced to Europe by the Romans. The Roman Emperor Nero (AD37–68), was served with a pottage of leeks to enhance the great voice he believed he had.

In this simple dish, which is prepared mostly in Istanbul, the leeks are cooked in oil and eaten when they reach room temperature. Olive oil dishes such as this, using a variety of vegetables, rank high in Turkish cuisine. Nowadays, many of these dishes are part of the *mezzé*.

Ingredients
5–6 tablespoons extra virgin olive oil
1 large onion, finely chopped
500g (1lb 2oz) leeks, sliced lengthways into 2cm (¾in) pieces
1 teaspoon sugar
1 small carrot, cubed
1 small carrot, shredded
1 teaspoon salt, or to taste

Heat the oil in a pan and sauté the onion and leeks over medium-high heat for 6–8 minutes. Sprinkle with sugar, add the cubed and shredded carrots, stir and sprinkle with salt. Cover and simmer over low heat for 20 minutes. Turn off the heat and keep it covered until it reaches room temperature.

Çerkez tavuğu

CIRCASSIAN CHICKEN

A fine dish with a nutty taste, this travelled with the captive Circassian slaves who bewitched the Ottoman sultan with their beauty and food. I guarantee it will become a favourite dish of yours, too.

This dish relies very much upon the flavour of the chicken and the quality of the walnuts. It is not an economical dish but it is worth trying for a special occasion. Before eating, squeeze over some lemon juice to lift the flavour. This is an excellent buffet dish. Traditionally, this is eaten warm or cold and is served as part of a *mezzé*. In this recipe I have used pine nuts instead of bread, however, 2–3 slices of bread with crusts removed, or a mixture of bread and pine nuts may be used.

Serves 10.

For the chicken
1 chicken about 1.8kg (4lb), with the skin on
1.75 litres (3 pints) water
bouquet garni consisting of 1 cinnamon stick, 1 celery stick, 1 onion studded with 4
*   cloves, 4 cardamoms, 8 black peppercorns, 1 sprig of parsley*
1½ teaspoons salt

For the sauce
140g (5oz) mixture of almonds and pine nuts
200g (7oz) walnuts
2 large cloves of garlic
1½ teaspoons salt, or to taste
juice of ½ large lemon
200ml (7fl oz) milk
250ml (9fl oz) stock
55g (2oz) bread with crusts removed

For the garnish
1–2 tablespoon walnut oil
1 teaspoon chilli flakes or powder
8 walnut halves (approximately)
2 lemons, cut into pieces

Cut the chicken in half and rub it all over with salt and lemon, then rinse thoroughly. Put the chicken in the pan with water. Skim the foam as it forms on the surface of the water. Bring to the boil, add the bouquet garni, cover the pan and reduce the heat to medium. Simmer for about 1 hour, or until tender. About 20 minutes before the end of cooking, sprinkle with salt. When the chicken is cooked, transfer it to a plate.

Strain the chicken stock, measure the amount for the sauce and leave the remaining stock on the side in case you need later to thin the consistency of the sauce (what is left over can be used for soups). Divide the chicken meat lengthways into strips, discarding the skin and bones. To make the sauce, place the almonds and pine nuts, walnuts, garlic, salt, lemon juice, milk, stock and bread in a food processor. Blend until a smooth, creamy texture. Remove and spread so that it covers the chicken strips.

To garnish, warm the walnut oil but do not allow to smoke, add the chillies or cayenne pepper and stir once. Drizzle over the chicken mixture and sauce, sprinkle over the walnuts and serve with pieces of lemon.

Patates salatası

POTATO AND DILL SALAD

This simple and refreshing salad is served in Turkey as an hors d'oeuvre or an addition to a buffet. I ate it for the first time when I lunched at my friend's house in one of the Princes Islands. The table was set beneath a huge, spreading tree in a beautiful walled garden and was laid with an assortment of *mezzé* dishes, including this salad.

I serve *Patates salatası* as a starter with a bowl of olives. The recipe is enough for 5, but remember to leave it to stand for at least 15 minutes before serving, allowing enough time for the flavours to develop. You can use mayonnaise or oil if you prefer. To deepen the flavour of the potatoes, peel, grate, then mix them while still warm with 1½ tablespoons of olive oil and follow as below.

Ingredients
2 potatoes (about 350g / 12oz)
3 baby cucumbers (about 225g / 8oz)
3 tablespoons extra virgin olive oil
3 tablespoons yogurt
1 large garlic clove, crushed
55g (2oz) dill, finely chopped
1¼ teaspoons salt, or to taste

Cook the potatoes in boiling water until just tender. Remove from the water, peel and shred. Also shred the cucumber and leave in a sieve to drain. Blend thoroughly the rest of the ingredients. Stir the potatoes into the yogurt sauce along with the cucumber. Leave to marinate in a cool place for at least 15 minutes, then serve.

Etli ekmek

DEEP-FRIED LAMB PASTRIES

This dish is typical of Turkish cuisine. It makes an ideal starter for 8, allowing two portions for each, or could be one of a selection of other dishes such as Rice and mushrooms with dill, Tomato and walnut salad or Aubergine dip (page 23). For a light finish, serve *Mamounieh* (page 140) with Turkish coffee or fresh mint tea.

For the dough
275g (9½oz) flour
¾ teaspoon salt
1 teaspoon quick-rising yeast
150ml (5 fl oz) warm water, or as necessary

For the filling
350g (12oz) minced lamb
75g (2½oz) onions, finely chopped
1 teaspoon salt
¼ teaspoon black pepper
a pinch cayenne pepper (optional)

Combine the flour, salt and yeast in a bowl. Add the water, mixing thoroughly until all ingredients are blended together. Knead for 5 minutes or until it is smooth and elastic. Sprinkle the dough on both sides with a little flour and place in the bowl. Cover with a towel, keeping away from draughts, and allow 1–1½ hours for it to rise. Just before it is ready to use, thoroughly mix all the filling ingredients and the cayenne, if using. (If preferred, sauté the lamb beforehand in ½ tablespoon of oil.)

Divide the dough into 4 portions. Take one portion at a time and flatten it as thin as possible with a rolling pin over a lightly floured surface. Cut out circles with a biscuit cutter and spread the lamb mixture over one half of each circle. Fold the pastry over and pinch the edges to seal. Lightly prick with a fork and deep fry in hot oil until a deep golden colour. Remove and drain on kitchen paper. Serve hot.

Turkey

Main courses

Kaḡıta levrek

SEA BASS EN PAPILLOTE

A speciality of Istanbul, which is famed for its fish dishes, this is a star for three important reasons: it is very tasty, simple to prepare, and it presents beautifully. Any ingredient – lamb, chicken, fish or even fruit – can be prepared *en papillote*. This dish serves as a main course and is a blessing for a busy schedule. An 18th-century recipe uses fresh vine leaves, layering them with the other ingredients and adding a few sour grapes for flavour.

Serves 4.

Ingredients

2 medium size sea bass (about 1kg / 2¼ lb), each cut into 2 fillets

1 teaspoon salt

extra virgin olive oil

2 tomatoes (about 285g / 10oz), sliced

1–1½ lemons, cut into 8 slices

a few parsley leaves (about 30g / 1oz)

1 large green pepper, cut into 8 strips

Prepare 4 rectangles of greaseproof paper. Rinse the fish fillets and pat dry with kitchen paper. Sprinkle with ½ teaspoon salt and set aside. Take one sheet of greaseproof paper, brush with oil and place the fish on top. Put 2 slices of tomato on the fish, then 2 slices of lemon, a few parsley leaves and 2 strips of pepper. Sprinkle with the remaining salt and close the *papillote* by folding the edges of the paper together to enclose the fish.

Repeat with the other fillets. Sprinkle the top of the *papillotes* with a little water. Cook in a preheated oven at 180°C (350°F/gas mark 4) for 15–18 minutes. Serve hot with boiled potatoes and invite each guest to open their own *papillote*.

Siveydiz yoğurtlu

LEEKS WITH YOGURT

Yogurt is an important ingredient in Turkish cuisine as well as in Arab cooking. It is widely believed that the nomads with their flocks of sheep and goats discovered the formula for the preparation of yogurt. It is very common in the Levant to use a wooden spoon when cooking with yogurt, as it is thought to prevent curdling.

Although it is served as a main dish, this unusual dish from south-east Turkey is eaten as a soup.

Ingredients
450g (1lb) lamb, cubed
700ml (1¼ pints) water
1¾ teaspoons salt, or to taste
bouquet garni, consisting of 1 cinnamon stick, 1 celery stick and black peppercorns
1.3kg (3lb) leeks, finely sliced
1 teaspoon cornflour
1 teaspoon water
600ml (1 pint) thick yogurt
1 egg
30g (1oz) butter
fresh garlic leaves, or a whole head of fresh garlic, sliced

Put the lamb and water in a large pan. Bring to the boil and skim. Sprinkle with salt and add the bouquet garni. Cover and simmer over low heat for 35–40 minutes or until the meat is tender.

Before adding the leeks to the meat, you might need to transfer the meat into a larger pan. Add the leeks and cover the pan so that they reduce in size. When the leeks have reduced in size and the liquid has started boiling, cover and simmer for 20 minutes.

Mix the cornflour with 1 teaspoon of water. Stir this into the yogurt, along with the egg, then strain and set aside. Melt the butter in a medium-size frying pan. When it is hot, add the garlic and sauté for 1–2 minutes or until transparent.

Add the yogurt to the leeks and meat and stir with a wooden spoon (you might need to turn the heat up) until it boils. Add the garlic. Reduce the heat to low and leave to bubble uncovered for a further 1–2 minutes. Serve hot with Burghol vermicelli.

Musakka

AUBERGINES, LAMB AND TOMATOES

This is very different from the Greek *musakka*, which is baked with white sauce and cheese. There is also a Lebanese version suitable for vegetarians that uses chick peas and is eaten at room temperature, as its name indicates: in Arabic *musakka* means 'cooled'.

This Turkish one is very tasty and satisfying. It makes a perfect main course. With it serve a light starter such as the Lebanese *Tabbouleh* (page 17) or the Turkish *Kısır salatası* (page 217). To end the meal offer the soothing Pumpkin dessert (page 271).

Ingredients
extra virgin olive oil
4 aubergines (about 1.3kg / 3lb), cut in 1cm (½in) rounds
350g (12oz) minced lamb
2 tablespoons finely chopped parsley
1½ teaspoons salt, or to taste
¼ teaspoon black pepper
675g (1½lb) red tomatoes, peeled and sliced in rounds

Preheat the grill leaving the baking pan underneath. Remove the pan and place in it sufficient oil to coat both sides of the aubergines. (You will need to grill the aubergines in batches.) Return the pan to the grill and cook the aubergines for 3–4 minutes or until they are golden brown. Turn them over to brown the other side. Repeat with others until all are ready.

In a frying pan, sauté the lamb in 1 tablespoon of oil until golden brown. Stir in the parsley, turn off the heat and sprinkle with salt and black pepper. Stir well.

Arrange a layer of tomatoes in a medium-size pan. Cover with two layers of aubergines. Spread the lamb on top and cover with the remaining aubergines and then the remaining tomatoes. Cover the pan, place over low heat and simmer for 30–40 minutes. Turn the heat off, cover with a thick towel and leave to stand for 10–15 minutes to allow the flavours to blend. Serve hot on its own or with rice.

Frik pilâv

FRIK WHEAT, CHICK PEAS AND BURGHOL

This speciality of south-eastern Turkey is a highly flavourful dish that is traditionally made with butter. The richness of the ingredients gives a wonderful flavour, especially when you top the hot *pilâv* with 1–2 tablespoons of yogurt.

The two ingredients that may be unfamiliar to you are the *frik* (burned green wheat, known as *freekeh* in Syria and Lebanon) and the pepper paste, which is similar to tomato paste in texture but is made with Turkey's sweet red peppers. The two ingredients can be easily purchased from Turkish and Lebanese delicatessens. If *frik* is unavailable, substitute with coarse burghol for the whole dish.

This is a satisfying winter dish that has been added to my repertoire of main courses. Nevertheless, in summer it makes a very soothing lunch when topped with chilled yogurt.

Serves 6.

Ingredients
5 tablespoons extra virgin olive oil or butter
450g (1lb) onions, finely chopped
1½ tablespoons sweet red pepper paste
3 tablespoons tomato concentrate
1 large tomato, peeled and cubed (optional)
1 litre (1¾ pints) water
2 teaspoons salt, or to taste
225g (8oz) frik
¼ teaspoon black pepper, or to taste
170g (6oz) chick peas, soaked overnight and pre-cooked
170g (6oz) coarse burghol

Heat the oil or butter in a pan and over medium heat sauté the onions for 5 minutes or until translucent. Stir in the pepper and tomato pastes. Add the fresh tomato, if using, water and salt. Bring to the boil over high heat, add the *frik*, reduce the heat to low, cover and simmer for 15 minutes. Sprinkle with the black pepper and add the chick peas and burghol. Return to the boil, cover and simmer over a low heat for 6–8 minutes or until the water has been absorbed.

Turn off the heat, cover the pan with a thick towel and leave to stand for 10–15 minutes so that the flavours amalgamate. Serve with yogurt.

Ali nazik

AUBERGINE PURÉE AND LAMB

The aubergine is the king of the Turkish table, which boasts more than 40 ways of preparing the vegetable. I recall a visit to the local market at Antalya, where I was struck by eye-catching strings of dried aubergines hanging over the stalls like chandeliers. Their colour was a deep purple and made me wish that my kitchen in London had enough room for a whole string of these vegetables along with chillies and sweet peppers. It is wonderful how such a flavourful dish can be produced so quickly. It is a lovely main course that is easy to prepare.

Ingredients
2 aubergines about 900g (2lb)
2½ teaspoons butter
1 teaspoon oil
150g (5½oz) onion, finely chopped
225g (8oz) minced lamb
¾ teaspoon salt, or to taste
¼ teaspoon black pepper

For the sauce
1 garlic clove, finely crushed
500ml (16fl oz) yogurt
½ teaspoon salt

To garnish (optional)
2 tablespoons diced red sweet peppers
1 tablespoon finely chopped parsley

Prick the aubergines in several places. Put them on a baking sheet and place under a preheated grill 10cm (4in) away from the source of the heat. Grill for 20–30 minutes or until the skin is blackened and blistered and the pulp is soft, turning them once. A quicker method is to place the aubergines on a grid over a gas flame.

Meanwhile, heat 1 teaspoon of the butter and the oil in a medium-size frying pan. Add the onions and lamb, and sauté for 6–8 minutes or until they are cooked through. Sprinkle with ½ teaspoon of the salt and the pepper. Stir well and keep warm.

When the aubergines are ready, remove from the grill and peel. Mash the pulp with a fork. Melt the remaining butter in a frying pan and add the mashed aubergines. Sauté for 2 minutes and sprinkle with the remaining salt. Remove and place in a serving dish. Place the meat mixture on top. Mix the garlic with the yogurt and salt and pour over the meat. Garnish with the diced red peppers and parsley, if using.

Kalkan balığı tavası

TURBOT WITH LEMON AND SAFFRON

I have eaten the best fish in Istanbul, where there is a wide variety of seafood from the Black Sea, the Aegean, the Marmara, the Mediterranean and the Bosphorus. Fish are caught and sent straight to the market-sellers, who display them on wooden stalls. The visitor to a fish market in Istanbul will be struck by the freshness of its beautifully laid-out fish. Not far away there are several fish restaurants; they are packed for lunch or dinner since the Turks love fish. Turbot has delicious meat, is low in fat and rich in nutrients. As a general rule, fish is eaten simply, grilled or fried.

Ingredients
4 turbot fillets (about 450g / 1lb)
2 teaspoons salt
2½–3 lemons, sliced into medium-size rounds
300ml (10½ fl oz) water
½ tablespoon saffron

Sprinkle the fillets of fish with salt. Place a layer of lemons in a non-metallic dish. Spread the fish evenly over the top and cover with another layer of lemons. Combine the water with the saffron and pour this over the lemons and fish. Put a plate over the fish and weight this down with something heavy. Refrigerate for 8 hours or, better still, overnight.

The following day, remove the fish, dry between kitchen paper and cook on a gridiron or under the grill. Serve hot with grilled aubergines and rice or *kilyos pilari* (see page 211).

Somon-balığı külbastısı

SALMON WITH ALMOND SAUCE

I remember a visit to the market in Antalya where I couldn't resist buying some red mullet, a favourite fish of mine. Before I did, though, my Turkish friend, Gülfem, asked the fishmonger's neighbour, who runs a little restaurant, whether he would cook them for me, and he accepted. I thought that was wonderful, to be able to choose your fish and eat it sitting in the busy market, surrounded by the most beautiful fruit and vegetables you ever saw.

This dish is prepared with salmon but any other fish can be used. I found out that in the Caspian sea it is possible to find that rarity, a white salmon. Salmon is an oily fish, rich in omega-3 oils that are important for a healthy heart. This is a simple recipe to prepare, which keeps the full flavour of the salmon. If the meal is served in winter, lentil soup would make a good starter. I suggest ending the meal with *Kanafeh* (see page 79) for dessert.

For the salmon
4 salmon fillets
½ teaspoon salt
a pinch of black pepper
6–8 bay leaves

For the sauce
55g (2oz) blanched almonds
1 garlic clove, crushed
15g (½oz) bread, crusts cut off and soaked in 50ml (2fl oz) water
3 teaspoons extra virgin olive oil
¾ teaspoon salt
50ml (2fl oz) lemon or vinegar or a mixture of both

To garnish (optional)
green chillies, finely diced

Sprinkle the salmon with salt and pepper, place the bay leaves on top of the fish then layer them one on top of the other. Leave in a cool place.

Place all the sauce ingredients in a food processor and blend to a creamy consistency. If you prefer a thinner sauce, add a little extra water, and blend again for a second.

Grill the salmon or sauté with a mixture of the remaining olive oil and 1 teaspoon of butter for 2 minutes on each side, or as necessary. Serve hot with the sauce on top or on the side. Garnish with finely diced green chillies, if using.

Enginar tavuğlu dolması

ARTICHOKES WITH CHICKEN

This magnificent dish is a speciality of the Aegean coast. While eating this in a restaurant in Istanbul, a man in his mid-60s approached my table. He repeatedly thanked the chef, who was sitting with me, for the wonderful food he had prepared, and then tried to kiss the chef's hand in token of respect and appreciation for the hands which prepared the food he had just eaten. The chef insisted that a verbal 'thank you' would suffice.

This recipe presents beautifully as a main course.

Ingredients
8 artichokes
water
1 tablespoon extra virgin olive oil
juice of 1 medium lemon

For the filling
1 teaspoon olive oil
1½ teaspoons butter
1 medium-size chicken breast, cut into 1cm (½in) pieces or strips
¼ teaspoon salt
¼ teaspoon black pepper
50ml (2fl oz) milk
50ml (2fl oz) lemon juice
15g (½oz) dill or parsley, finely chopped

For the sauce
1 tablespoon butter
1 tablespoon flour
90ml (3½fl oz) milk, or chicken stock
1 egg yolk
1 teaspoon lemon juice
1 teaspoon cream
a pinch of nutmeg (optional)

Cut off the stems of the artichokes and trim the tips of the leaves. Place the artichokes in a pan and cover with water, adding the oil and lemon. Bring to the boil, cover and simmer on medium-low heat for 30–40 minutes or until tender. Drain, but reserve the liquor. (Simmering the artichokes in this way makes it easy to remove the leaves.)

Snap all the leaves off each artichoke until you reach the base. Gently scoop out the choke and discard. Place the artichoke hearts in one layer in a baking dish. Pour the artichoke liquor into the dish so that it comes halfway up the artichoke hearts.

For the filling, heat the olive oil and butter in a frying pan. When hot, add the chicken and sauté until lightly browned. Sprinkle with salt and pepper. Add the milk and lemon juice. Cover and simmer over medium-low heat until the juices have evaporated. Turn the heat off. Stir in the dill or parsley straight away and fill the artichoke hearts with the mixture.

To make the sauce, heat the butter in a small pan, add the flour and stir for about 30 seconds. Gradually add the milk or chicken stock, or a mixture of both, whisking constantly. Now add the egg yolk, lemon and cream while still whisking, until the mixture slightly thickens. Sprinkle with nutmeg, if using.

Pour the sauce over the chicken pieces to cover. Bake in a preheated oven at 180°C (350°F/gas mark 4) for 15–20 minutes or until the top is golden brown. Serve hot.

Pastirmali kuru fasulye

PASTIRMA WITH BEANS

When I ate this very tasty and nutritious Turkish dish in Istanbul, the French *cassoulet* came to mind, not surprisingly, for in the 19th century, French influence was strong in the Ottoman Empire on many areas of life, including food.

Pastirma is beef or veal that has been preserved using a paste of spices known as *àeme*, which is made of garlic, fenugreek and cumin. You can make a vegetarian version of this dish using mild chilli peppers or sweet peppers to lift its taste.

This recipe is simple and makes an excellent main dish for friends, family or a big party. Choose a light starter and a refreshing dessert, such as baked apples topped with vanilla ice cream, to end the meal.

Ingredients
285g (10oz) haricot beans
1.3 litres (2¼ pints) water
170g (6oz) onion, finely chopped
3–4 tablespoons extra virgin olive oil
4 slices of **pastirma**
1 garlic clove, sliced
2 mild or hot chillies, halved
500g (1lb 2oz) tomatoes, peeled and chopped
1 teaspoon tomato purée
1½ teaspoons sugar
1½ teaspoons salt, or to taste

Place the beans and water in a pan and bring to the boil. Skim then continue to boil vigorously for 2 minutes. Reduce the heat to low, cover and simmer for 10 minutes. Add the onion, cover again and leave to simmer for 1 hour or until the beans are very soft.

In the meantime, heat the oil in a frying pan. When it is hot stir in the *pastirma* and garlic. Add the chillies, the fresh tomatoes and the tomato purée, sprinkle with sugar and salt. Stir well, bring to the boil, and simmer on a low heat for 5 minutes.

Add this mixture to the beans in the pan, bring to the boil, cover and simmer as before on low heat for 10–15 minutes or until all the flavours have blended together. Turn off the heat and leave covered for 5 minutes. Serve hot on its own or with rice.

Hünkâr beḡendi

RULER'S AUBERGINE

Most probably this dish was embraced by the ruler of the country, hence the name. It is rich, filling and easy to make. The aubergines and the meat can be prepared ahead of time and reheated before serving. The meat is at its best when simmered until really tender to harmonize with the texture of the aubergine purée.

This is a delicate dish, perfect to serve as a main course for 5.

For the meat
3 tablespoons extra virgin olive oil
500g (1lb 2oz) diced lamb
285g (10oz) onions, finely chopped
1 tablespoon tomato purée
225g (8oz) tomatoes, peeled and finely chopped
1 teaspoon salt, or to taste
a pinch of black pepper
a pinch of white pepper
450ml (15fl oz) hot water
bouquet garni consisting of 2 bay leaves and 1 celery stick

For the aubergines
3 aubergines (about 985g / 2lb 3oz)
3 tablespoons lemon juice
30g (1oz) butter
1 tablespoon flour
90ml (3½fl oz) milk
½ teaspoon salt, or to taste
a pinch of sugar

Heat the oil in a pan. When it is hot, sauté the lamb and onions on a high heat for 5 minutes, stirring occasionally. Reduce the heat to medium or medium-low and continue to sauté for a further 10 minutes, or until the juices released by the meat and onions coat the pan, the liquid has evaporated and the meat and onions are nicely browned. Stir in the tomato purée and tomatoes and, using a wooden spoon, stir the juices with the meat. As the tomato juices start to bubble, allow to simmer for 2 minutes. Sprinkle with salt and the black and white pepper. Add the water and bouquet garni, bring to the boil and reduce heat to low. Cover and simmer for 1 hour, or until meat is tender.

In the meantime, grill the aubergines over a gas flame or in the oven (following the recipe for Aubergine dip on page 23) until they are blackened on all sides. Hold each aubergine upright and peel the skin with a sharp, pointed knife. Then slice off the top and place the pulp in a bowl. Repeat with the remaining aubergines. Add the lemon juice and beat with a sharp knife (in rather the same way as you beat eggs with a fork) until you obtain a smooth texture that still keeps the character of aubergines.

Melt the butter in a medium-size pan and when it becomes hot, add the flour and stir for 30 seconds. Stir in the aubergines for 2–3 minutes, then add the milk, salt and sugar. Allow to simmer for a few minutes, stirring occasionally. Spread the aubergine mixture on a serving dish, place the meat over the top and serve immediately.

Etli güveç

LAMB AND VEGETABLE STEW

This wonderful stew is bursting with flavour. In Turkey, it is served in summer when vegetables are bountiful and cheap. The stew can be made with chicken instead of lamb, or without any meat at all. When it is made without meat, sprinkle a little oregano and flaked, dried chillies over the top to enhance the flavour. A healthy and tasty stew depends very much on the freshness of the ingredients. As the celebrated chef, Paul Bocuse, once said: 'A good cuisine begins in the local market.' This dish proves his point.

This recipe serves 5, with rice, or burghol pilaff.

Ingredients
500g (1lb 2oz) lamb, cubed
10 small onions
12 garlic cloves, peeled
450g (1lb) potatoes, peeled and cubed
8 whole black peppercorns
4 mild chilli peppers
500g (1lb 2oz) aubergines, cubed
900g (2lb) tomatoes, peeled and quartered
2½ teaspoons salt
1–2 tablespoons extra virgin olive oil or butter

Preheat the oven to 180°C (350°F/gas mark 4). Spread the lamb over the base of a heavy-bottomed, ovenproof dish. Spread the onions on top and then the garlic. Now layer with the potatoes. Sprinkle the peppercorns all over, and dot with the chillies. Next spread over the aubergines, top with a layer of tomatoes and sprinkle with salt. Drizzle the olive oil all over the tomatoes. Cover, place in the preheated oven and cook for 2–2¼ hours. Serve hot.

Tonlu pilaki

TUNA IN A FRAGRANT PARSLEY SAUCE

This is a dish not to be missed. Layering the tuna with the other ingredients ensures that it retains its unique taste. It also protects the fish, which has a dry texture, from the effects of high heat. It can be prepared in advance and baked just before serving. It is a joy to have a dish that is healthy and easy to prepare, yet also very presentable. As a starter, *Kibbeh al-hammam* (page 96) is perfect.

Ingredients
1½ teaspoons sea salt
4 slices of tuna (about 450g / 1lb)
150ml (5fl oz) extra virgin olive oil
450g (1lb) onions, finely sliced
1 whole head of garlic, sliced
2 tablespoons tomato purée
45g (1½oz) parsley, finely chopped
175ml (6fl oz) water
2½ tablespoons organic cider vinegar
2 potatoes sliced into 5mm (¼in) rounds and fried
1–2 carrots sliced into 5mm (¼in) rounds and steamed

Sprinkle 1 teaspoon of salt over the tuna and set to one side. Heat the oil in a large frying pan and, when hot, add the onions and sauté over medium heat for 2–3 minutes. Then add the garlic, reduce heat to medium-low and sauté with the onions for 5–6 minutes further or until both are translucent. Stir in the tomato purée, the parsley and water. Bring to the boil, reduce the heat to low, cover and simmer for 1 minute. Turn off the heat, stir in the vinegar and sprinkle with the remaining salt. Preheat the oven to 180°C (350°F/gas mark 4).

Place the fried potatoes in one layer in a baking dish, top each slice with a slice of carrot and a little less than half the onion mixture. Arrange the tuna pieces over the top and cover with the remaining onion mixture and its liquor. Bake for 18–20 minutes. Remove and serve immediately.

Karnıyarık

AUBERGINES WITH MINCED LAMB

This is one of the best aubergine dishes that I have ever come across. It is easy to make, presents beautifully and melts in the mouth. Serve with a dish of rice to make it even more nourishing and comforting.

There is a story to illustrate the popularity of the dish. One day a man came to visit a close friend in Istanbul. When the friend saw him coming, he ran and gave him a big hug and asked him how he was. The man replied that life was difficult, whereupon his friend took pity on him and said, 'Come, come, it's lunch time. Let us go up and eat.'

Inside the house, the friend's wife was stirring a dish in a corner of the room that served also as a dining and a sitting room. Pans hung from the ceiling amid ropes of onions and garlic. The man sat with his host round the table and ate a most delicious dish, *Karnıyarık*. When he had eaten, the visitor whispered into his friend's ear, 'Do you think it is possible to have the recipe because what I ate is so delicious.'

'Of course,' the friend replied, and his wife gave him the details. Before the man left, his friend said, 'Look, there is the butcher. Tell him I sent you and he will take care of you.' When the man left the butcher's shop, with the meat wrapped in paper in one hand and the recipe safely guarded in his pocket, a dog jumped on him, grabbed the meat bag and ran. The man shouted after him, 'Dog, you may have taken the meat but you're unlucky because the recipe is still here with me.'

Karnıyarık is, indeed, an excellent main course.

Ingredients
8 baby aubergines (about 375g / 13oz)
4 tablespoons extra virgin olive oil
1 tablespoon pine nuts
85g (3oz) onions, finely chopped
150g (5½oz) minced lamb
1 teaspoon salt, or to taste
a pinch of black pepper
350g (12oz) tomatoes, peeled and sliced

Peel the aubergines then cut in half lengthways, keeping the stem intact. Make a slit along the aubergines but do not cut right through. Put the olive oil in a frying pan and, when hot, sauté the aubergines over medium-high heat until lightly browned and soft. Remove with a slotted spoon, allowing the oil to drip back into the pan. If necessary, add more oil to the same pan, then sauté the pine nuts, stirring constantly. When the pine nuts begin to change to a golden colour, add the onions and the lamb. Sauté, stirring occasionally, until the meat is cooked through and browned and the onions have softened. Sprinkle with ½ teaspoon of salt and the pepper. Take 1 aubergine at a time, gently fill the slit with some of the meat mixture, and repeat with others.

In a medium-size pan, arrange a bed of tomatoes, put the stuffed aubergines on top, and cover with another layer of tomatoes. Sprinkle with the remaining salt. Cover the pan and place over a low heat to simmer for 30–40 minutes. Serve hot with rice.

Domatesli balık

COD WITH TOMATOES

Cod is a fish that adapts well to various sauces. This sauce is taken from an old Turkish recipe book, and it seems that this dish has been prepared since the late 16th century. It is easy to do and looks impressive with its colourful medley of tomatoes laced with onions. This makes an excellent main dish. Accompany it with a light starter such as *Kısır salatası* (page 217). For the dessert, Rice pudding with lemon zest (page 75) would round off the meal nicely.

Ingredients
4 pieces of cod (about 450g / 1lb)
1¾ teaspoons salt, or to taste
100ml (4fl oz) extra virgin olive oil
500g (1lb 2oz) onions, sliced
a large handful of chopped parsley
400g (14oz) tomatoes, peeled and quartered
150ml (5fl oz) water
50ml (2fl oz) cider vinegar

Sprinkle the cod with 1 teaspoon of salt and leave aside. Heat the oil in a frying pan and, when it is hot but not smoking, add the onions and sauté for 5–6 minutes, or until golden brown. Stir in the parsley and sauté with the onions for half a minute more.

Turn off the heat, remove half the onions and spread over a baking pan that can take the 4 pieces of cod in one layer. Place the cod pieces over the bed of onions and cover with the remaining onions and sauce. Place the tomatoes over the onions and sprinkle with the remaining salt. Combine the water with the vinegar and pour all over. Put the baking dish in an oven preheated to 180°C (350°F/gas mark 4) and cook for 18–20 minutes. Remove and serve immediately.

Türlü

VEGETABLE STEW

Since vegetable dishes prepared in olive oil are usually eaten cold, this dish is customarily cooked in summer when the vegetables are abundant. Still, this can be served hot as a light main dish with *Burghol bi shaariyeh* (page 108) all year round. To end this light meal, an apricot pudding with nuts is perfect.

Ingredients
5 tablespoons extra virgin olive oil
255g (9oz) onions, finely chopped
1 whole head of garlic (about 75g / 2½oz), sliced
170g (6oz) French beans, halved
590g (1lb 6oz) aubergines, cubed
115g (4oz) carrot, cut into 2cm (¾in) slices
1 green pepper, cut into 1cm (½in) slices
255g (9oz) courgette, cut into 2.5cm (1in) strips
285g (10oz) okra
1–2 mild red chillies, halved
2 teaspoons salt, or to taste
¼ teaspoon black pepper
4 large peeled tomatoes, sliced

Heat the oil in a pan and, when it is hot, add the onions, garlic and beans. Sauté over a medium heat for 4–5 minutes, or until the onions and garlic are translucent and are almost golden brown. Spread the aubergines over the top. Add a layer of the carrots, green pepper, courgettes and okra. Place the chillies randomly over the okra and sprinkle with salt and black pepper.

Cover and simmer over low heat for 1 hour. Add the tomatoes, cover and simmer for a further 30 minutes. Turn off the heat, cover the pan with a thick towel and leave to stand for 10 minutes to allow time for the flavours to blend.

Midye pilav

MUSSELS WITH RICE

Nearly everywhere you go in Istanbul you find a starter of mussels stuffed with rice, which is eaten at room temperature.

This dish, where the mussels are not stuffed but cooked with the rice, is adapted from an 18th-century cookery book. I was inspired to try it after dining at a restaurant in an unspoiled spot by the sea. When we arrived by chance at the restaurant, it was full and we had to wait outside for a while. Within minutes, we were led to our table which had been set over an Oriental carpet in the middle of the street! The dish was offered as a starter. However, it is quite filling and could easily be served as a main dish. With it a chilled *Firin Sütlac* (page 275), is a delectable and comforting end to a meal.

Ingredients
30–40 fresh mussels
100ml (4fl oz) extra virgin olive oil
2 tablespoons pine nuts
500g (1lb 2oz) onions, chopped
225g (8oz) tomatoes, chopped
1½ teaspoons salt, or to taste
700ml (1¼ pints) water
285g (10oz) rice, rinsed
2 tablespoons currants, soaked for 20 minutes
¼ teaspoon allspice
¼ teaspoon cinnamon
a pinch of black pepper

Scrape the mussel shells clean of any filaments and rinse thoroughly. Discard any that aren't fully closed. Heat a little of the oil in a pan, and sauté the pine nuts until golden. Remove with a slotted spoon and set aside. Heat the remaining oil, then add the onions and sauté for 6–8 minutes or until golden brown. Stir in the tomatoes, leave for 1–2 minutes, sprinkle with salt and add the water. Bring to the boil, reduce the heat to low, cover and simmer for 5 minutes.

Add the pine nuts and all the other ingredients. Return to the boil, cover and simmer over low heat for 10 minutes or until the water has been absorbed. Turn off the heat, cover with a thick cloth and leave the pan to stand for 10 minutes before serving.

Kıymalı ekmek

BREAD WITH MINCED LAMB

This dish couldn't be simpler. It doesn't even require the preparation of any dough, because all you need is pitta bread – or any other bread of your choice. It's wonderful either as a starter or a main dish. A perfect accompaniment is a salad rich in fibre and anti-oxidants, such as *Fattouche* (see page 18); you can omit the bread of the *Fattouche* since this dish already contains some. To finish the meal, the unusual *Elmali muhallebi* (page 278) would be excellent.

Serves 2.

Ingredients
1 tablespoon extra virgin olive oil
1 onion (about 115g/4oz), finely chopped
225g (8oz) minced lamb
2 tablespoons tomato purée
8–10 tablespoons water
½ teaspoon salt, or to taste
freshly grated black pepper
a pinch of cinnamon
1 pitta bread, cut into 4–6 triangles
300ml (10fl oz) yogurt
1 small clove garlic, crushed
a pinch of salt

To garnish
a few pine nuts

Heat the oil in a frying pan, add the onions and lamb and sauté over a medium heat for 3–4 minutes, or until the meat loses its red colour. Mix the tomato purée with the water and stir into the lamb and onion in the frying pan. Sprinkle with salt, black pepper and cinnamon.

Place the bread on a baking sheet and spread with the meat mixture. Bake in a preheated oven at 180°C (350°F/gas mark 4) for 15 minutes, or until the bread is toasted. In the meantime, mix the yogurt with garlic and salt. Top each portion with 1 tablespoon of yogurt and a few pine nuts. Serve hot.

Levrek buğulama

POACHED SEA BASS

This delicious and nutritious main course from the capital city, Istanbul, can be cooked and served in no time at all. For an exotic feel, have an array of Levantine starters to begin the meal such as the Aubergine dip from Lebanon (page 23). This dish can be baked in the oven or simmered over a low heat in a covered dish for 15 minutes.

Ingredients
2 medium-size sea bass (about 1kg / 2¼ lb), cut into 4 fillets
100ml (3½ fl oz) extra virgin olive oil
200g (7oz) mushrooms, finely sliced
1 green pepper, cut into thin strips
450g (1lb) tomatoes, peeled and cut in small pieces
1¼ teaspoons salt, or to taste
¼ teaspoon of black pepper
1 lemon, finely sliced
2–4 bay leaves

To garnish
a large handful of parsley, finely chopped

Rinse the fish, dry between kitchen paper and place in a medium-size shallow pan. Heat the oil in a frying pan and add the mushrooms and green pepper. Sauté over a medium heat for 3–5 minutes, then add the tomatoes and sauté for another 5 minutes, sprinkling with salt and pepper. Remove and spread over the fish fillets in the pan. Place the lemon slices and bay leaves on top.

Bake in the uncovered dish in a preheated oven at 180°C (350°F/gas mark 4) for 15 minutes. Garnish with parsley and eat either warm or at room temperature.

Kadınbudu köfte

LADY'S THIGH MEATBALLS

A lovely lamb dish with a sensual title, this was often prepared in the palace kitchen during the time of the Ottoman Empire. Its name is a perfect indication of how delicious it is.

Serve as a main course for 5 with steamed green vegetables and boiled potatoes.

Ingredients
extra virgin olive oil
2 small onions (about 170g/6oz), finely chopped
450g (1lb) minced lamb
55g (2oz) cooked rice
1 teaspoon salt, or to taste
¼ teaspoon of black pepper
2 eggs
flour

Heat 2 tablespoons oil in a frying pan, add the onions and half the lamb and sauté over medium heat until all the moisture released from the lamb has evaporated and the meat has browned. Remove and mix with the remaining raw lamb, the rice, salt and pepper and 1 egg. Knead thoroughly until it forms a soft dough. Take a small portion from the dough and form into an oval shape. Dip into the flour, shaking off excess. Repeat with the remaining dough. Beat the remaining egg in a small bowl.

Heat 2.5cm (1in) of oil in a frying pan. When it is very hot, dip the meatballs into the beaten egg and drop into the oil. Fry until nicely browned all over. Drain on kitchen paper. Serve with vegetables.

Mantı

PARCELS OF MINCED LAMB

The Tartars in Turkey were famed for making succulent *Mantı*. The dough is prepared in the same way all over Turkey but the filling changes from region to region. In Kayseri, a city in mid-Anatolia, they make small parcels; larger portions are made in other regions of Turkey and may be stuffed with rice and parsley. This is a tasty dish, especially when eaten with yogurt and tomato sauce.

This recipe serves 10 as a main dish and makes about 130 tiny parcels, which can be poached or baked.

For the sauce
2 tablespoons of extra virgin olive oil or butter
5 tomatoes, peeled and finely chopped
1½ teaspoons sugar
2–3 garlic cloves, finely chopped
1 teaspoon dried mint
2 teaspoons finely chopped dill (optional)

For the dough
400g (14oz) flour
1 egg
2 teaspoons salt
1 tablespoon vinegar
cold water

For the filling
225g (8oz) minced lamb
1 onion (about 100g / 3½oz), finely grated
½ teaspoon salt
¼ teaspoon black pepper
a pinch allspice (optional)
600ml (1 pint) meat stock, if baking

To garnish
yogurt

To make the sauce, warm the oil or butter in a small pan, add the tomatoes, sugar and garlic, and leave to simmer over a low heat for 4 minutes. Add the mint and the dill, if using, and continue to simmer for a further 5 minutes.

To make the dough, combine the flour, egg, salt and vinegar in a bowl. Gradually add the water and mix with your fingers to form a pliable dough. Knead for 5 minutes, cover with a wet napkin and leave to rest for 1 hour.

To make the filling, combine all the ingredients and the allspice, if using, in a bowl. Divide the dough into 2 or 3 portions. Take one portion at a time and roll it out thinly over a lightly floured surface. Cut into equal squares about 2.5cm (1in). Place a little of the meat mixture in the centre of each square. Bring together the opposite sides of the square of dough and press to secure. Repeat with the remaining dough.

To poach, have ready a pan of slightly salted, boiling water. Drop the parcels into the water, stirring now and again to prevent them sticking to one another. Remove after 2–3 minutes and serve as mentioned below. To bake, put the parcels in a buttered ovenproof dish and place in a medium-hot oven for 10–15 minutes or until slightly golden brown. Remove, cover with 600ml (1 pint) meat stock and return to the oven. Bake for 20 minutes or until the stock has all been absorbed.

Serve the parcels in separate soup dishes. Top with a little of the tomato sauce and garnish with 1 tablespoon of yogurt.

Desserts

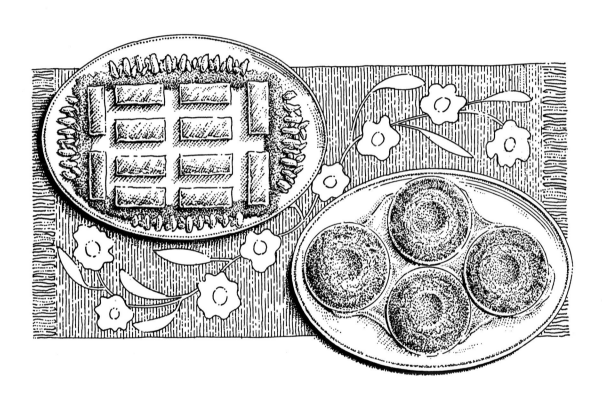

Kabak tatlısı

PUMPKIN DESSERT

This dessert can be enjoyed all year round. It takes a short time to prepare and is a pleasure to cook for family and friends. Be careful not to burn the pumpkin under the grill.

Nothing beats the flavour of the delicious *kaimak*. However, if unavailable, clotted cream or mascarpone are excellent substitutes. For a rounder flavour, blend the cream with a little of the syrup that is released from the pumpkin. Serve over the pumpkin or at the side.

Ingredients
4 medium pieces of pumpkin, peeled
sugar
a handful of walnuts, finely ground
1 tablespoon unsalted pistachios, finely ground (optional)
kaimak, *mascarpone or clotted cream*

Place the pumpkin pieces in a pan. Cover fully with sugar (this helps to release their liquid). Put the lid on the pan and leave overnight. The following day, place the pan over low heat, cover and leave to cook for 20–30 minutes, or until the pumpkin pieces are soft. Gently transfer them to a baking tin. Drizzle a little of the resulting syrup over the pumpkin and reserve the rest. Caramelize for a few minutes under a very hot grill. Remove and allow to cool.

Serve each piece of pumpkin on a plate, sprinkle with walnuts or pistachios, if using, for a touch of colour. Place a dollop of *kaimak*, mascarpone or cream on top. Pour over the remaining pumpkin syrup.

Kaymaklı kuru kayısı

APRICOTS STUFFED WITH CREAM

The apricot is a healthy fruit rich in carotene. The French writer, Bernard le Bovier de Fontenelle, lived to be 100 following the advice of his grandmother to eat a lot of apricots – but she probably didn't mean with cream!

This dessert can be offered at any time – either after dinner with coffee or in a buffet. I use mascarpone as *kaimak* is not always obtainable. A little of the apricot syrup that is released during cooking is stirred into the cream to enrich the flavour. Save the remaining syrup to use in fresh or dried fruit salad.

Ingredients
400g (14oz) sugar
600ml (1 pint) water
450g (1lb) dried apricots, soaked overnight
1 tablespoon lemon juice
6 heaped teaspoons of **kaimak, mascarpone or clotted cream**
30g (1oz) pistachios, finely ground (optional)

Heat the sugar and water in a pan and stir to dissolve. Allow to simmer over medium heat for 10 minutes, then drain the apricots and add to the syrup. Bring to the boil, allow to simmer for 10–12 minutes over a medium heat or until the apricots have softened and the water has thickened to a syrupy consistency. Turn the heat up for a few minutes. Add the lemon juice and cook for 1 minute. Transfer the apricots to a side dish using a slotted spoon and allow to cool.

Mix the cream with 2–3 tablespoons of the cooked apricot syrup. When the apricots have cooled, split and fill with cream. Sprinkle with ground pistachios, if using, and serve.

Keskül

ALMOND MILK PUDDING

A refreshing dessert, again easy to make, that may be enjoyed any time of the year and for any occasion. Rich and creamy milk puddings are often prepared in the Levant. This one uses ground almonds and vanilla, which reflects the European influence. This dessert has become a firm favourite of mine. It is simple yet sophisticated in flavour and all my friends love it.

Ingredients
100g (3½oz) blanched almonds
700ml (1¼ pints) milk
30g (1oz) cornflour
100ml (4fl oz) water
170g (6oz) sugar
¼ teaspoon vanilla essence, or 1 vanilla pod

To garnish
1–2 tablespoons coarsely ground almonds
1–2 tablespoons coarsely ground unsalted pistachio
1 tablespoon fine coconut flakes

Place the blanched almonds and 250ml (8fl oz) milk in a blender. Blend for 5 minutes or until almonds are smooth and creamy. Transfer to a pan with the remaining milk.

Mix the cornflour with the water, strain over the milk mixture and stir to blend. Now put the pan over a medium heat while stirring constantly in the same direction with a wooden spoon until it boils. Add the sugar and the vanilla essence or pod. Bring back to the boil and keep stirring for another 5 minutes or until the milk thickens and coats the spoon. Remove from the heat and pour into individual serving bowls. Chill and garnish with ground almonds, pistachio and coconut.

Katmer

FILO, CREAM AND PISTACHIO

I watched this dessert being made at the restaurant of Hakki and Meral Ozturk. The owner showed me around his beautifully equipped basement kitchen. All the men working there were busy making their own speciality. One was slicing meat; another was preparing a huge amount of *kibbeh* dough. The owner himself demonstrated the dessert for me in a quiet corner of the kitchen.

Katmer may be heavy on calories but a little goes a long way.

Ingredients
85g (3oz) butter, melted
*1 **yufka** or filo*
5 heaped tablespoons mascarpone
5 heaped tablespoons ground pistachio
4 heaped tablespoons icing sugar

Brush about 1–2 tablespoons butter over a *yufka*, or filo. Dot the mascarpone on the pastry in 5 places, like a domino. Sprinkle with the ground pistachio and sugar, reserving a little of both for the garnish, and drizzle with the remaining butter. Fold in all the sides of the *yufka* or filo to form the shape of the back of an envelope. Bake in a preheated oven at 180°C (350°F/gas mark 4) for 15–20 minutes or until golden. Immediately sprinkle the remaining icing sugar and pistachio. Eat warm or cold.

Firin sütlac

MILK PUDDING, RICE AND MASTIC

This healthy, smooth-textured dessert can be served warm or cold. It is easy to digest, making it suitable for children, the elderly and invalids. The recipe was given to me by a Turkish housewife who is an excellent cook. Turkish rice can be obtained from Turkish or Lebanese delicatessens.

Ingredients
1 litre (1¾ pints) milk
55–75g (2–2½oz) rice
85g (3oz) sugar
¼ teaspoon pieces of mastic
1 egg yolk

Rinse the pan but do not dry. Add the milk and rice, and place over low heat. Stir occasionally and leave to simmer gently for 1½ hours. Five minutes before the end of cooking, stir in the sugar. Gently crush the *mastic* pieces with ¼ teaspoon sugar. Sprinkle over the milk and stir. Turn off the heat and pour the pudding into a deep baking dish or 4 small heatproof bowls.

In a cup, thoroughly mix the egg yolk with 5–6 tablespoons of the cooked rice pudding. Smooth the surface of the pudding with a little of the egg mixture. Place under a hot grill for 4–5 minutes or until nicely caramelized. Remove and serve warm or chilled.

Ayva tatlısı

QUINCE DESSERT

I tasted this dessert at the Feridun Ugüviü restaurant. It was heavenly and I was delighted to be offered the recipe. However quinces are prepared, the result is always delicious. As a teenager I used to love eating raw quince sprinkled with salt. Apparently quince jelly (*ayva perverdesi*) was among dozens of great Turkish dishes served at the circumcision celebrations of the sons of Suleiman the Magnificent. King François of France had such a fondness for a quince paste that his eyes would fill with tears while eating it.

Quinces are not widely available in the U.K. these days. If you are lucky enough to have a quince tree in your garden, do try this splendid dessert.

Ingredients
3 quinces (about 565g / 1lb 4oz)
200g (7oz) sugar
150ml (5fl oz) hot water
6 cloves

For the stuffing
100g (3½oz) sugar
1 clove
quince seeds
75ml (3fl oz) water
100ml (4fl oz) lemon juice

To garnish
mascarpone (4 tablespoons, or to taste)

Peel, halve and core the quinces. Remove the seeds and reserve them to use in the stuffing. Place 4 quince halves in a pan, divide the sugar between them and fill their hollows. Add the water and cloves and bring to a boil over a medium-high heat. Reduce the heat to low, cover and simmer for 50 minutes or until quinces are soft.

Shred the remaining 2 quince halves and place them in a saucepan with the sugar, clove and quince seeds. Heat until the sugar melts and bubbles. Add the water and lemon juice and leave to simmer for 30 minutes or until the quince mixture thickens and caramelizes.

Place the halved quinces on an oven tray. Reserve the syrup that was released during cooking. Fill the hollow of each quince with the quince stuffing. Drizzle over a little of the reserved syrup and place under a hot grill for 4 minutes or until the top is golden brown. Remove, drizzle over the remaining syrup, chill and serve garnished with the mascarpone.

Irmik helvası (portakallı)

SEMOLINA AND PINE NUTS HELVA

This is a famous dessert in Turkey where it is often served after funerals. It is also fed to the army, as it is delicious, filling and economical. I fell for this wonderful recipe after tasting it in a popular restaurant in Istanbul. The following day, Sevil Develier, the restaurant owner's wife, gave me the recipe. Fortunately, like most Turkish recipes, it is of the utmost simplicity. If you have a large family, prepare it for Sunday lunch or serve it when friends come for tea.

This recipe serves 7–10 and can be made with plain milk or flavoured with orange.

Ingredients
255g (9oz) butter
170g (6oz) pine nuts
500g (1lb 2oz) fine semolina
1 litre (1¾ pints) milk
590g (1lb 5½oz) sugar

Heat the butter in a pan. When it is hot, stir in the pine nuts, cook for 5 seconds until golden then add the semolina. Cook for 1 hour over low heat, stirring occasionally. Halfway through cooking the semolina, put the milk in another pan with the sugar and place over a low heat. Stir the sugar with a wooden spoon to dissolve and allow to come to boiling point. If you are using the orange juice, replace 200ml (7fl oz) of the milk with the juice. Add the semolina mixture to the boiling milk and leave to bubble for 5 minutes. Turn off the heat, cover the pan with a lid, then a thick towel and leave for 1 hour. Separate the semolina with a fork and serve warm.

Elmalı muhallebi

APPLE PUDDING

This is a modern version of a sophisticated Turkish dessert. It can be adapted for any occasion and can be prepared in advance. I find that the only time-consuming part of the recipe is in the preparation of the apples, which need to be sliced very thinly. The cinnamon and walnut mixture gives the pudding its great depth and character.

This recipe serves 6–8 and can be eaten warm or chilled.

Ingredients
675g (1½lb) apples, peeled
3½ tablespoons sugar
150ml (5fl oz) water

For the filling
85g (3oz) walnuts, coarsely ground
½–¾ teaspoon cinnamon

For the muhallebi
1 egg yolk
½ teaspoon vanilla essence or pod
4½ tablespoons sugar
55g (2oz) flour, sifted
600ml (1 pint) milk
30g (1oz) melted butter

Slice the apples thinly. Place one third of the apples in a layer in a wide, shallow pan. Sprinkle with 1¼ teaspoons sugar and a little water. Make another layer of apples and repeat as before. Finally, add the remaining apples, sugar and water. Place the pan, uncovered, over a low heat. Leave to cook for 40 minutes or until the apples have softened and the base has caramelized. Spread the walnuts evenly over the apples and sprinkle with the cinnamon.

Mix the egg yolk with the vanilla, sugar and flour. Then gradually add the milk to the egg mixture and whisk until it is smooth. Place over medium heat, stirring constantly until it thickens. Stir in the butter and cook for 1 minute more. Pour the thickened milk over the apples. Serve warm or chilled.

Havuçlu kek

CARROT CAKE

There's no question about it – this cake is definitely a Western influence. I was given the recipe by a Turkish lady and found it particularly interesting because it contains no butter. It is excellent to eat with morning coffee or at tea time. Spreading the slices with apricot or quince jam makes it more delicious still.

It serves 6–8.

Ingredients
4 eggs
150ml (¼ pint) maple syrup, or 225g (8oz) sugar
125g (4½oz) walnuts, coarsely chopped
170g (6oz) carrots, grated
1 teaspoon cinnamon
250g (8½oz) flour, sifted
2 teaspoons baking powder

Preheat the oven to 180°C (350°F/gas mark 4). Lightly butter a medium-size cake tin and sprinkle all over with flour, then shake off the excess. Put the eggs, maple syrup or sugar in a bowl and mix thoroughly. Stir in the walnuts, carrots and cinnamon. Gradually mix in the flour and baking powder, stirring in the same direction for 2 minutes.

Pour into the cake tin, shaking it gently to distribute the mixture evenly. Place in the preheated oven and bake for 40–45 minutes. Remove and leave for 5 minutes to cool, then unmould. Serve at room temperature.

GLOSSARY

Burghol

Wheat that has been boiled, dried and cracked into coarse, medium and fine varieties. Coarse and medium burghol are used in pilaffs and stuffings; fine burghol for *Kibbeh*, *Tabbouleh* (page 17) and many other recipes that appear in this book. Burghol is low in fat, rich in B vitamins, and is white or light brown in colour. I use the white variety for the mountain potato *Kibbeh*, to match the colour of the potato. Burghol is also used to make *Kibbeh al-samak*, a dish that is cooked in the coastal towns of Lebanon. A delicacy prepared by the orthodox during Lent, it combines fish with burghol, coriander, onions and seasonings, and is then baked in the oven. In the U.K., burghol wheat is usually known as 'bulghar'.

Cardamom

An expensive spice that belongs to the ginger family. It has a very distinctive flavour and is used in marinades or stock. Cardamom helps to freshen the taste and was used to ward off any rank flavours of fish, meat and chicken. It is also the ingredient used in Arabic coffee. Cardamom has long been known as an aid to digestion and chewing fresh pods is an excellent way of masking the flavour of garlic.

Cassia

In 1000 BC the Phoenicians used to import cassia from Arabia. Cassia bark, one of the ancient spices, comes from a type of laurel tree. Both the bark and ground cassia have a deep flavour and fragrance that suit savoury and dessert dishes of the Middle East. Cassia should not be mistaken for the more expensive cinnamon. Although it comes from the same family, it has a sweeter flavour and is lighter in colour. The recipes in this book use it as a substitute for cinnamon.

Cinnamon is an essential spice in the Lebanese kitchen. It is also used as a panacea – a drink made of the bark is given to the nursing mother to help produce more milk and to relieve flatulence. Cinnamon was introduced to the Middle East by the Phoenicians and the inhabitants of the Arabian peninsula, and its medicinal properties were greatly valued by the Greeks and the Romans. The Roman Emperor Nero is said to have burned the palace with a year's stock of cinnamon to honour his wife – who was assassinated on his orders. This spice was very expensive in those days and was then used as an incense.

Coriander

An aromatic herb with a powerful taste, it is used extensively, fresh and dried, in many Lebanese and Syrian savoury dishes as a garnish or to enhance the flavour. At one time dried coriander was used in the Ottoman Palace cuisine, but it has now vanished from the Turkish table.

Cumin

A small fragrant plant yielding pink or white flowers. Cumin has a strong flavour and is used ground in soups and dishes made with grains and pulses. It also aids digestion and prevents flatulence.

Foul moutammam

This is a popular breakfast salad in Lebanon and Syria. It also comes as a part of a *mezzé*. *Foul moutammam* is a combination of *foul medammas* and chick peas. *Foul* is the Arabic name of the brown bean, a variety of the broad beans native to the Mediterranean region. The bean comes in two sizes; the large size is generally used in Syria, and the small size in Lebanon. It varies in colour from pale brownish-beige to dark brown. *Foul moutammam* is a nutritious vegetarian and economical meal. It is no wonder that it has been the food of the poor since the pharaohs' time. It is rich in protein, B vitamins and fibre, and aids digestion. *Foul moutammam* is drizzled with oil and, depending on the country and personal taste, sprinkled with cumin. It is eaten by taking a piece of round, flat Arabic bread in three fingers of your right hand, and scooping up some of the beans, chick peas, their sauce and the inevitable white onions. *Foul* and chick peas are sold dried in Lebanese or Cypriot grocers health shops and many supermarkets. To prepare, soak overnight and cook in fresh water and a touch of oil.

Kaimak

A thick cream made from buffalo's milk, similar in taste and consistency to clotted cream, and served with desserts in Turkey. When *kaimak* is not available, clotted cream or mascarpone can be used.

Kama

Middle Eastern truffle, beloved by the Syrians. *Kama* grows underground, and has a short season in the spring so its supply is small and rare. Good *kama* depends on the weather: the more thunder and lightning the better and more obtainable it will be. It comes in two colours: dark brown, which has a better flavour, and white. *Kama* has a distinguished taste and is delicious whichever way it is cooked – in a salad, sautéed, stewed or skewered and cooked over charcoal. The Syrians are very proud of their *kama* recipes, which are most unusual. A guest is honoured when offered a *kama* dish or when receiving it as a gift. *Kama* needs to be well cleaned to rid it of the sand that clings to it. A top Damascene chef told me that today, women even wash *kama* in the washing machine. Canned *kama* is on sale in Lebanese and Syrian grocery stores.

Kashkaval

A sheep's milk cheese, originally from the Balkans and popular as far afield as Greece and also the Lebanon, where it is known as *kashkawan*. *Kashkaval* is pale yellow, with a pleasantly mild flavour, similar to the Spanish *manchego*.

Kibbeh arnabieh

A most delicious medley of *kibbeh* shells, chick peas and onions, all swimming in a flavourful tahini sauce. This tahini sauce uses the juice of Seville oranges, which grow in the Lebanon, to give the whole dish its unique flavour. *Kibbeh arnabieh* adorns the table to honour a guest when Seville oranges are in season from winter to early spring. The juice is used instead of lemon to flavour *houmous*.

Kibbeh samak

A mixture of cracked wheat, fish, coriander, onions, salt and pepper, all kneaded together to make a soft dough. This dough is spread over a mixture of cooked onions and pine nuts, and flavoured with the threads of that lovely, but expensive, spice, saffron.

Kishk

A staple wheat burghol that is processed with milk and yogurt and left to ferment for several days. It is dried in the sun and ground either in the traditional way, between the fingers, or by machine, to a medium-fine powder. This very healthy dish is eaten with bread for breakfast, providing warmth in cold weather.

Ma'al-zahr

Orange flower water is the distilled essence of the Seville orange blossoms. It is highly fragrant and used in most Lebanese desserts and in the famous white coffee. It is not so common in Turkey although an 18th-century cookery book on Turkish cuisine mentions it very occasionally.

Ma'al-ward

Rose water. Another fragrant water, which is distilled from special kinds of rose petals, is known in Arabic as *ward el-jouri*. Also used in many Arabic and Turkish desserts. Rose water has a sweeter flavour than orange flower water.

Mahlab

A mild fragrant spice obtained from the kernel of the wild black cherry. The ground kernels are used to lift the taste of certain sweet pastries. *Mahlab* is best bought whole and ground before use.

Mastic miskee

A resin obtained from the small evergreen tree of *Pistacia lentisius*. Mastic, or *miskee*, as it is called in Lebanon and Syria, comes in small, round, pale yellow pieces, which are slightly translucent. The resin gives a fragrant, distinctive flavour to milk puddings, ice cream, and chicken or meat marinades. Mastic should be used in moderate quantities because too much can make the dish taste bitter. Because of its chewy texture, grind in a mortar with a little sugar or salt, depending on whether the recipe is savoury or sweet. With a pestle gently and firmly move your hand clockwise until you obtain a medium-fine, powder-like texture. Mastic is found in Middle Eastern shops.

Mezzé

An assortment of appetizers presented in small dishes. A ritual that appears all over the Levant and is accompanied with an alcoholic drink called arak (raki in Turkey). Although *mezzé* can be a meal in itself, a main dish always follows, generally a mixture of grilled chicken and meat, or fish. It is said that *mezzé* originates from the Arabic words *mazmaza ol youmazmez* – nibble or to nibble.

Mouloukhieh or Jews' mallow – *Corchorus olitorius*

A plant that grows in Lebanon, Syria and Egypt. The dark green leaves are used whole to cook with lamb in a stew, or finely chopped and added to a stock of meat and/or chicken. The Druze, a religious minority found in Syria, Lebanon and Israel, refrain from eating it – especially the religious sheikhs. The reason is thought to be that the Fatimid Egyptian Sultan, Al-Hakim bi-Amr Allah, deified by the Druze faith, prohibited his people from eating it. Some people believe that the reason behind its prohibition may be that the plant is said to be an aphrodisiac.

Osfour

Osfour consists of deep, orangy-yellow threads that come from the petals of the flowers of the safflower plant. The plant originated in Africa and Asia. *Osfour* is known as saffron bastard. In fact, it has nothing to do with saffron. Unlike the strong-flavoured and expensive saffron, *osfour* has a mild flavour and gives a yellowish colour to food and a pleasant taste without overpowering it. *Osfour* is on sale in Middle Eastern shops.

Pomegranate syrup

Called in Arabic *rubb* or *debs al-rumman*, it is made from the juice extracted from the pomegranate, and can be either sweet, sweet and sour, or completely sour. Usually, the sour or sweet-and-sour seeds of the pomegranate are boiled until reduced down to a burgundy brown colour and to a thickness which varies from country to country, depending on the intended use. Pomegranate syrup has a delicious taste and is used to flavour savoury dishes and salads. A syrup made from the sweet pomegranate is used for drinks.

Soapwort – Saponaria officinalis

A perennial European herb with light pinkish flowers, its root is used both to make soap and a dip called *natef*, eaten with *karabije Halab*, a dessert. The dip is made by soaking, then boiling, the root, which is whisked to produce a white foam.

The Greek physician, Dioscorides, is said to have used the root as a medicine. It is a known diuretic and expectorant and should be used with caution. (Known in Lebanon and Syria as *chirch al-halaweh*.)

Sumac

Comes from a non-poisonous shrub that grows wild in the Levant. The unripened, moist, dark red berries grow in clumps. They are picked, dried in the sun and the seeds are ground to obtain a medium-fine powder that is burgundy in colour. It provides a very pleasant sour taste and is used in salads, *zaatar*, marinades of chicken or meat, and fried eggs. In the past, sumac was very useful because it was a substitute for lemon juice, especially when lemons were out of season and expensive. The Romans made use of it as well. Sumac, uncommon in the cuisine of the west, can be bought from Lebanese, Syrian or Turkish shops.

Tahini

The cream extracted from the sesame seed. Tahini is rich in vitamins and minerals, but has a high calorie content. It is the essential ingredient used to make *houmous*, sauces, certain savoury dishes as *mouhabbaleh*, in desserts and an accompaniment to carob molasses, a famous sweet delicacy. The colour of tahini varies from one brand to another. The best type for dishes of the Levant is Lebanese.

Taro or calocasses

A tuber vegetable, with little flavour, used as a meat or potato substitute in stews. (Known in Lebanon as *kelkass*.)

Verjuice

Known in Arabic as *Assir al-hussrom*, it is a juice pressed from tiny, unripe green grapes. In Syria it is used sometimes as a souring agent instead of lemon juice, and gives a distinguished flavour to stews and stuffed vine leaves. Bottles of verjuice are found on sale in Middle Eastern food stores.

Zaatar

A mixture of the dried, crushed thyme, sumac, sesame seeds and sea salt combined with olive oil to make the Lebanese breakfast dish, *Mankoushi*. *Mankoushi* is baked in public bakeries exactly like Italian pizza, except that the dough is smothered with *zaatar*. In Aleppo in northern Syria, *zaatar* has additional ingredients added to it, such as pistachio, anise seeds and cumin. In Damascus, some add thin shavings of coconut. *Zaatar* is on sale at Middle Eastern groceries.

FOOD SUPPLIERS

Archie
14 Moscow Road
London W2
Tel: 020 7229 2275

Athenian Grocery
16a Moscow Road
Bayswater
London W2 7AX
Tel: 020 7229 6280

Green Valley
36 Upper Berkeley Street
London W1
Tel: 020 7402 7385

Halim
493–497 Green Lanes
Haringey
London N4
Tel: 020 8340 8090

Middle East Food Market
383–385 Uxbridge Road
Acton
London W3
Tel: 020 8752 0678

Reza
347 Kensington High Street
London W8
Tel: 020 7603 0924

Soloman's
247 Elgin Avenue
London W9
Tel: 020 7624 2957

Zen
27 Moscow Road
London W2
Tel: 020 7792 2058

GENERAL INDEX

INDEX OF RECIPES
AND INGREDIENTS